MW01285186

TELL AHMAR ON THE SYRIAN EUPHRATES

TELL AHMAR ON THE SYRIAN EUPHRATES

FROM CHALCOLITHIC VILLAGE TO ASSYRIAN PROVINCIAL CAPITAL

GUY BUNNENS

With contributions by

*Cristina Baccarin, Vanessa Boschloos, Deborah Giannessi,
Elizabeth Hendrix, Andrew S. Jamieson, Adelheid Otto,
Silvia Perini, Arlette Roobaert, John M. Russell*

OXBOW | books

Oxford & Philadelphia

Published in the United Kingdom in 2022 by
OXBOW BOOKS
The Old Music Hall, 106–108 Cowley Road, Oxford, OX4 1JE

and in the United States by
OXBOW BOOKS
1950 Lawrence Road, Havertown, PA 19083

© Oxbow Books and Guy Bunnens 2022

Hardcover Edition: ISBN 978-1-78925-838-7
Digital Edition: ISBN 978-1-78925-839-4 (epub)

A CIP record for this book is available from the British Library

Library of Congress Control Number: 2022935313

Printed in Malta by Melita Press

Typeset in India by Lapiz Digital Services, Chennai.

For a complete list of Oxbow titles, please contact:

UNITED KINGDOM
Oxbow Books
Telephone (01865) 241249
Email: oxbow@oxbowbooks.com
www.oxbowbooks.com

UNITED STATES OF AMERICA
Oxbow Books
Telephone (610) 853-9131, Fax (610) 853-9146
Email: queries@casemateacademic.com
www.casemateacademic.com/oxbow

Oxbow Books is part of the Casemate Group

Front cover: Ivory plaque depicting a procession of servants carrying provisions (C O.1708; Aleppo M 10982).
Back cover: Tell Ahmar seen from the north-west after the closure of the Tishrin Dam (Author's own).

Contents

Foreword

The archaeological site of Tell Ahmar played a non-negligible role in the interregional relations of the ancient Near East, due to its position at an important crossing point of the Euphrates and at the intersection of routes connecting Upper and Lower Mesopotamia with Anatolia and Syria-Palestine.

The site was first excavated by a French expedition led by François Thureau-Dangin, from 1929 to 1931. More recently, as the building of a dam – the "Tishrin Dam", about 40 km downstream from Tell Ahmar – was threatening the site, the decision was taken, in full agreement with the Syrian Directorate General of Antiquities and Museums, to undertake salvage excavations at the site. An archaeological expedition placed under the author's direction worked at the site from 1988 to the completion of the dam in 1999 under the auspices of the University of Melbourne, then, as the site was not completely inundated, from 2000 to 2010 as part of the *Mission archéologique de l'Université de Liège en Syrie* led by Professor Önhan Tunca.

The present study intends to offer a synthesis of the discoveries made at Tell Ahmar from the beginning of its exploration until the present time, essentially by the French and Australian/Belgian expeditions, which obtained significant as well as complementary results. Archaeological data will be presented in the chronological order of the historical periods they belong to and, whenever possible, supplemented by written evidence with the double aim to outline the slow progression of a local site from the status of a Chalcolithic village to that of a provincial capital of the Assyrian empire and, at the same time, to outline its role as an intermediary between Mesopotamia and the regions to the west of the Euphrates.

Secondarily, this study also intends to present the essential discoveries of the Australian-Belgian mission before they are fully published, so that they become available for further research.

A few inserts by various scholars give complementary information on specific problems or explain the general context of some finds. In order to make the text as light and accessible as possible, endnotes and technical discussions are kept to a strict minimum. Illustrations, unless otherwise specified, are by the author.

The site is referred to by its Arabic name Tell Ahmar. Although it has been common practice in scholarly literature to call it Til Barsib, ancient names that we know were used to designate the site (Masuwari, Til Barsib, Kar-Shalmaneser), all date from the first millennium. It is therefore more appropriate to use them only when the context allows it.

All dates, unless otherwise specified, are before our era.

Acknowledgements

Australian and Belgian research at Tell Ahmar was made possible thanks to the assistance of many persons and institutions. My thanks go first to the former Department of Middle Eastern Studies of the University of Melbourne and to its chairman Professor Takamitsu Muraoka, who gave encouragement and support to the project and provided it with the means to start in 1988. They also go to the Research Department of the University of Melbourne, to the Australian Research Grants Scheme and its successor the Australian Research Council, as well as to the Ian Potter Foundation who all contributed to keeping the project going. Thanks are also due to the Department of Classical and Near Eastern Studies of the University of Melbourne for the support it gave to the excavations.

In Belgium my gratitude goes to Professeur Önhan Tunca, director of the *Mission archéologique de l'Université de Liège en Syrie*, who, in 2000, included the Tell Ahmar project in its research programme and gave financial support to the excavations.

Special thanks are due to the Syrian Directorate General of Antiquities and Museums and to its successive directors, among whom Afif Bahnassi, Ali Abou Assaf, Sultan Muhesen and Bassam Jamous, who gave unfailing support to the project. I cannot omit the directors of the Archaeology Department of the Directorate General of Antiquities and Museums, Adnan Bounni and Michel al-Maqdissi, as well as their colleague Nessib Saliby. The Directorate of Antiquities in Aleppo, especially its directors Wahid Khayata and Nadim Fakesh, together with their colleagues Mohammed Muslim, Hamido Hammade, Nasser Sharaf and Yussef Kanju, also gave unfailing support to the project. The representatives of the Directorate General of Antiquities and Museums, who assisted us in the field, are too numerous to be thanked individually. May they find here the marks of my gratitude.

Archaeology is a collective endeavour and is possible only with the assistance of many co-workers, all volunteers in the case of Tell Ahmar, whose enthusiasm and commitment are essential to the success of a project. They are too many to be all named here, but I would like to express special thanks to Lia Abbate, Cristina Baccarin,

Thomas Genty, Michelle Glynn, Geoffrey Irvin, Andrew S. Jamieson, Alan Lawrie, Jenny Leimert, Martin Makinson, Leah McKenzie, Sarah Myers, Silvia Perini, Jeremy Smith, Madeleine Trokay, Virginia Verardi, Gregory Wightman.

From 1994 to 2002, John M. Russell joined the expedition with a team first from Columbia University (New York) and then from the Massachusetts College of Art and Design (Boston). He took responsibility for completing research in Area E and conducting a geophysical survey that led to test probes in Area CJ. He must be warmly thanked for his contribution to the project.

The map and grid of the site were drawn up by Russell Clarke in 1988 and 1989, with the assistance of Brigitte Wolf. Brigitte Wolf came back in 1997 to draw up a plan of the eastern part of the tell. Both deserve special thanks.

I may not omit the inhabitants of Tell Ahmar, many of whom worked in the excavations. In the course of time, links were created, which went beyond a formal working relationship. The guardian of the site, Usama Jassem, was especially helpful, not only in his task of guardian, but also, and perhaps mainly, in the assistance he gave to resolving the practical problems that every archaeological expedition working in a small village, cut off from the outside world, has to face.

The expedition could not have worked efficiently without its cook Abou Yaqoub – and his successor Ali Mohammed Abbas – whose talent contributed to the morale of the team, nor without its driver, Mohammed Abbas, who, for most of the time, was our sole link with the outside world.

Two long-time friends – Tsolag Tenguerian, too early departed, and Abdallah Hadjar, retired engineer and an archaeology enthusiast – gave an invaluable support to the expedition, either by solving countless material problems or by giving moral support in difficult times.

Lastly, there is no word to thank my wife Arlette Roobaert. Not only did she take the responsibility of part of the field work, but she also paid meticulous attention to the administration of the expedition and she efficiently contributed to loosening the tensions that may arise between persons working in often demanding conditions.

Abbreviations

CHLI
J.D. Hawkins, *Corpus of Hieroglyphic Luwian Inscriptions*, I, *Inscriptions of the Iron Age*, 3 vols, Berlin 2000.

PNA
The Prosopography of the Neo-Assyrian Empire, 6 vols, ed. K. Radner, Helsinki 1998–2011.

RGTC
Répertoire géographique des textes cunéiformes, Wiesbaden 1974–2017.

RIMA
Royal Inscriptions of Mesopotamia. Assyrian Periods, 3 vols, ed. A.K. Grayson, Toronto 1987–1996 (the texts are available on the web site <http://oracc.museum.upenn.edu/riao/corpus/>

RINAP
Royal Inscriptions of the Neo-Assyrian Period, ed. G. Frame, 6 vols, Winona Lake (IN)/University Park (PA) 2011–2021 (the texts are available on the web site <http://oracc.museum.upenn.edu/rinap/index.html>).

RlA
Reallexikon der Assyriologie und vorderasiatischen Archäologie, ed. E. Ebeling, B. Meissner, W. von Soden, D.-O. Edzard & M.P. Streck, Berlin-New York 1928–2018.

SAA
State Archives of Assyria, ed. S. Parpola, Helsinki 1987–.

Til-Barsib
F. Thureau-Dangin & M. Dunand, with the assistance of L. Cavro & G. Dossin, *Til-Barsib*, Bibliothèque archéologique et historique 23, 2 vols, Paris 1936.

Prologue

The site and its exploration

Tell Ahmar – the "Red Hill" in Arabic – is the modern name of an archaeological site on the east bank of the Syrian Euphrates river, about 20 km to the south of the ancient city of Carchemish and the modern Syrian–Turkish border (*Fig. 1*). Its name is probably due to the colour of bricks which, as we shall see in Chapter 5, consolidated the flanks of the Acropolis at the time of the Assyrian domination when a palace stood on top of the hill. These bricks were

probably still visible in the nineteenth century, before the first explorations of the site had started.

In Antiquity the site was designated by several names. In the first half of the first millennium, it was called Masuwari in Luwian, Til Barsib (probably an Aramaic name), and Kar-Shalmaneser in Assyrian. Earlier names are unknown, although David Hawkins has suggested that Luwian Masuwari might derive from Mazuwati,[1] a city

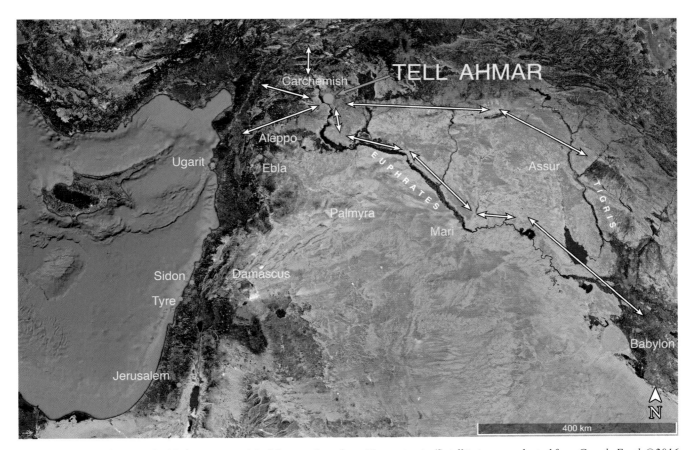

Fig. 1. Tell Ahmar between the Mediterranean, Asia Minor and northern Mesopotamia (Satellite image, adapted from Google Earth ©2016 Basar/Soft). The white arrows show important communication routes converging in the Tell Ahmar/Carchemish region.

mentioned at the time of the Hittite king Suppiluliuma I in the fourteenth century.

1. Tell Ahmar in its natural environment[2]

Tell Ahmar stands on the edge of a natural terrace overlooking the floodplain of the river (*Fig. 2*), which is now completely covered by the waters of the Tishrin Dam reservoir. To the east of this terrace a plain extends over about 25 km from north-west to south-east and about 7 km from south-west to north-east in the area of Qumluq and Beddayeh to the north-east of the site (*Fig. 3*). It is closed to the north by a narrowing of the valley near Carchemish and, to the south, by a constriction immediately downstream from Qara Qozaq. To the east, it is bounded by the plateau of Upper Mesopotamia.

The annual rainfall, that oscillates between 200 mm and 400 mm, places the site in a border zone between arid and semi-arid areas, where dry farming is possible but precarious.

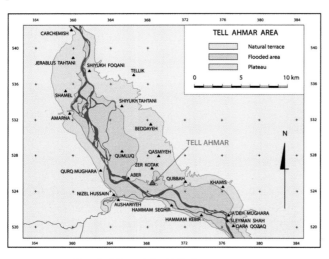

Fig. 2. Map of the Tell Ahmar region.

Fig. 3. The Tell Ahmar region seen from the SE in 1968, near Ja'deh Mughara.

a. Morphology of the site

The tell is the oldest part of the site, but, at the apogee of its existence in the eighth and seventh centuries, the settlement extended far beyond the artificial hill and covered an area of slightly less than 60 hectares in which three sectors can be identified (*Fig. 4b*).

The tell was the main sector, occupied from the sixth millennium down to the end of Antiquity. In the first millennium, it served as an acropolis and will therefore be referred to as the "Acropolis". Both the pre-Assyrian and the Assyrian rulers had a palace erected there, dominating the surrounding sectors. In the early first millennium the occupation expanded to a second sector, the natural terrace extending to the west of the Acropolis, which we shall call "Middle Town". Today it is occupied by the modern village (*Figs 7* and *8*). At the beginning of the Assyrian period the occupation further expanded to a third sector, a natural depression to the north, north-east, and east of the Acropolis. It will be called "Lower Town".

A semi-circular rampart, probably built in the first decades of the Assyrian occupation, surrounded the whole site. Although it has been almost entirely levelled by the villagers, it is still clearly visible on satellite photographs (*Figs 4a* and *5*). We do not know if a rampart protected the site to the south. However, it is not likely that the settlement extended to the river's flood plain, as we shall see below (pp. 107–108)

Before the first archaeological excavations started in 1929, the tell had the shape of an elongated oval, about 230 ×120 m. Today it is slightly larger, because the French archaeologists dumped the dirt from their excavations on the north and south sides of the tell (*Figs 6a* and *9*). The highest point was 346 m above sea level according to the 1:50,000 *Hammam Serhir* map of the *Forces françaises du Levant* and about 25 m above the surrounding plain according to the French expedition. French excavations lowered the top of the tell by a few metres. Some of their trenches, considerably eroded, were still visible in 2010. The building of the Tishrin Dam has considerably damaged the site. The Lower Town is now under water and the tell, together with part of the Middle Town, forms a promontory in the dam's lake (*Figs 5* and *6c*).

b. The site and the river

Tell Ahmar stands in a privileged position, which offers not only an easy access to water but also a wide view over about 25 km of the river's valley. This advantage has been dramatically confirmed during the recent civil war when conflicting forces took Tell Ahmar as an observation post.

However, not everything was advantageous in this position. The river, which flows from west to east here, has always been unstable. It frequently shifted bed, still in the recent past. Before the building of the Tishrin Dam, it was flowing opposite Tell Ahmar at the foot of the cliffs

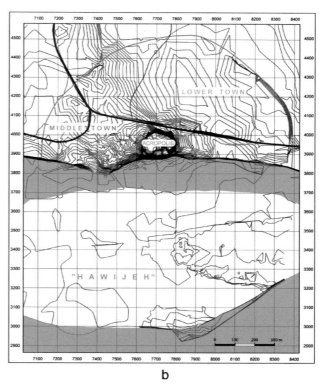

a   b

Fig. 4. Tell Ahmar– morphology of the site: a) Corona satellite photo taken in 1969 (Corona Atlas of the Middle East *[Center for Advanced Spatial Technologies, University of Arkansas/U.S. Geological Survey]). The semi-circular rampart of Tell Ahmar is clearly visible; b) map of Tell Ahmar and the river (after Clarke & Wolf's topographic survey). The blue areas show the approximate location of the two branches of the Euphrates before the north branch dried up.*

overlooking the right bank. On the contrary, at the time of the French excavations (1929–1931), the river was split into two branches, one flowing at the foot of the tell (*Fig. 9*), the other at the foot of the cliffs on the opposite side. The north branch must have dried up at the beginning of the 1960s according to the testimony of the villagers. Parallel channels are distinctly visible on the satellite photograph of Figure 4a, which show that the river shift must have occurred in several stages. Moreover, catastrophic river floods could occur unexpectedly in the spring due to snow melting in Turkey. The current, always fast in the river, is especially violent at the time of the flood and can be held responsible for the erosion of the southern part of the Acropolis. Judging from the plan of the preserved part of the Assyrian palace (*Fig. 161*), which must have covered the entire surface of the Acropolis, the tell lost about a quarter or a fifth of its area. The date of the erosion is impossible to determine.

c. Tell Ahmar at a crossroads

It is not just in its relation to the river that Tell Ahmar was privileged. It was also ideally located in the communication network of ancient Western Asia (*Fig. 1*). Placed at the apex of the so-called Fertile Crescent, in northern Mesopotamia,

Fig. 5. Satellite photo taken in 2016 (after Google Earth [©2016 CNES/Atrium]). The Lower Town is under the waters of the Tishrin Dam reservoir but the line of the rampart is still visible. The Middle Town and the Acropolis form a kind of peninsula.

and close to the Anatolian plateau, it was in an ideal position to play a role in the exchanges between Mesopotamia and Syria-Palestine as well as the Mediterranean, to the west, and Anatolia, to the north-west.

a

b

c

Fig. 6. Tell Ahmar seen from the east at three moments of its history: a) 1931: The trenches and dump from the French excavations are distinctly visibile (photo: Georges Dossin archives); b) 1989: The dump from the French excavations tends to merge with the original hill; houses have been built on top of the tell; c) 2000: The tell stands above the waters of the Tishrin Dam lake.

Fig. 7. The Middle Town and the modern village seen from the Acropolis in 1931 (photo: Georges Dossin archives). The house of the French expedition stands in the foreground. It has been built in the local technique of "beehive" constructions with domed roofs. In front of the house, rails of the so-called voies decauville, on which small waggons were pushed to evacuate the dump from the excavations, have been piled up.

At first sight, however, the valley's configuration does not seem to have offered ideal conditions to travellers using the road that linked Assyria to the west. When they arrived at Tell Ahmar, they saw only white cliffs which formed a wall that a donkey or camel caravan could not have crossed without facing great difficulties. A special feature, however, helped turn this obstacle into an opportunity. The cliffs are cut by a gap at some distance upstream, through which the Sajur river flows into the Euphrates. Travellers could go through this gap and follow the river banks to get to the plain of inner Syria. The obstacle thus became an advantage. The cliffs protected the site from aggressors coming from the west and the narrowness of the gap allowed for controlling circulation in the passageway. On the other hand, as the site was situated at some distance from the Sajur confluence, it could manage to use this distance as a buffer zone protecting it against any danger that could have come from this direction. At the confluence itself, two strongholds were guarding the passageway according to Shalmaneser III's inscriptions. One, ancient Mutkinu on the left bank of the Euphrates, may have been located at Tell Aber, just opposite the Sajur confluence, or at a site in its vicinity such as Qumluq. Both were excellent observation posts. The other, ancient Pitru, was on the right bank of the river. It is almost surely modern Tell Aushariyeh, which is ideally placed to control circulation coming from both east and west.

The road going from Aleppo to Urfa and northern Mesopotamia was still taking this route in modern times. Gertrude Bell came this way on her journey along the Euphrates.[3] A frail boat carried men, animals and cars across the river towards Tell Ahmar. The French expedition followed

Fig. 8. The Middle Town and the modern village seen from the Acropolis in 1968. The "beehive" houses have been abandoned. The house in the foreground stands at the place where the French expedition's house must have been.

Fig. 9. Tell Ahmar at the time of the French excavations (photo: Maurice Dunand archives, courtesy of Patrick Michel and Dominique Torrione, Archives administratives et patrimoniales, Université de Genève). The dump from the excavations is thrown on the slope of the tell and falls in the Euphrates, a branch of which is still flowing at the foot of the hill.

the same path in the late 1920s and early 1930s (*Fig. 10*). When the Melbourne excavations started in 1988 a ferry was still operational in the area although it was doomed by the bridge newly built at Qara Qozaq, a few kilometres downstream.

The Euphrates navigability has been questioned.[4] However, it can hardly be put in doubt if one remembers the wine jars shipped from Carchemish or Emar to Mari[5] or the boats made for Sennacherib at Til Barsib and used against Elam.[6] Both were possible only if the river was navigable.

Tell Ahmar's role as a crossing point is well illustrated by two letters of Assyrian officials. Inurta-ila'i, who could have been a governor of Kar-Shalmaneser, wrote to the king:

> On the 30th of Adar (XII), the interpreter […] and the emissaries of Que – with them 1 wooden carriage, 3 mules and 3 men – crossed the river and spent the night in Kar-Shalmaneser. They [are coming] to the Palace to greet (the king).[7]

Elsewhere, the crown prince Ululayu, future Shalmaneser V, wrote to the king:

> The emissaries of Commagene, Carc[hem]ish, Ma[r]qasa, Sam'al, Ashdod and Moab have come, but they have passed through Til-Barsib and Guzana without my permission.[8]

Whatever the point of departure in the West, be it in Anatolia (Que [*i.e.* Cilicia], Commagene, Marqasa [modern Marash], Sam'al [*i.e.* Zincirli]) or Palestine (Ashdod, Moab), the journey to Assyria had to go through Tell Ahmar.

d. Natural resources

An advantage of Tell Ahmar was its position on the edge of a fertile plain where agriculture was possible, although, as we saw above, significant variations from year to year made living conditions uncertain. Only the adoption of motor pumps in recent times allowed for an intensification of agricultural production.

Fig. 10. The car of the Thureau-Dangin expedition boarding the ferry (photo: Georges Dossin archives).

Another means of subsistence was fishing. Still today the villagers draw part of their subsistence from fishing in the Euphrates, either for their own consumption or for selling to retailers who regularly visit the village. Besides agriculture and fishing, natural resources also includes the native poplar, *Populus euphratica*, groves of which were still growing near the modern village Ja'deh Mughara before the completion of the Tishrin Dam. Poplar logs could be used locally in the construction of houses, as was shown by the excavations, but they could also be traded. Limestone was also abundant, especially on the right bank of the Euphrates opposite Tell Ahmar and basalt was readily available on the plateau to the east of Tell Ahmar. It is surely the place of origin of the material used in the carving of statues and reliefs as well as in the manufacture of the many domestic implements found in the excavations.

Less usual was a particular kind of stone available in a place called Kapri-Dargilâ,[9] from where Sennacherib imported blocks that were used to fashion vases:

> Moreover, turminabandû, as much as is needed (for making) burzigallu-bowls, (a stone) that had never been seen before, revealed itself at Kapri-Dargilâ, which is on the border of the city Til-Barsib.[10]

The identification of this stone is a matter of debate, although Roger Moorey made an extremely plausible suggestion more than 20 years ago when he noticed that the word *turminabandû* had been carved on the edge of slabs made of reddish breccia, which were used in the pavement of the Ishtar Gate at Babylon at the time of Nabopolassar and Nebuchadnezzar II.[11] He thus assumed that reddish breccia was the type of stone to which the word *turminabandû* was referring and, as a confirmation, he reported that reddish breccia was available near Birecik, *i.e.* not very far from Til Barsib. In this regard, it is worth mentioning that two stelae from Tell Ahmar were carved out reddish breccia. One was the small Ishtar stele now in the Louvre (*Fig. 179*), the other the Moon-God stele recovered from a modern house in the village during the renewed excavations (*Fig. 180*). Pending a petrographic analysis of the slabs from Babylon and of the stelae from Tell Ahmar, it can be assumed that these stelae were made with the stone that Sennacherib called *turminabandû*.

2. Discovery and exploration of Tell Ahmar

a. First explorations

Tell Ahmar attracted the attention of archaeologists for the first time in 1908. In March of that year, David G. Hogarth, keeper at the Ashmolean Museum in Oxford, set on an exploration journey in the region of Carchemish.[12] Collecting information on the sites in the near vicinity of Carchemish, he heard that "writing like nails" could be found in some places, one being Tell Ahmar opposite the Sajur.[13] He decided to go there and started recording all visible antiquities. Among the most impressive remains he saw were the large stele of the Storm-God now kept in the Aleppo museum (Storm-God stele B, *Fig. 134*) and the two inscribed lions that were guarding the east gate of the city (*Figs 147–149*). He also had the opportunity of making the first comprehensive description of the site. Not least among his merits was his, albeit hypothetical, identification of Tell Ahmar with Til Barsib known from Assyrian sources.

The following year, in February 1909, Gertrude Bell, who would play a major role in the creation of Iraq, undertook a long journey along the Euphrates. She stopped at Tell Ahmar at the express demand of Hogarth who wanted to get more photographs and squeezes of the antiquities he had seen the previous year but in such weather conditions that he could not manage to get good enough documents.[14] Actually, some of Bell's photographs were published in Hogarth's report.

Gertrude Bell seems to have taken great pleasure from her stay at Tell Ahmar. She writes:

> Then I came in to tea and found my tents pitched below the Tell and above the village. The broad Euphrates sweeps slowly past the Tell and I have just watched the sun set beyond the white cliffs of his other bank. I doubt whether there is anyone in the world so happy.[15]

The place must have been very attractive indeed, as it is the very place where the Thureau-Dangin expedition erected its house several years later (*Fig. 7*).

David G. Hogarth is associated with another major step in the discovery of Tell Ahmar, namely the definitive identification of the site with Til Barsib. In 1911, when the Germans were building the railway to Baghdad, he decided to undertake archaeological excavations at Carchemish, some 20 km to the north of Tell Ahmar. There may have been more than a coincidence in his choice. Not only the railway was going through the archaeological site, but the tell of Carchemish overlooked the exact place where a bridge was carrying the railway across the Euphrates. Hogarth, as much concerned with archaeology as with building the British empire, may have thought that it was a good observation point to watch the progress of the work as well as the circulation on the railway. The expedition consisted of three members. Besides Hogarth himself, there was an epigrapher, R. Campbell Thomson, and a young archaeologist, Thomas E. Lawrence, future "Lawrence of Arabia". Hogarth did not stay long at Carchemish and left the excavations under the supervision of his two colleagues. It seems that Hogarth, disappointed by the results of the Carchemish excavations, was considering the possibility of transferring his research to Tell Ahmar.[16] At the end of the excavation season, he told his two colleagues to go there to get more information. Campbell Thompson copied and deciphered the inscriptions of the two lions of the east gate of Tell Ahmar. As the inscriptions specify that the lions were erected at Kar-Shalmaneser – the Assyrian name of Til Barsib – Hogarth's hypothesis of the identification of Tell Ahmar with Til Barsib was confirmed.

On the eve of the First World War, all the information that could be obtained from a survey of the site had been gathered. The next step would be formal excavation. This was done after the war, when Syria had been placed under French mandate by the League of Nations.

b. The French excavations

Tell Ahmar did not attract much attention from the French authorities until 1925, when Paul Perdrizet visited the site and explained its potentialities in a letter that René Dussaud read to the French *Académie des inscriptions et belles lettres* on 16 October.[17] The first investigations started two years later, in 1927. François Thureau-Dangin, who was visiting the Jezireh with Joseph Darrous, from the Antiquities authority of Aleppo, spent a few days at Tell Ahmar. From the 17th to the 25th of May, with the help of a dozen of *tirailleurs sénégalais*, he exposed a stele of king Esarhaddon at the foot of the tell (*Fig. 178*) and a fragmentary inscription of Shalmaneser III near the modern cemetery. At about the same time Darrous transferred to Aleppo the monuments described by Hogarth. In the following year, while he was conducting excavations at Arslan Tash, Thureau-Dangin, in the company of Joseph Darrous, Georges Dossin and Father Barrois, stopped a second time at Tell Ahmar on the way back from a Sunday trip along the Euphrates. He heard that villagers had just found fragments of a carved black stone. It turned out that these fragments belonged to a second Storm-God stele, now in the Louvre (Storm-God stele A, *Fig. 133*). As the lower part of the stele was missing, Thureau-Dangin went back to Tell Ahmar on the following day, but he could not find the missing piece.[18]

Regular excavations started in 1929. From 1929 to 1931, three excavation seasons were conducted at the site, totalling seven months of work (*Figs 11* and *12*). François Thureau-Dangin was assisted by Maurice Dunand, who had already worked with him at Arslan Tash. In 1931, Georges Dossin, young professor at the University of Liège in Belgium, joined the expedition. The results of their work was published in *Til-Barsib*.

Thureau-Dangin made impressive discoveries. Most of the effort concentrated on the Acropolis where four essential discoveries must be mentioned. One was a palace, Neo-Assyrian in its conception, which covered the entire surface of the tell.[19] This palace was especially worthy of attention because of the paintings that covered its walls.[20] As the techniques of the time did not allow them to be deposited in their entirety, only pieces were removed and an architect, member of the *Institut français d'archéologie et d'art musulman de Damas*, Lucien Cavro, who had already made copies of the mosaics of the Umayyad mosque of Damascus, was entrusted with copying them to a 1:1 scale. The second discovery was a group of constructions that were dated to the "Aramaean period", or, in modern terminology, to the Iron Age II.[21] However, if some parts of this level were effectively Iron Age II in date, others belonged to the Middle Bronze Age (below, p. 68). Thirdly, immediately below the so-called "Aramaean level", the French archaeologists uncovered a large chamber tomb that they called the "Hypogeum".[22] Lastly, in a deep sounding conducted down to the virgin soil on the south-east slope of the tell, they collected pottery sherds in the tradition of the Ubaid period, dating back, for some of them, to the sixth millennium.[23]

Another excavation trench was opened on the site of the east gate, or Lion Gate, where the two inscribed lions, whose decipherment led to the definitive identification of Tell Ahmar with Til Barsib, had been erected. Its excavation was placed under Georges Dossin's supervision.[24]

Additionally, in the Middle and Lower Towns, several trenches were opened without apparently returning satisfactory results as only reliefs coming from these trenches were published.[25] Some of these trenches were still visible in 2010 between the village and the cemetery.

Fig. 11. François Thureau-Dangin recording the pottery from the Hypogeum (photo: Maurice Dunand archives, courtesy of Patrick Michel and Dominique Torrione, Archives administratives et patrimoniales, Université de Genève).

Fig. 12. François Thureau-Dangin deciphering the inscription carved on Esarhaddon's stele A in the storeroom of the old Aleppo Museum (photo: Georges Dossin archives). The sculpture in the middle of the photo is the large Storm-God stele B now on display in the inner courtyard of the museum (Fig. 135).

c. The Australian and Belgian excavations

The Melbourne University expedition worked at the site from 1988 to 1999, until the Liège University expedition took over from 2000 to 2010. Both could benefit from the collaboration of an American team led by John Russell, first from Columbia University (New York) then from the Massachusetts College of Art and Design (Boston), from 1994 to 2002. The American archaeologists completed the excavation of Area E, conducted an electromagnetic survey of the western part of the site and of its vicinity, and started excavating the CJ extension of Area C. A British–German team placed under the supervision of Arnulf Hausleiter and the late Anthony Green also joined the Australian and Belgian expedition. They conducted a surface survey of the Middle and Lower Towns in 1999 and 2000.

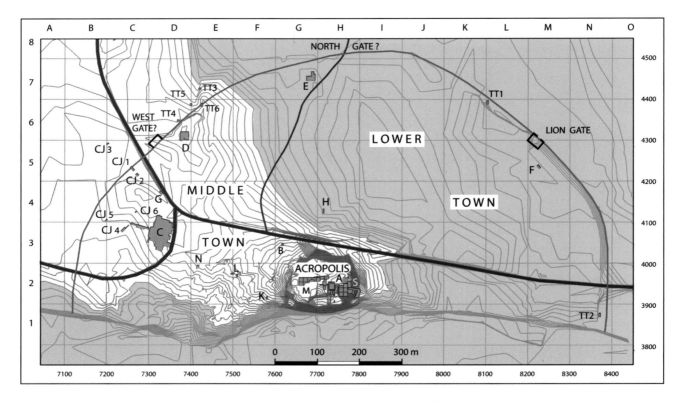

Fig. 13. Plan of Tell Ahmar with indication of the excavated areas (after Clarke & Wolf's topographic survey). The excavated areas are shown in red. The blue zone marks the part of the site that has been flooded by the waters of the Tishrin Dam reservoir.

The Australian–Belgian excavations obtained significant results in several fields. They were able to shed light on little known, if not entirely unknown, periods in the history of the site. For instance, only the Hypogeum was known for the Early Bronze Age. The renewed excavations were not only able to give a context to the Hypogeum but they also uncovered a temple and a small street from the same period. The Middle and Late Bronze Age occupations were totally unknown until the renewed excavations exposed a house and an architectural complex – administrative building and storage structure –, both dating from the Middle Bronze Age II, as well as another house dating from the Late Bronze Age. A better understanding of the so-called *niveau araméen* of the French excavations could be achieved by noting that it amalgamated levels extending from the Middle Bronze to the Iron Age. Our knowledge of the Iron Age was further extended by the identification of a Middle Assyrian presence, which made the transition between the Late Bronze and Iron Ages and by the discovery of an Iron Age II pebble mosaic under the Assyrian palace. Lastly, the exploration of Neo-Assyrian residences, especially in Areas C and E in the Middle and Lower Towns, complemented the picture that could be drawn from the study of the palace on the Acropolis.

A few correlations could be made between the plans of the French excavations, as they were published in *Til-Barsib*,

and the vestiges exposed by the renewed excavations. They concern the Hypogeum, unfortunately not very precisely located on the plan of the French excavations, a few rooms of the so-called Aramaean level – which actually belong to a Middle Bronze Age building – the north-east corner of Room XLV of the Assyrian palace and the massive mud-brick pillar assumed by the French excavators to be a support of the Assyrian palace. As for absolute elevations, the correlation was made through the threshold of the Hypogeum, which was 13.01 m in the French system and 101.51 m in the system of the renewed excavations, which is based on an arbitrary reference point.

The Australian–Belgian excavations also recognized two stratigraphic sequences on the tell. In trench A15, below the monumental chamber tomb for which the name "Hypogeum" will be kept, strata extending from Late Chalcolithic to Early Bronze Age I/II (fifth to early third millennium) were identified. The second sequence was recognized in the eastern part of the tell, at the junction of Areas A and S. It starts in the Early Bronze Age IV (second half of the third millennium) and ends with the Neo-Assyrian period represented by the north-east corner of Room XLV of the Assyrian palace (eighth/seventh century).

Figures 13 and 14 show the location of the excavation trenches of the Australian-Belgian expedition.

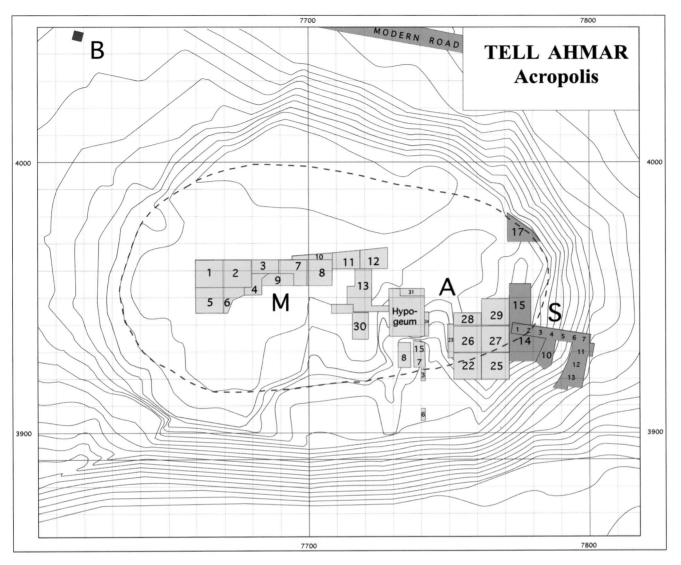

Fig. 14. Map of the tell, or Acropolis, of Tell Ahmar (after Clarke's topographic survey). The dashed line marks the approximate limits of the tell at the level of the Assyrian palace before the French archaeologists dumped the dirt from their excavations on the sides of the hill.

Notes

1   See below, p. 74.

2   J. Gaborit, *La Vallée engloutie: Géographie historique du Moyen-Euphrate (du IVe s. av. J.-C. au VIIe s. apr. J.-C.)*, 1, *Synthèse*, Beirut 2015, gives a useful description of the geographical features of the Euphrates (see especially pp. 21–22 for the hydrological regime of the river and pp. 30–34 for a description of the section of the river where Tell Ahmar stands).

3   G. Bell, *Amurath to Amurath*, 2nd ed., London 1924, p. 23.

4   The various aspects of the question, historical as well as geographical, are reviewed by J. Gaborit, *op. cit.* (n. 2), pp. 54–64.

5   G. Chambon, *Les archives du vin à Mari*, Florilegium Marianum XI = Mémoires de NABU 12, Paris 2009, pp. 18–19.

6   RINAP 3/1, Text 34, 23–24.

7   Translation M. Luukko in SAA 19, No 54, p. 61.

8   Translation M. Luukko in SAA 19, No 8, p. 10.

9   J.N. Postgate, Kapri-Dargilā, *RlA* 5/5–6 (1980), p. 400.

10   Translation A.K. Grayson and J. Novotny in RINAP 3/1, Text 17, VI, 57–61, p. 140.

11   P.R.S. Moorey, *Ancient Materials and Industries: The archaeological evidence*, Oxford 1994, p. 344.

12   D.G. Hogarth, Carchemish and its neighbourhood, *Liverpool Annals of Archaeology and Anthropology* 2 (1909), pp. 177–83.

13   D.G. Hogarth, *Accidents of an Antiquary's Life*, London 1910, pp. 160–161, 171–176.

14   G.L. Bell, The east bank of the Euphrates from Tell Ahmar to Hit, *Geographical Journal* 36 (1910), pp. 513–18; ead. *op. cit.* (n. 3), pp. 28–31

15 Letter dated 17 February 1909 (formerly available at <http://www.gerty.ncl.ac.uk/letter_details.php?letter_id=1649>).

16 Letters of T.E. Lawrence to his family, dated 16 April and 16 May 1911 respectively (formerly available at <http://www.telstudies.org/writings/letters/1911/>).

17 *Comptes rendus des séances de l'Académie des inscriptions et belles lettres*, 1925, pp. 268–269.

18 A report on Thureau-Dangin's first visits to the site can be found in F. Thureau-Dangin, Tell Aḥmar, *Syria* 10 (1929), pp. 185–205.

19 *Til-Barsib*, pp. 8–42 (M. Dunand); below, pp. 117–127.

20 *Til-Barsib*, pp. 42–74 (F. Thureau-Dangin); A. Thomas, *Les peintures murales du palais de Tell Ahmar: Les couleurs de l'empire assyrien*, Dijon-Paris 2019.

21 *Til-Barsib*, pp. 84–96 (M. Dunand).

22 *Til-Barsib*, pp. 96–119 (M. Dunand); below, pp. 19–29.

23 *Til-Barsib*, pp. 120–124 (M. Dunand).

24 *Til-Barsib*, pp. 125–132 (G. Dossin); below, pp. 105–107.

25 *Til-Barsib*, pp. 133–165 (*passim*) (F. Thureau-Dangin).

Part One

Tell Ahmar from its origins to the end of the second millennium: East meets West on the Euphrates

The site of Tell Ahmar was first occupied in the sixth millennium. For most of its history, down to the end of the second millennium, it was in the midst of a flow of cultural, economic and political exchanges going to and from Mesopotamia and regions situated further west.

In the first stages of its existence, Tell Ahmar found itself on the fringe of the expansion area of the Ubaid culture which, originating in southern Mesopotamia, extended to the west in the sixth millennium and still affected the local communities of the Euphrates valley in the first half of the fifth millennium. Then, in the second half of the fifth millennium, Late Chalcolithic communities operated the transition to the so-called first urban period which, from the mid-fourth millennium onwards, saw another movement originating in southern Mesopotamia – the so-called Uruk expansion – create urban settlements in the Euphrates valley, apparently without including the local communities within their operating system.

In the early third millennium, at the beginning of the period commonly called Early Bronze Age (c. 3000–2000), the Uruk settlements had vanished and local communities continued their village life. At the same time, strong polities emerged, both in Mesopotamia and in the West. This trend – the so-called second urban period – culminated in the second half of the third millennium when powers such as Ebla in northern Syria, Nagar in northern Mesopotamia, Mari further down the Euphrates, and Kish and Akkad in southern Mesopotamia were dominating the interregional relations of ancient Western Asia. Tell Ahmar found itself in the border zone between great political powers and in the middle of movements that originated both in the East and the West.

In the first half of the second millennium, during the period conventionally referred to as Middle Bronze Age (c. 2000–1600), the situation did not significantly change for Tell Ahmar. It was still in the border zone between eastern and western powers. Amorite dynasties had seized power in great centres of northern Syria and Mesopotamia. Most relevant to Tell Ahmar were the kingdom of Yamhad, centred on Aleppo, which sought to extend its grip on regions to the east of the Euphrates, and Carchemish, which, although it was not yet as powerful a state as it would be a few centuries later, nonetheless played a significant role in the region. Towards the south, the most important centre was the river harbour of Emar near modern Meskene.

Around 1600, a crisis marked the end of the Middle Bronze Age. The Late Bronze Age (c. 1600–1200), although not always easy to distinguish from the previous period on the cultural level, was marked by noticeable political changes. Syrian polities passed under the authority of foreign powers. First, in the Late Bronze Age I (c. 1600–1400), the Hurrian state of Mittani, whose capital may have been at Tell Fekheriye on the Habur, extended its dominance over most of northern Syria. Mittanian cuneiform tablets were found at Tell Bazi, another site of the Tishrin Dam area. Later, in Late Bronze Age II (c. 1400–1200), the Hittites replaced the Mittanians. Carchemish became a regional capital from which a Hittite viceroy ruled Northern Syria. Towards the end of the Bronze Age, the Assyrians made their first appearance in the Euphrates region.

All these developments left recognizable traces in the material culture of Tell Ahmar.

1

Tell Ahmar and the origins of urban life

1. First contacts with Mesopotamia (c. 5500–3500)

The earliest evidence for a human occupation of the site of Tell Ahmar comes from à deep sounding of the French expedition and from one of the excavation trenches of the renewed excavations. Painted pottery sherds, possibly from the Late Neolothic Halaf period and definitely from the so-called Ubaid period, had been collected by the French archaeologists in levels lying directly on the bedrock (see below p. 16).[1] They can be dated to the sixth millennium. These sherds were found in a trench situated on the edge of the tell to the south of the Early Bronze Age temple and the Middle Bronze Age House S3 both excavated during the renewed excavations. In the course of these, another trench of the French excavations was reopened to the south of the monumental tomb called the Hypogeum and at a much lower level. Research in this trench, called trench A15, yielded sherds from the period following the Ubaid, namely the Late Chalcolithic, and, more specifically, the Late Chalcolithic 1–2 (c. 4500–3900), sometimes called Late Ubaid or Post-Ubaid. Unfortunately, it has not been possible, for safety reasons, to reach the virgin soil. Late Chalcolithic remains were found over a surface that was only 4 × 6 m in size and made even smaller by a modern pit, the bottom of which was only reached in the lowest level, Stratum A15/9.

The pottery recovered from this trench was characterized by a rather large number of painted sherds decorated in the Ubaid tradition (*Figs 15* and *16*). Decoration consisted of simple geometric patterns usually applied on the upper part of the body. Shapes did not show many variations. Bowls were the most frequent form.

Pottery was not the only feature of the Ubaid tradition identified at Tell Ahmar. Architecture gave another example. A structure, probably a tripartite house (House A9), was recognized in Stratum A15/9 (*Figs 17* and *18*). (The use of digit 9 in both cases is coincidental.) Such houses consisted of a long central room on either side of which extended two lines of smaller rooms. Typical of the Ubaid culture, this kind of construction was set to considerably develop in the following Uruk period.

House A9 was only partially exposed. It extended further west in the unexcavated zone. Only the eastern end of the central room (marked 2 on the plan), as well as of two side rooms (1 and 3 on the plan) have been excavated.

Fig. 15. Late Chalcolithic 1–2 painted pottery.

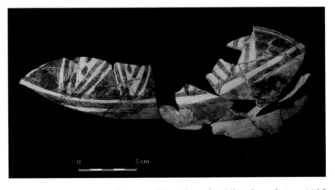

Fig. 16. Fragments of a round bowl in the Ubaid tradition (A15 PL124).

The north wall of Room 1, almost entirely destroyed by the large modern pit, was nothing more than a trace in the ground. Another building, whose nature is unknown, lay a few metres to the east entirely within the unexcavated area. Only the outer face of one of its walls was sticking out of the baulk. A small wall linked the two constructions.

Tripartite houses represent a first differentiation in architecture, which would correspond to an increasing differentiation in the social fabric. Ubaid societies are often defined as "chiefdoms", that is societies among which an individual, or a group of individuals, assume a pre-eminent role in the political organization of society and manage to concentrate part of collective resources in their hands. Tripartite houses would be the material sign of this concentration of power and wealth. However, it cannot be ruled out that tripartite houses were not specifically associated with a social group but were intended to accommodate ceremonial or religious activities, which were of concern to the entire society, such as meetings of the family heads or the practice of ancestor worship.

Be that as it may, the high status of the Tell Ahmar tripartite house seems to be confirmed by the pottery that was recovered from it. It consisted essentially in small bowls, that is vessels used to consume food rather than preparing or preserving it. Banquets may have been organized in the house, so that, as Deborah Giannessi observes (see below), it may have been used as a representative area.

Besides pottery, two objects coming from this house deserve a mention. One is an awl or punch made of flint (*Fig. 19*), the other a diamond-shaped flat object carved out of a fine grain black stone (*Fig. 20*). One of its sides was decorated with a geometric pattern. As it was perforated, it was most likely used as a pendant.

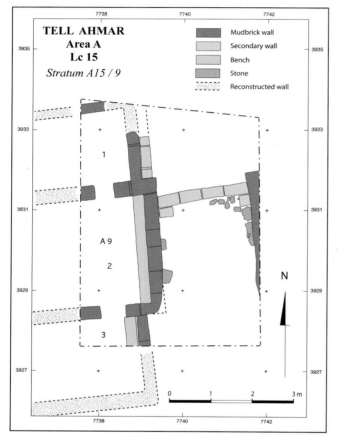

Fig. 17. Trench A15, Stratum A15/9.

Fig. 18. Trench A15, Stratum A15/9 (looking N).

Fig. 19. Trench A15, Stratum A15/9: Flint awl or punch (A15 O.24).

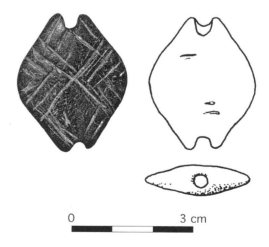

Fig. 20. Trench A15, Stratum A15/9: Black stone pendant (A15 O.25) (drawing: Jack Cheng).

The chronology of Stratum A15/9 raises a difficulty. According to Deborah Giannessi, who is preparing the publication of the pottery, the material from this stratum should be dated to the Late Chalcolithic 1–2 (c. 4500–3900), but a charcoal sample from this stratum yielded a much earlier C[14] date, towards the end of the sixth millennium.[2] However, as C[14] dates correspond to the death of the organic material analysed, it is not impossible that the piece of wood was older than its context. It is also possible that the "real" date lies in between, in the first half of the fifth millennium.

The Chalcolithic occupation at Tell Ahmar must have been significant. The Ubaid levels explored by the Thureau-Dangin expedition were about 3 m thick and the post-Ubaid levels uncovered by the renewed excavations were 1 m metre thick. On the other hand, it seems that the Ubaid period was the first occupation period at Tell Ahmar, as it was lying directly on virgin soil. Tell Ahmar thus finds its place among the many Ubaid sites that, contrary to sites of the preceding Halaf period, had a long life, until the end of Antiquity in the case of Tell Ahmar.

Few contemporary sites were excavated in the Tell Ahmar area, so that it is difficult to evaluate the site's role in the life of its region. Two more Chalcolithic sites – Tell Aber to the west[3] and Tell Kosak Shamali to the south-east[4] – were explored, both on the east bank of the Euphrates. A tripartite house may have been found at Tell Aber, more-or-less contemporary with the house at Tell Ahmar.[5]

It is interesting to note that the three sites were on the left bank of the Euphrates, all near a river crossing. Both Tell Aber, whose name means "crossing", and Tell Ahmar were opposite the confluence of the Sajur with the Euphrates. We saw above the importance of such a location (see Prologue). As for Tell Kosak Shamali, it was situated opposite Qalaat Nejem, a medieval fortress on the right bank of the river, which was commanding another river crossing. It is therefore possible that Tell Ahmar had already taken advantage of its position to control the traffic along and across the Euphrates.

Whatever the solution adopted for these problems, Tell Ahmar made its debut on the international stage as a member of the Ubaid culture in the sixth millennium and continued to exist in the fifth millennium as a member of the local Late Chalcolithic cultures, among which it may have enjoyed a special status if the hypothesis of a tripartite house could be confirmed.

Late Chalcolithic pottery (Deborah Giannessi)

The ceramics from the earlier levels excavated at Tell Ahmar during the new excavations belong to the so-called Late Chalcolithic period, which is dated in northern Mesopotamia from c. 4500 to 3100, a long time span divided in subphases LC1 to LC5[1] according to the changes and variations of the cultural materials, and mainly the ceramic evidence. During the Late Chalcolithic period some new and characteristic elements in ceramic production appeared, like the widely diffused Chaff Ware tradition with its characteristic so-called Coba bowl (*Fig. a*), a globular bowl with plain rim, which takes its name from the site where it was first identified, namely Coba Höyük/Sakçagözü, in the region of Gaziantep in south-eastern Turkey. Chaff Ware ceramic was made from paste with significant straw temper, and used in different types of pottery production, from painted ware to the common or cooking ware with a wide distribution from the Levant to southern Anatolia, the Middle Euphrates and the western Zagros. The development of a ceramic technological process of cheap production reflects new socio-political dynamics which promoted a trend towards standardization and mass production of pottery which reached a peak at the very beginning of the third millennium with the advent of urbanization.[2]

However, elements of continuation with the previous period, the Ubaid, are also still visible, like fine Painted Ware, easily recognizable from the rest of the ceramic (*Figs 15* and *16*). The Ubaid painted pottery, and its culture, spread from south Mesopotamia to the northern regions, from Iraq to Iran, Syria and southern Anatolia from c. 5300 to 4300 BC, being adopted by the local communities which reproduced it with some variations within different regional frameworks. Painted Ubaid Ware has mostly brown/black painted decoration with a large variety of motifs, like festoons, waves, chains, rhomboids, ladder, dots, cross-hatching, horizontal bands, alone or in a composite design covering primarily the upper part of the vessel. Naturalistic and zoomorphic figures also occur but are more rare. Typical shapes are globular bowls with plain, slightly everted or inturned rim, bell-shaped bowls and jars with high or medium neck everted rim. Within this repertoire with its local variations of shapes and motifs in space and time,

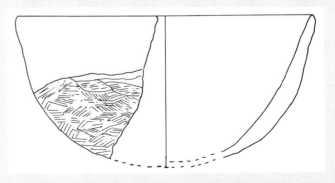

Fig. a. Coba Bowl (drawing: Deborah Giannessi).

the painted Ubaid-like pottery types remain constant over a very long period until the very end of the so-called Late Chalcolithic period in the late fourth millennium and are thus a hallmark of these late proto-historic phases in Greater Mesopotamia.

Late Neolithic/Halaf and Ubaid: the first villages

The earliest ceramics at Tell Ahmar were found during the excavations by Thureau-Dangin, just above virgin soil. They include painted Ubaid style ceramics,[3] bell-shaped bowls, densely decorated with a large variation of motifs, rhomboids, festoons, ladder, cross-hatching and zig zag. The excavator dated the whole sequence (3 m deep) to the Ubaid period, but the deepest levels reached (quotes 0,23 and 0,13 in the French excavation terminology) seem to belong to an earlier Halaf horizon, represented by a few sherds with characteristic motifs of this period, like the so-called "dancing ladies"[4] or the bucranium.[5] The limited evidence does not allow a precise dating but shows that occupation at Tell Ahmar reaches back well into the sixth millennium.

Late Chalcolithic 1–2: climax of village societies

The renewed excavations collected, in trench A15, c. 1500 diagnostic sherds, in particular from the floor of Stratum A15/9, the deepest excavated.[6] This material shows two distinct ceramic traditions. The oldest tradition, from Strata A15/9 to A15/7, belongs to a homogeneous cultural horizon of Late Chalcolithic 1–2, and can be dated to c. 4500–3900.

In this group, the painted pottery of Ubaid tradition is represented by c. 13.5% of the collected sherds, of which 85% come from bowls. The high frequency of bowls and the near absence of vessels for food processing in Stratum A15/9 give some indications about the functions of the excavated rooms, apparently mainly used for consumption of meals, and quite likely a representative area.

The Painted Ware (*Fig. b, Fig. c1–4*) is in general of very fine paste, of green, buff or orange colour with infrequent small grits. The dominant shapes are globular bowls with plain or inturned rim, but there are also a few jars with the classic everted collar typical of this period, with mostly brown/black decoration, but in a few cases also with red paint. Decoration follows the most standard patterns of the tradition, horizontal bands, swags, and cross-hatching motifs.

Although the Chaff Ware is a very characteristic pottery type of north-west Mesopotamia during the Late Chalcolithic periods it makes up only 2% of the sherds collected at Tell Ahmar (*Fig. a*), showing a marginal role of this ceramic type, as also documented in the other two nearby sites of the period, Tell al-'Abr and Tell Kosak Shamali.[7]

The local ceramic tradition of the Middle Euphrates is represented by Simple Ware, with mainly globular bowls, but with more variations of the shapes of the rim than in the painted group: inturned, plain, everted, beaded rim and channelled rim. The polishing of the vessels was mostly done with a wet cloth but some rougher vessels were also scraped with a flint tool, a characteristic of this period, and found both in Tell Ahmar and in Tell al-'Abr and Kosak Shamali.

Ceramic materials often show some connections to regional or international networks of distribution. Thus at Ahmar long distance contacts are revealed by imported ceramic types, like a few examples of red or black burnished ware. The sherds come from jars with everted neck (*Fig. c6*) or miniature bowls, of medium fine paste, grey or black, and covered with a thick burnished layer, vessels which probably arrived in Ahmar with their contents from northern regions.[8]

Fig. b. Late Chacolithic pottery sherds (photograph: Deborah Giannessi); 1) painted sherd; 2) Grey Ware; 3) Reserved Slip Ware.

In general, the homogeneous ceramic horizon between Strata A15/9 and A15/7 shows a continuous occupation of the site, with a more intense use in Stratum A15/9, while the pottery reflects a progressive standardization and selection of shapes and decorative motifs characteristic of the Late Chalcolithic period.

The Late Chalcolithic 4: towards urban societies

The second ceramic tradition identified in the Late Chalcolithic levels by the renewed excavations include features of the previous phases but also reflects a new cultural and chronological framework suggesting a *hiatus* with the previous occupation. Indeed, in Stratum A15/6 the local ceramic horizon continues from the previous cultural horizon, now mostly represented by the Simple (*Fig. c5*) and Cooking Wares, but also by the characteristic Painted Ware (*Figs b1 and c1*), while Uruk pottery types appear as a new feature.

During the fourth millennium, the Uruk culture in southern Mesopotamia began a still poorly understood expansion towards the north, using the Euphrates River as a connection. New and more standardized vessels appeared. An archaeologically very visible reflection of this cultural diffusion is the wide distribution of very roughly made conical bowls, referred to as Bevelled Rim Bowls. The function of these bowls has been hotly debated, and most recently attributed to bread production.[9] At Tell Ahmar, a few Bevelled Rim Bowls were found (*Fig. d*).

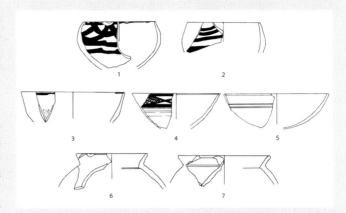

Fig. c. Most common shapes in the Tell Ahmar Late Chalcolithic ceramic repertoire (drawing: Deborah Giannessi).

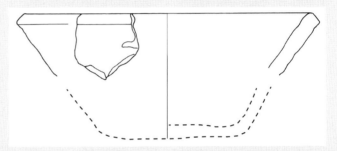

Fig. d. Bevelled Rim Bowl (drawing : Deborah Giannessi).

Two other characteristic Uruk-related types are attested at Tell Ahmar by a few examples. The first is Grey Ware, a fine pottery of grey colour mostly used here for small vessels, like hammer head bowls (*Fig. b2*) or small everted rim jars. The second is Reserved Slip Ware, a ceramic with a decoration technique which consisted in partially removing a thick layer of the slip applied on a common ware, making a decoration on the surface of oblique lines of different colours from red/pinkish to white (*Fig. b3*).

The appearance of these elements in the Upper Euphrates is first attested during the so-called Middle Uruk period, or, in northern terminology, Late Chalcolithic 4, dated to c. 3600–3400.

From the ceramic evidence, it is clear that Tell Ahmar has a long prehistoric occupation which underlines its key role in the Middle Euphrates region. Current evidence from these early societies is still very limited but will hopefully be augmented by future investigations.

Notes

1   The chronology follows that first established in the Santa Fe congress (*Uruk Mesopotamia and its Neighbors: Cross Cultural Interaction in the Era of State Formation*, ed. M. ROTHMAN, Santa Fe 2001), and more recently upgraded in *After the Ubaid, Interpreting change from the Caucasus to Mesopotamia at the Dawn of Urban Civilization (4500–3500)*, ed. C. MARRO, Varia Anatolica XXVII, Paris 2012.

2   S. MAZZONI, Gable seals from Tell Afis: A group of Chalcolithic stamps across Syria and Anatolia, ed. F. BALOSSI RESTELLI, A. CARDARELLI, G. M. DI NOCERA, L. MANZANILLA, L. MORI, G. PALUMBI & H. PITTMAN, *Pathways through Arslantepe, Essays in Honour of Marcella Frangipane*, Rome 2020, pp. 327–335.

3   *Til-Barsib*, fig. 19 and pls xxxv–xxxvi.

4   *Til-Barsib*, pl. xxxvi, Nos 27–28.

5   *Til-Barsib*, pl xxxvi, No 29 (middle sherd).

6   Detailed analysis of the materials is in progress by the author and will be part of a future publication.

7   Y. YAMAZAKI, The terminal Ubaid assemblage of Tell Al-'Abr and its identity, in *After the Ubaid, Interpreting change from the Caucasus to Mesopotamia at the Dawn of Urban Civilization (4500–3500)*, ed. C. MARRO, Varia Anatolica XXVII, Paris 2012, pp. 183–204.

8   Tell Kosak Shamali further south on the Upper Euphrates, in Sector B levels 6–5, also produced burnished ware, red or grey, with the same shapes and in similar ceramic context. The level there is dated to the post-Ubaid phase, c. 4400. Y. NISHIAKI, T. KOIZUMI, M. LE MIERE & T. OGUCHI, Prehistoric Occupations at Tell Kosak Shamali, the Upper Euphrates, Syria, *Akkadica* 113 (1999), pp. 13–68. In particular see figs 13–14.

9   D.T. POTTS, Bevelled-Rim Bowls and bakeries: Evidence and explanations from Iran and the Indo-Iranian borderlands, *Journal of Cuneiform Studies* 61 (2009), pp. 1–23; J.-L. MONTERO-FENOLLOS & J. SANJURJO-SÁNCHEZ, Nuevas investigaciones sobre la cerámica de Uruk en el Medio Éufrates sirio: Los cuencos con borde biselado o bevelled rim bowls, *Aula Orientalis* 34 (2016), pp. 293–311.

2. The first urban period (c. 3500–3000)

Immediately above the Late Ubaid strata, Stratum A15/6 of trench A15 yielded material associated with the culture of the Middle Uruk period.

The Uruk period was the time when a society based on agropastoralism was progressively replaced by a much more sophisticated socio-economic system. Cities were created in which all sorts of specialists – such as administrators, warriors, priests, craftsmen, traders – were concentrated. The phenomenon started in southern Mesopotamia and is linked with the site of Uruk which gave its name to the period.

The Uruk civilization seems to have been the first to start an expansion movement implying colonization, which reached its climax in the Late Uruk period, c. 3500–3000. A series of settlements were founded in northern Syria by people coming from southern Mesopotamia. Habuba/Kannas[6] and Jebel Aruda,[7] on the right bank of the Euphrates downstream from Tell Ahmar, are among the most famous and the largest of these settlements. Closer to Tell Ahmar, Jerablus Tahtani,[8] Nizel Hussain,[9] at the mouth of the Sajur, and Tell Aber,[10] opposite the Sajur, also yielded Uruk material. The North-Syrian Euphrates seems thus to have been very attractive to Uruk explorers.

Unfortunately, remains from Stratum A15/6 do not amount to more than a few walls that do not form intelligible structures. Contrary to those excavated at Habuba/Kannas and Jebel Aruda, they were not built with the typical elongated mud-bricks often designate by the German word *Riemchen*. Tell Ahmar was not directly involved in the vast expansion movement of the Uruk civilization.

3. A time of transition (c. 3000–2500)

In the first half of the third millennium, a new urban civilization progressively emerged in northern Syria, but not

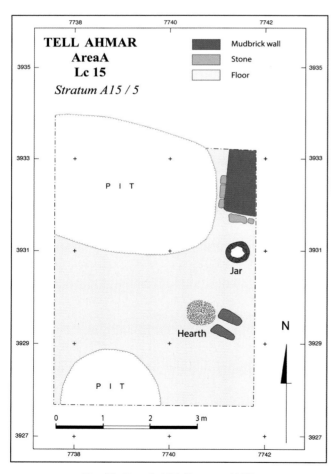

Fig. 21. Trench A15, Stratum A15/5.

Fig. 22. Trench A15, Stratum A15/5 (looking NE). The depression on the left was caused by the digging of a modern pit.

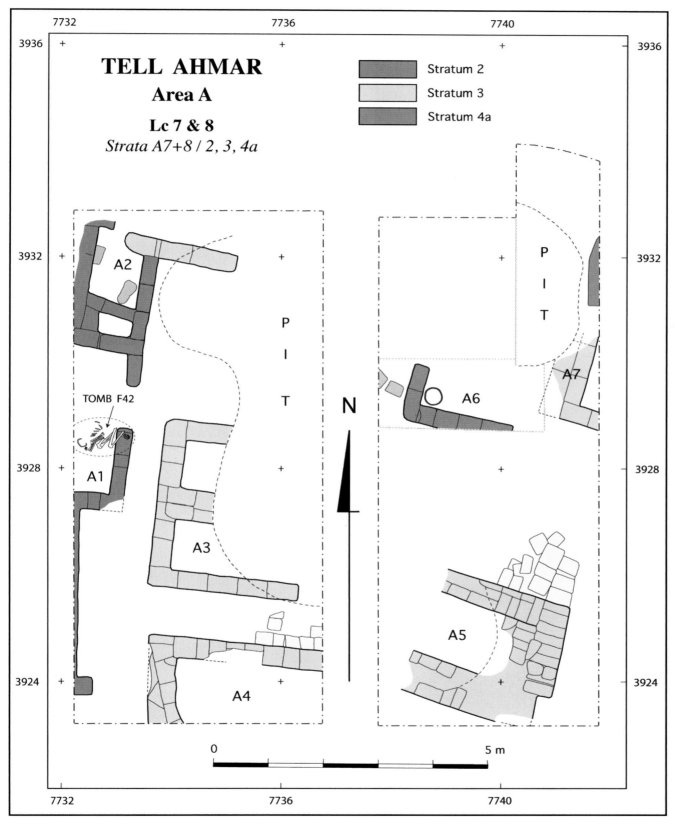

Fig. 23. Trench A7+8: Early Bronze Age I/II strata. Trench A15 was opened in the NE part of the excavation.

Fig. 24. Trench A7+8: In-ground burial A8 F42 of the Early Bronze Age I/II (north to bottom).

Fig. 25. Trench A7+: Burial A8 F42,Reserved Slip jar (A8 PL24) (drawing: Andrew S. Jamieson).

as a result of foreign interference, as was the case in the Uruk period. It was a local development that did not reach its climax until the second half of the third millennium.

The entire third millennium is usually referred to as the Early Bronze Age. However, one should not be misled by the name "Bronze Age". It does not herald a big turn in the socio-economic organization, stemming from a major technological progress, a kind of "Bronze Revolution". The phenomenon progressed slowly and bronze did not enter common use until well into the third millennium. No sudden and dramatic transformation affected Syrian society. Actually, a new terminology has been proposed to avoid the reference to the bronze technology. The ARCANE (*Associated Regional Chronologies for the Ancient Near East and the Eastern Mediterranean*), which recommends adoption of chronological sequences specific to every region of Western Asia in the third millennium and uses for the Tell Ahmar region a sequence termed "Early Middle Euphrates" (EME). It consists of six periods (EME 1 to EME 6)[11] which, in broad terms, correspond to the traditional periodization that includes Early Bronze Age I to III, IVa and IVb as well as the Intermediate Bronze Age. For the sake of consistency – there is no substitute for Middle Bronze Age, Late Bronze Age and Iron Age yet – the traditional terminology is used here.

At Tell Ahmar, the transition to the Bronze Age started in Stratum A15/5 (*Figs 21* and *22*), where a carefully smoothed floor was associated with a hearth and a sunken jar. In the north-east corner of the trench, a thick mud-brick wall was visible.

Later strata were excavated on a larger area including trenches A7 and A8 which were opened before research concentrated on the northern half of A7 renamed A15. There results from this that Stratum A15/4a and Stratum A7+8/4 are one and the same stratum. Strata A7+8/4 to A7+8/2 dated from the Early Bronze Age I/II and were characterized by the reemergence of small constructions (Buildings A1 to A7 on the plan) (*Fig. 23*).[12] Of Stratum A7+8/1, whose remains were probably removed by the

older excavations, almost nothing was found. Only an in-ground burial can be mentioned (Tomb A8 F42). An adult had been laid down in flexed position, turned towards the south, although his head, placed to the west, was turned towards the north as if the deceased had been looking backwards (*Fig. 24*). A Reserved Slip globular jar had been deposited near the feet of the body (*Fig. 25*). The Reserved Slip, typical of the Uruk period (*Fig. b3, p. 16*), survived at the beginning of the Early Bronze Age. The tomb was probably dug under a house whose walls were visible in the west baulk.

4. The second urban period (c. 2500–2000)

In the Early Bronze Age III and IV, Syria reached a new level of intense urbanization.

At Tell Ahmar, four excavated areas revealed significant vestiges of this period (*Fig. 26*). The first was a funerary complex, of which the burial chamber had been exposed by the French expedition, which called it the "Hypogeum" (*l'hypogée*). The tomb, on the southern edge of the tell, was included in Area A of the renewed excavations. The second discovery, further west, in Area M, consisted of two rooms of a massive building called Building M10. Thirdly, to the east of the Hypogeum, a small street lined with modest constructions was winding up on the southern side of the tell (trenches A22, A25, A26). Lastly, the remains of a temple came to light on the south-eastern slope of the tell, in Area S. All these constructions were perhaps associated with a large mud-brick terrace that might have contributed to consolidating the southern flank of the tell.

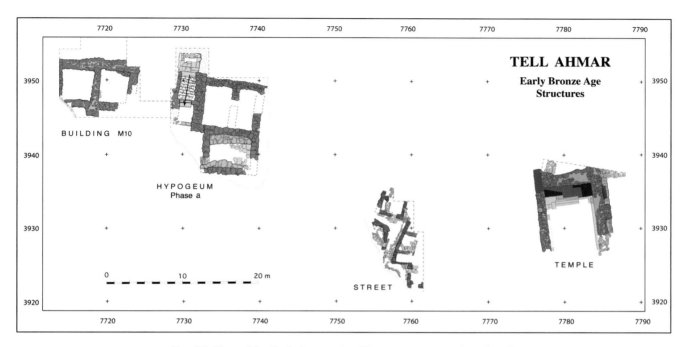

Fig. 26. Plan of the Early Bronze Age IV remains excavated on the tell.

a. The Hypogeum Complex

The large burial chamber excavated by the Thureau-Dangin expedition[13] was still visible when excavations resumed at the site in 1988 (*Fig. 27a*)· It has thus been possible to study its structure and investigate its context, essentially to the north as this was the only sector, in the close vicinity of the Hypogeum, that the French expedition had not already excavated. The description below draws heavily on the stratigraphic study conducted by Crisitina Baccarin who is in charge of the final publication of the Hypogeum Complex.[14]

Research quickly revealed that the Hypogeum, contrary to what had been believed for a long time, was not an isolated tomb but only part of a larger architectural complex with more structures to the north and north-west. It was also discovered that the earliest floor of these structures was more-or- less at the same elevation, c. 101.20 m, as the floor of the Hypogeum itself (*Fig. 27b*). In other words, and for at least a part of its history, the Hypogeum did not deserve its name. It was an almost entirely above-ground construction, which only progressively became buried.

Five components made up the entire complex (*Fig. 28*). First was the tomb itself consisting of a large rectangular chamber whose exterior dimensions were about 7.40 m long from east to west and 6.40 m wide from north to south. The second component was a large room to the north, c. 6.50 × 4.00 m on the inside, subsequently divided into two smaller rooms. Thirdly, to the north-west, a flight of stairs (*Fig. 30*) went down to the fourth component, another approximately square chamber (c. 2.70 × 2.00 m on the inside). Lastly, a space – covered room or open court – extended to the east of both the Hypogeum and the North Room(s). It had been considerably damaged by previous excavations.

The Hypogeum stood as an autonomous unit in this ensemble. Its walls were not bound with those of the other structures. The wall that, to the north-west of the Hypogeum, separated the North Room from the stairs rested against the north-west corner of the Hypogeum. It was not structurally connected to the adjacent walls either, but, as its function was to isolate the stairs from the North Room(s), it must have been built at the same time as they were. The North Room used the wall of the Hypogeum as its southern limit. It is only in a later stage, when the room was divided into two units, that a wall was built against the wall of the Hypogeum. Moreover, the North Room's east wall, although it was in line with the Hypogeum's east wall, was not bonded to it. Lastly, the north wall of the North Room(s) was continued by the north wall of the space to the east so that they both formed another autonomous structure. Nonetheless, the co-existence of all these elements as early as the first phase (Phase HC/d) was established, as we saw above, by the presence of floors at the same absolute elevation, c. 101.20 (*Fig. 27b*).

The period of use of the complex must have been rather long, because four construction phases – of which two have been subdivided into two sub-phases – have been identified. They are designated from top to bottom, that is from the latest to the earliest, as Phases HC/a, HC/b, HC/c, HC/d. The radiocarbon analysis of two pieces of charcoal from North Room 2 in Phase HC/a gave the following dates: 2455–2196 cal BC[15] and 2290–2131 cal BC.[16] A third sample of charcoal from the stairs, possibly but not surely from Phase HC/a, was dated to 2459–2276 cal BC.[17]

The Hypogeum, which, as we just saw, was structurally independent from the rest of the complex erected around it, thus seems to have been the first to be built. It may even have been the only one for some time and, if this is correct, it might represent a Phase HC/e, not otherwise attested. Unfortunately, archaeology gives no clue to solve the problem. On the other hand, the Hypogeum does not seem to have ever been reopened after its first use because the bodies and objects that had been deposited in the chamber showed no sign of having been displaced. It is quite likely that the Hypogeum was used only once and remained the focus of the entire complex throughout its existence.

The floor of the Hypogeum, slightly convex, was paved with large irregular limestone slabs. The entrance was through the west side. The structure consisted of four straight walls forming a kind of box inside which two additional walls, set against the north and south sides of the encasing structure, were built in such a way that each layer of stone was slightly projecting over the lower one so as to form a corbelled vault (*Fig. 27*). All these walls were made of large, roughly hewn stones. Large thick slabs, resting on the inner walls, covered the chamber.

The bodies, probably of two adults, had been deposited on the floor in the eastern part of the chamber (*Fig. 29*). They were damaged by the fall of some of the covering slabs. Remarkably, a large number of bones of Capridae were mixed with the human bones, possible leftovers of food offerings.

Bronze objects had been deposited on the floor towards the middle of the chamber, which included three small bowls, eight dagger blades, nine pins or awls, two mirrors, seven axes, one pick, one rein-guide, and a ring. One of the axes was decorated with two pairs of lions facing one another on either side of the socket (*Fig. 31*). The rein-guide consisted of two rings above which two equids – donkeys or wild-asses – were facing each other (*Fig. 32*). It strongly reminds of a rein-guide in electrum, with only one equid, found by Leonard Woolley in Queen Pu-abi's tomb in the so-called Royal Cemetery at Ur.[18]

More than a thousand complete pots had been piled up in the north-west corner of the tomb, leaving just a narrow passageway in front of the entrance (*Figs 29 and 33*). Almost all the pottery types in use in the North-Syrian Euphrates valley in the second half of the third millennium

a

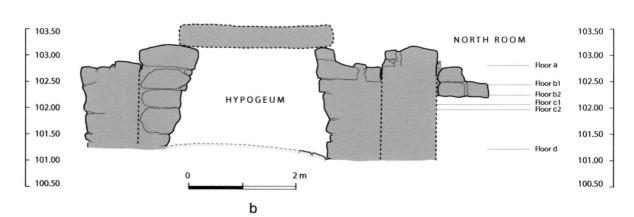

b

Fig. 27. The Hypogeum: a) The remains in 1989 (looking west); b) S–N section (after Greg Wightman's drawing).

were represented in this collection. A few were especially worthy of notice due to their shape or decoration. One, for instance, had the shape of a bird with a long neck and a globular body (*Fig. 34*). A tube inside the vessel had its mouth fixed at the foot, which allowed the container to be filled when it was held upside down. When the vessel was back to its normal position the liquid could no longer flow out through the tube. It had to be poured through the neck and head of the bird that served as a spout. Another vessel, with an opening covered by a strainer that was integral

part of the object, combined animal and human features (*Fig. 35*). The spout was in the shape of an animal head. The body, legs and tail of an animal were roughly suggested by clay strips applied on the side of the vessel. The handle was shaped like a female figurine with a thick and short kilt. The figure was bent in such a way that it looked like supporting the rim of the vessel, over which its plait was passing (*Fig. 35b*). Two jugs were decorated with a male figure seated at the place of the spout. One was a grotesque figure through the mouth of which the liquid contained in the jug could be poured (*Fig. 36*). The other, almost entirely broken away, has been restored on the model of the first one. However, enough of the human figure was preserved to show that water was flowing, not through its mouth, but through its penis (*Fig. 37*).

The monumentality of the burial, as much as the abundance of its offerings, has made the Hypogeum an exceptionally impressive relic of the past with no equivalent until now.

Contrary to the Hypogeum, the North Room and the stairs underwent several modifications. The entrance to the North Room, of which the paved threshold has been found, was near the north-west corner of the room in Phase HC/d (*Fig. 28*). In Phase HC/c2, the entrance was still at the same place, but, in Phase HC/c1, it seems to have been transferred towards the north-east corner (*Fig. 38*). At the same time, a curving wall, whose stone base has been discovered, closed the room to the north-west. It is probably to Phase HC/c1 that the six child burials, found in the eastern half of the room,[19] must be assigned. Two were jar burials (F19.81, F19.120). Another two were shaft graves of which the sides had been consolidated with mud-bricks (F19.74, F19.113). The last two were just pits (F19.116, F19.127).

The modesty of the burials contrasted with the abundance of the material deposited in them. One of the burials included more than fifteen vessels (F19.113) (*Fig. 39*).

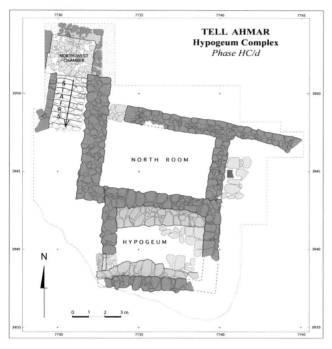

Fig. 28. Hypogeum Complex: Plan of the earliest phase (Phase HC/d).

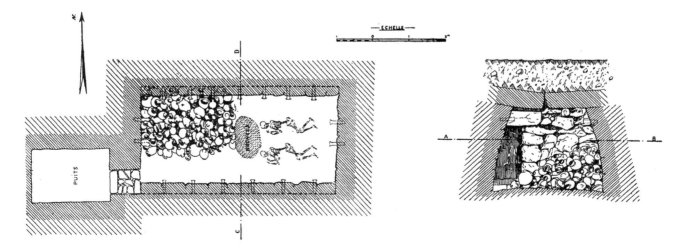

Fig. 29. The Hypogeum: French expedition's plan (after Til-Barsib, *fig. 28, p. 98).*

Fig. 30. *Hypogeum Complex: Stairs leading down to the North-West Chamber (looking S).*

Fig. 31. *The Hypogeum: Decorated axe, viewed from both sides (Louvre AO 15777) (photo: Georges Dossin archives).*

Puzzling installations were associated with these tombs. Two depressions in the shape of an inverted cone, with a coating of granular pinkish white plaster, had been placed on either side of the group of burials. One was more than 32 cm in diameter (F19.117), the other, with a flat bottom, about 45 cm (F19.122) (*Fig. 40*).

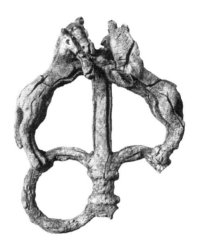

Fig. 32. *The Hypogeum: Bronze rein-guide (photo: Georges Dossin archives).*

Fig. 33. *The Hypogeum: Pottery accumulated in the NW corner of the tomb at the time of discovery (photo: Georges Dossin archives).*

Fig. 34. *The Hypogeum: Bottle in the shape of a long-necked bird (Aleppo M 7565) (photo: Anwar Abd el-Ghafour).*

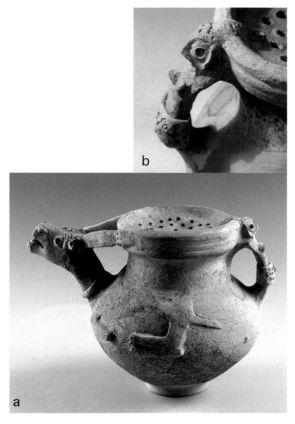

Fig. 35. The Hypogeum: Jug with a strainer (Aleppo M 7581: a) Side view (photo: Anwar Abd el-Ghafour); b) handle in the shape of a female figurine.

Fig. 36. The Hypogeum: Jug with a spout in the shape of a male figure (Damascus M 7582): a) side view; b) spout.

In Phase HC/b2, a new wall was built against the north wall of the Hypogeum and a partitioning wall divided the North Room in two halves, at least in its southern part (*Fig. 41*). In Phase HC/b1, the partitioning wall was slightly shifted to the east (*Fig. 42*). Lastly, in Phase HC/a, this part

Fig. 37. The Hypogeum: Jug similar to that of Fig. 36 (Aleppo M 7583) (photo: Anwar Abd el-Ghafour).

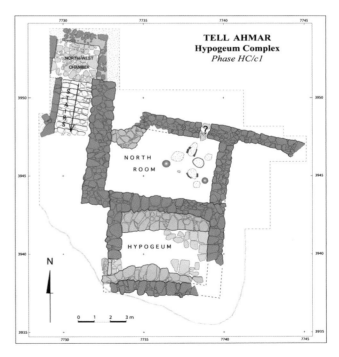

Fig. 38. Hypogeum Complex: plan of Phase HC/c1. The dotted pattern shows the location of child burials and the orange circles the conical depressions associated with the burials.

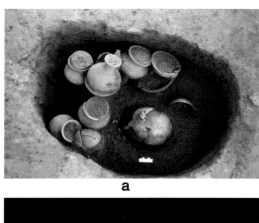

a

b

Fig. 39. *Hypogeum Complex: Child burial A19 F113; a) The skull appears above the small scale; b) pottery from the burial.*

Fig. 40. *Hypogeum Complex: Conical depression F19.122 associated with the child burials.*

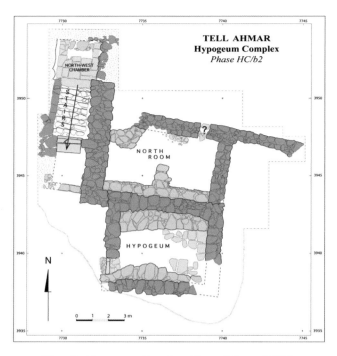

Fig. 41. *Hypogeum Complex: Plan of Phase HC/b2.*

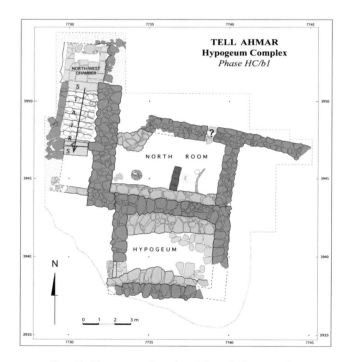

Fig. 42. *Hypogeum Complex: Plan of Phase HC/b1.*

of the complex was entirely rebuilt and the north wall, the only preserved wall of the North Rooms in this phase, was moved further north (*Fig. 43*). As the bottom of this wall was at the same absolute elevation as the top of the covering slabs of the Hypogeum, we may assume that the burying

process of the tomb had been completed. The Hypogeum was now entirely underground.

The staircase, in Phases HC/d, HC/c2, and HC/c1, was made of ten steps of irregular basalt blocks. In Phase HC/b2, three steps of limestone were added at the top end of the staircase, towards the south and, to the north, another block of limestone covered the two lowest basalt steps to form a kind of threshold at the entrance to the North-West Chamber whose floor was raised and covered with a new pavement. Phase HC/a may have been marked by another extension of the stairs. The plan of the so-called *niveau araméen* of the French excavations, shows, in its Room 16, a kind of pavement.[20] However, the stones that form this pavement are placed in parallel rows of two or three blocks each and the north edge of each of these rows is indicated by a thicker line as to suggest a shadow. All this reminds more of stairs than of a pavement. The published report says nothing about this installation, but the combination of the plan drawn by the French excavators with that of the renewed excavations shows that these stones were almost exactly in line with the stairs that were leading to the North-West Chamber (*Fig. 43*). They were about the same width, the lines of stones were about the same dimension, and they were placed immediately to the south of a line of stones exposed by the renewed excavations at some distance to the south of the stairs. So many similarities cannot be fortuitous. It is therefore very likely that five steps, possibly six counting the line of stones found to the south of the stairs, must be added to the already known stairs. The

space extending in-between may have been a kind of landing. The absolute elevation of these steps is not shown on the plan of the French excavations, but, as they were found, as well as the Hypogeum, during the exploration of the *niveau araméen*, there is no difficulty in assuming that they belonged to Phase HC/a, the last phase of the Hypogeum.

We should refrain from thinking that, instead of forming the last occupation phase of the Hypogeum Complex, the walls of Phase HC/a would belong to a later construction which would have covered the Hypogeum, because there is a direct link between the walls and the burial. As we saw above, the wall that stood between the stairs and the North Room(s) played a crucial role in the structure of the complex. Now, as it happens, the wall was still in use during Phase HC/a as is shown by its association with the north wall of the North Rooms. There follows that the Hypogeum as well as the other components of the complex were still part of the same architectural ensemble in Phase HC/a.

b. Building M10

Two rooms of a building, called Building M10, dating from the Early Bronze IV have been exposed a few metres to the west of the Hypogeum Complex, in trench M13 (*Fig. 43*).

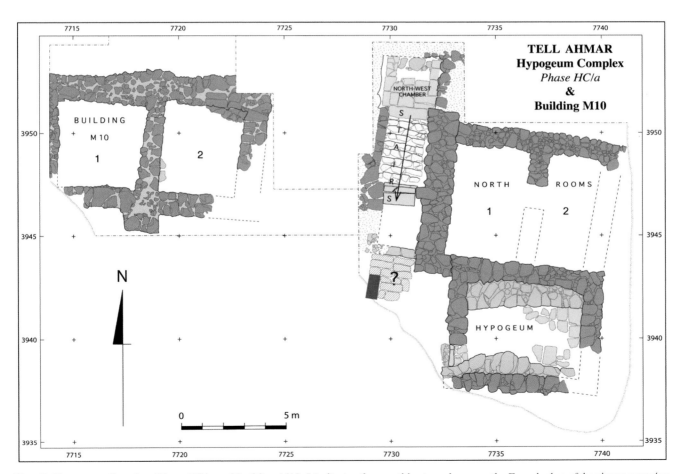

Fig. 43. Hypogeum Complex: Phase HC/a and Building M10. ? *indicates the possible steps shown on the French plan of the* niveau araméen.

Unfortunately, the space that extended between Building M10 and the Hypogeum Complex had been removed by earlier excavations so that any stratigraphic correlation between the two constructions had been deleted.

The two rooms were about 4 × 4 m in size for the west room and 3.50 × 4 m for the east room. Only the stone base of the walls was preserved. As the west wall of the west room could not been exposed over all its width, it is possible that the building extended in this direction. The absence of doorways and of floors associated with these walls may indicate that they were only foundations.

Similarities can be observed between Building M10 and the Hypogeum Complex. The two rooms of Building M10 were in line with the North Rooms of the Hypogeum Complex during Phase HC/a. The width of the rooms was almost the same, about 3.50/4 m, in both constructions, and the space between the two constructions was also about the same size as the rooms. Moreover, the construction technique, which associated roughly hewn stones of various sizes, was common to both buildings. Lastly, the two buildings were approximately at the same absolute elevation. The bottom of the north wall of the eastern room of Building M10 was at 102.90 m and that of the north wall of the North Rooms of the Hypogeum Complex at 102.88 m. The proximity of both constructions, together with their orientation, size, construction technique, and elevation, strongly suggest that they both belonged to the same architectural structure.[21]

The Hypogeum Complex would thus have been considerably extended in its last phase of occupation.

c. Function of the Hypogeum Complex

What was the significance of the complex?

The first point of relevance is the complexity of the construction in which the Hypogeum was included. From the first phase (Phase HC/d) on, it is clear that, besides the Hypogeum, the North Room(s), and the North-West Chamber, the complex included at least one more space – courtyard or covered room – to the east, in the same

Fig. 44. Hypogeum Complex: Fragment of jar with a seal impression (A19 O.52).

alignment as the North Room(s). Nothing points to the existence of more rooms to the north, although this cannot be entirely ruled out. No architectural detail points to an extension towards the south either. The situation did not significantly change until the last phase, when the complex was enlarged by pushing slightly to the north the north wall of the North Rooms and, possibly, by building more rooms to the west.

The second point to consider is the nature of the complex. Was it a residential building or an entirely funerary complex?

The Hypogeum could have been the funerary vault of a prestige building. However, of all the components of the complex, only one, the North Room(s), could have had a domestic function as a food preparation area. The existence of child burials under the floor of the room raises no difficulty, as it was common practice to bury children under the floor of residential buildings. As for the other components, they are more problematic. The North-West Chamber could have been another funerary chamber, but no material has been discovered in it and its size, c. 2.50 × 2.50 m, was rather small for a monumental tomb. Actually, it is not impossible that it functioned as a kind of antechamber leading to another room situated to the west. The remains were not very well preserved on the western side but the existence of a doorway is possible. Anyhow, it is difficult to see what role this room might have played in a residential complex.

The space extending to the east of the North Room(s) does not allow firm conclusions either. It could have suited the needs of a residential building as much as those of a funerary complex. A fragment of the neck of a jar with a seal impression made before firing has been found in this space (*Fig. 44*). It could bear witness to the existence of an administrative system controlling the circulation of goods. Such a find could be made in a secular building as well as in a funerary complex.

As for the Hypogeum itself, contrary to a family burial, it does not seem to have been used on different occasions. At most, the presence of two bodies in the chamber could suggest the interment of a couple in two separate ceremonies. On the other hand, the large number of objects retrieved from the tomb by the French archaeologists does not seem to have resulted from the regular accumulation of offerings over time. On the contrary, everything seems to have been found in the place where it was initially placed, without any later disturbance. The Hypogeum seems to have remained intact throughout its existence, unlike the other components of the complex which underwent successive restructuring phases while their floors were rising. The sacrosanct nature that seems to have been that of the Hypogeum is best explained if its role was more symbolic than functional. It was the focal point of the complex and not a collective burial within a residential building. A ceremonial function for the Hypogeum and associated constructions is therefore the most likely possibility. Food offerings or banquets might have been prepared in the North Room(s).

It is probably no coincidence that five cist graves were excavated near the Hypogeum, to the east and south.[22] Their stratigraphic connections are not known. One, Tomb 3, was 1.25 m below the threshold of the Hypogeum, and another, Tomb 5, 1.25 m above the threshold. They could all be dated to the second half of the third millennium on the basis of the pottery they contained, but they may have belonged to different archaeological levels, possibly in connection with the various occupation phases of the Hypogeum Complex. Their presence in the close vicinity of the Hypogeum cannot be accidental. It can be assumed that they were dug there in order that the deceased could benefit from the aura, whatever its exact nature, emanating from a tomb of special significance. A symbolic function for the entire Hypogeum Complex would thus be confirmed.

Other monumental tombs were found in the Euphrates valley, notably, but not only, at Tell Banat[23] and Jerablus Tahtani.[24] The example of Jerablus Tahtani shows that these tombs were not necessarily associated with a large settlement and the White Monument at Tell Banat shows that they were not necessarily located in the heart of a political centre. The Ebla texts give evidence of a funerary cult of deceased kings in places rather far away from the capital, namely in Darib, possibly Tell Atareb about 30 km north of Ebla, and NEnaš, possibly Binish about 20 km east of Ebla.[25] The Tell Ahmar Hypogeum finds thus its place in a tradition that raised some burials to the rank of memorials for communities whose centre might have been remote from the memorial's location. Its position, on top of the tell and visible from a long distance must have enhanced its symbolic function.

d. A third millennium street or a tombs' alley?

About 15 m to the east of the Hypogeum, in trenches A22 and A26, remains of a street have been exposed in the course of the renewed excavations (*Fig. 45*). Its remains, found below a very poorly attested stratum – Stratum A22+26/1 – represent Stratum A22+26/2. Dating from the Early Bronze Age IV, it meandered on the slope of the tell, which was rather steep here, over more than 11 m. Its surface was littered with rubble mixed with pottery sherds (*Fig. 46*). The street was lined with small structures on either side. None was entirely preserved. To the west, the excavations conducted by the Thureau-Dangin expedition had removed everything during its exploration of the Hypogeum's surroundings. To the east, a large pit of unknown date had destroyed all remains from that time. To the south, erosion had taken away whatever might have existed there and, to the north, another trench of unknown date had destroyed the Early Bronze Age levels. Small blocks of stone protected the base of the walls against runoff water. Large, roughly hewn stones formed two or three steps near the south-west

corner of House A13. It then ran to the north, towards House A12, in front of which it turned left towards the trench of the French excavations.

One building deserves a special mention: House A13 on the eastern side of the street (*Figs 47* and *48*). Two construction or occupation phases were recognizable. In the lower phase (Phase A22+26/2b), an alignment of stones marked the southern limit of the house, just to the north of a retaining wall consolidating the constructed area which was higher than the street by a few dozen centimetres. A hearth consisting of pebbles was set against this wall. About halfway between the north and south walls an area of greyish soil mixed with small pebbles, oval in shape and about 1 × 1.5 m size, was surrounded by larger stones. In the upper phase (Phase A22+26/2a) another wall, indicated as "middle wall" on the plan, was erected less than a metre north of the south wall. The Phase A22+26/2b hearth was still in use, but the south wall seems to have been destroyed and its remains covered by the Phase A22+26/2a floor.

Two more features of Phase A22+26/2a deserve a comment. The first was an east–west alignment of long, flat and irregular stones to the north of the middle wall (shown in beige on *Fig. 48*). The last preserved stone of this alignment, to the west, was about 25 cm higher than the other stones and about 30 cm lower than a large stone placed within the west wall. It can be hypothesized that a third stone, now lost, filled the gap between them so that the stone in the wall may have served as a threshold from which one or two steps might have led down into the house. These steps would have been made necessary by the height of the threshold, the top of which was about 50 cm higher than the level of both the street and the floor of the house. Such a height was probably intended to protect the house against runoff water. At the other end of the alignment, towards the east, the last three stones were also set in such a way that they might have served as stairs, although it cannot be ruled out that this was due to post-destruction subsidence.

The other remarkable feature was a depression in the shape of an inverted cone, about 55 cm in diameter, discovered against the north wall, at about 1 m from the alignment of flat stones. This depression was very similar to the two conical depressions found associated with infant burials in the North Room of the Hypogeum Complex.

No material was discovered in the house except pottery sherds and three Corrugated Ware goblets. Two were placed against the northern edge of the possible lower step of the stairs leading into the house and a third near the south-east corner of the same stone. Two of these goblets were complete, indicating that they had probably been intentionally placed there.

Taken together, these features hardly fit a domestic building. Moreover, if Phase A22+26/2b is considered together with Phase A22+26/2a, we see that the oval surface of Phase A22+26/2b is surrounded by stones belonging

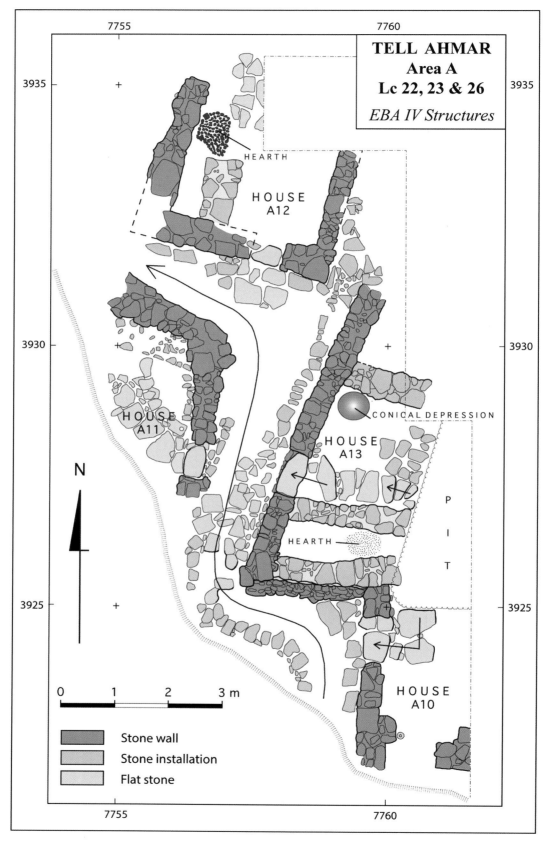

Fig. 45. Plan of the small street winding up the southern slope of the tell.

Fig. 46. The small street at the beginning of the excavation (looking S). The large stone on the left is the assumed threshold of the doorway to House A13.

Fig. 47. House A13 under excavation (looking W). The conical depression and the north wall have not yet been uncovered.

to Phase A22+26/2a (*Fig. 48*), as well as by a few stones further east, and by the conical depression against the north wall. Considering that conical depressions might have had a funerary function, that ceramic deposits were common in burials, and that the oval surface of Phase A22+26/2b was large enough to accommodate the dead body of an adult in flexed position, it is legitimate to wonder whether Phases a and b did not belong to one and the same installation and whether House A13 had not a funerary function. In such a case, the two phases would correspond not to two occupation phases but one occupation built in two times, Phase A22+26/2b having prepared the area for the installations of Phase A22+26/2a.

Another observation would confirm the funerary function of House A13. The overall conception of the house seems to reproduce, on a smaller scale, the internal organization of the core of the Hypogeum Complex. In both cases, a tomb would have been associated with a space where specific activities requiring the use of fire were performed. The space between the south and middle walls of House A13 would have played the same role in relation to the northern space as the North Room(s) of the Hypogeum Complex in relation to the Hypogeum itself.

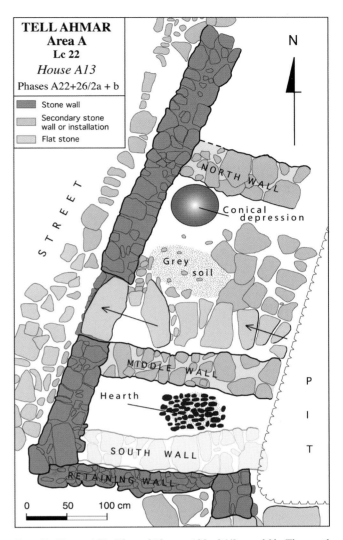

Fig. 48. House A13: Plan of Phases A22+26/2a and 2b. The south wall is shown in dimmed colour because it no longer existed in the last phase.

Fig. 49. House A12 (looking SE): The entrance threshold is visible at the top of the photo, to the left of the range pole. To the right is a wall enclosing a kind of recess. In the foreground is the pebble floor of a small hearth.

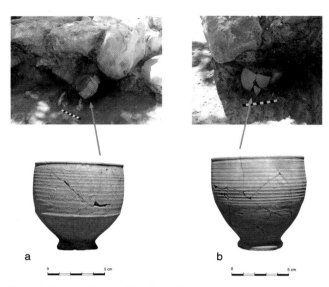

Fig. 50. House A12: Goblets buried against walls of the house; a) against the east side of the entrance (A26 PL47); b) against the exterior face of the west wall (A26 PL65).

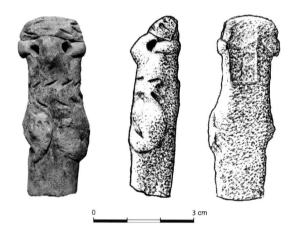

Fig. 51. House A12: Female terracotta figurine (A26 O.11) (drawing: Daniel Benette).

Fig. 52. House A12: Front part of a chariot model (A26 O.15) (drawing: Daniel Benette).

It must be admitted, however, that no human bone has been recovered from the oval surface nor from the soil accumulated above it. This might not be as decisive as it might seem because House A13 would not offer the only example of presumed burials void of bone remains. There are more examples in Area C (see below, pp. 191–192). Another difficulty would be the shallowness of the tomb. There are only 30 or 40 cm between the floors of Phase A22+26/2a and Phase A22+26/2b and the tomb could not have been dug below Phase A22+26/2b because the floor of an underlying stratum has been encountered only a few centimetres below the floor of Phase A22+26/2b. It is possible that a kind of barrow was erected above the burial. All in all, the funerary hypothesis remains the most plausible explanation of the function of House A13.

House A12, to the north of the street, offered analogies with House A13. Only the stone base of the west, south and east walls was preserved (*Fig. 49*). To the north the house had been destroyed by a later disturbance. The house was entered through a doorway placed in the axis of the street. To the left, when coming in, a small wall was enclosing a kind of recess in the south-west corner of the house. A hearth with a pebble floor was set to the north of it and, further north, a stone pavement made of irregular slabs extended beyond the preserved part of the walls. The floor consisted of carefully smoothed soil. Two features of House A12 made it comparable with House A13. One was a roughly circular pebble area marking the place of a hearth, very similar to the pebble area found in the southern part of House A13. Also similar was the deposition of two almost complete Corrugated Ware goblets, one inside the house against the wall to the east of the doorway, the other at the northern end of the west wall, against its outer face (*Fig. 50*). Their position as well as their good state of preservation suggest an intentional deposition, as was the case for the goblets of House A13. Could House A12 have been another funerary structure?

Two objects found on the floor of House A12 deserve to be mentioned. A small pillar-shaped terracotta figurine represented a possibly female figure holding its hands on its chest (*Fig. 51*). The face, roughly carved, had a large beaked nose and eyes indicated by two perforations. A few incisions represented the hair or a diadem and two rows of oblique incisions at the base of the neck were probably intended to represent a necklace. This kind of figurine was common in Upper Mesopotamia and in the Euphrates valley. The other object was a terracotta chariot or cart model, of which only the front part was preserved (*Fig. 52*). When complete, it must have had four wheels. There was a bench for the driver and the front plate was decorated with incisions in herringbone pattern.

To sum up, the street exposed to the east of the Hypogeum was running between small constructions, which, at least for some of them, may have had a funerary rather than domestic function.

Early Bronze Age terracotta figurines (Arlette Roobaert)

The Tabqa and Tishrin Dams, on the Syrian Euphrates, generated intense archaeological research, which greatly enhanced our knowledge of the history as well as of the material culture of the region. In particular, it brought to light objects that are illustrative of the daily life of the human societies that developed in the area. Among these are terracotta figurines, human or animal, which were found by the hundreds on all archaeological sites.

Recent studies showed that, in the Early Bronze Age, anthropomorphic figurines only appeared in large numbers in the second half of the third millennium, whereas animal figurines were produced since the beginning of the millennium.

These small objects are hand-modelled and of a rather coarse manufacture. Applied strips and pellets as well as incisions are used to indicate eyes, ornaments, and hair. Somewhat fragile, they are scarcely found complete.

Human figurines

The most characteristic type is a pillar-shaped figurine, slightly flaring towards the bottom to provide a stable base (*Fig. a*), with the arms bent on the chest (*Fig. b1*), or, occasionally, in the form of stumps (*Fig. a*). Anthropomorphic figurines are often found acephalous but it is also common to find isolated heads. The face features are very schematic, with a long beak-like nose and wide eyes made of applied perforated pellets (*Fig. b2–Fig. d*). The mouth is very seldom indicated, which makes the example of Figure e quite exceptional. On the contrary, the hairstyle is very elaborate, with a profusion of curls (*Figs b2, c, d2*), buns (*Figs c and d*), all different in form, plaits (*Figs a and d1*), and ponytails (*Figs b2 and e*).

Such a type, well attested along the Middle Euphrates, is found with many variations, especially in the rendering of the hairstyle, from Upper Mesopotamia until the Orontes valley. At Tell Ahmar it is represented by about fifteen figurines. Besides figurine A26 O.11, from Area A (*Fig. 51*), which may come from a funerary complex, a headless figurine (*Fig. a*) comes from Building M10, which might have been part of the last phase of the Hypogeum Complex. The other examples are associated with domestic contexts or come from later pits.

The emphasis placed on the head of the anthropomorphic figurines and, more specifically, on the eyes reminds us of the stone statues discovered in great numbers in the temples of the Diyala, especially at Tell

Fig. a. Pillar figurine (M13 O.34).

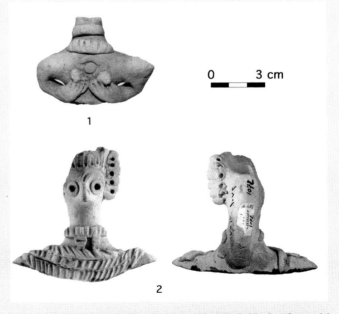

Fig. b. Upper part of pillar figurines (1: M7 O.28; 2: Aleppo M 7567, originally published in Til-Barsib, *p. 95 and pl. xxxiii/25).*

Fig. c. Heads with applied hair curls (1: A31 O.5; b: M6 O.2).

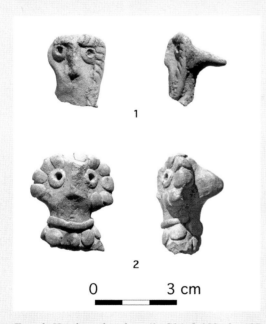

Fig. d. Heads with a bun (1: S14 O.153; 2: A27 O.142).

Asmar and Khafajeh,[1] in the first half of the third millennium, at a time for which terracotta figurines are not very well attested. There might therefore have been some kind of continuity, if not in the material, at least in the conception. However, the originality of the Syrian terracotta figurines lies in the remarkable variety of their hairstyles. From one site to the other, types are similar but never identical, which may result from local peculiarities. For instance, at Salenqahiyeh a frequent hairstyle consists of wide plaits on either side of the head, associated with various kinds of buns,[2] a type that is hardly attested at Tell Bi'a.[3] The stylistic diversity not only reflects the ingenuity of local artists but also the tastes of the time.

Why does the hairstyle and, to a lesser extent, ornaments take so much importance whereas the body is barely sketched out? Although the choice may be due to the plasticity of the clay, it is more likely that it reflects the desire of a society to draw attention to details which may seem trivial to us but which must have been significant at the time.

Although of a very relative artistic value and quite ordinary in appearance, the anthropomorphic figurines raise many problems that are not easy to resolve.

Male or female figurines?

The first and not the least of these problems concerns the sex of the figurines. Except for a few examples with a beard, the visible details hardly allow a decision concerning the sex.

The pillar figurines are usually assumed to wear a long gown covering the feet, which are never represented. Anatomic details are never shown, although on some examples the breasts are indicated either by applied pellets, sometimes perforated, or by applied cones (*Figs a and b1*). Does this attest an evolution that would evolve into the nude female figurines of the second millennium or does it result from the choroplast's concern with details? Be it as it may, in the second millennium, breasts marked by applied pellets can also occur on male figurines. Therefore, the presence or absence of breasts on third millennium figurines does not seem to be a decisive criterion to identify their sex. The variety of ornaments – one or more necklaces of various kinds, sometimes associated with pendants (*Figs a, b, d2, e*) – is not a decisive criterion either. Jewellery was not a feminine privilege at the time. Even though the diversity and complexity of the hairstyles induces us to see them as female representations, it must be emphasized that men could also have buns, as, for instance, Ishqi-Mari or Meskalamdug,[4] or hair locks framing the face, as the bearded worshippers from Tell Asmar, Khafajeh, and Tell Chuera. The most frequent posture, with the arms bent on the chest, with or without indication of the breasts, is no more decisive.

There is no unequivocal element that would allow assigning a figurine to one or the other sex. However, the trend at present is to see predominantly female representations in these figurines, except for some occasional types that, because of their hairstyle or particular posture, could be male.

Function of the figurines

Another problem is to determine who they represent and what they mean. They have been found in palaces as well as in more modest domestic structures, less frequently in temples, and very rarely in tombs. It must be observed that, at Tell Ahmar, the temple – which, admittedly, could not be entirely excavated – has yielded no figurines and that the third millennium tombs did not contain any.

Are they human or divine representations? In the first hypothesis, are they figures of worshippers, amulets, talismans, ex-voto offerings, or simply toys? If they are divine, which deities are represented? The god Dagan has been suggested for figurines with a pointed head-dress (opinions differ on whether it is a headgear or a hairstyle).[5] However, heads with a pointed headdress are found in various postures – with arms bent on the chest or with extended stumps – and they occur, depending on the sites, in completely different contexts.

Lastly, it is sometimes assumed that breakages are intentional and linked with magical rites.[6] Some scholars interpret the figurines as kinds of asexual spirits involved in rituals requiring the destruction of the figurine.[7] However, such a hypothesis is far from reaching unanimity. None of the interpretations suggested so far seem to apply to the figurines as a whole.

Fig. e. Head with the mouth exceptionally indicated (M13 O.46).

Animal figurines

Animal figurines are found in large numbers but are seldom complete. They include sheep, cattle and equids, sometimes dogs and, in rare instances, birds. A few specimens with a long neck are sometimes identified as gazelles.

Animal figurines are found on almost all Syrian archaeological sites. Tell Ahmar is no exception. Given their state of preservation – most often without head or legs – they have attracted little attention from scholars. However, they are beginning to arouse some interest, although it is very difficult to establish precise typologies. Their significance is also the subject of various theories. Are these figurines simply representations of domestic and wild fauna, or are they symbols of deities or divine forces? As with anthropomorphic figurines, the contexts in which they are found – houses, palaces, temples and, more rarely, tombs – do not provide a solution to the problem.

Since animal and human figurines are found in the same contexts, or even together, is there a common meaning to be attributed to them? Here again, opinions diverge. In fact, no study of the co-occurrence of theriomorphic and anthropomorphic figurines has yet been conducted. It would be likely to provide elements of an answer especially if it also takes into account other objects found in the same archaeological context.

Be they anthropomorphic or animal, the terracotta figurines of the third millennium raise more questions than they solve. The absence of written documents concerning them reduces all theories to hypotheses. However, it seems that research should include the study of the contexts specific to each site before venturing into generalizations. In any case, the number and diversity of human and animal figurines indicate that they were very popular and probably had different uses and meanings according to their context.

Notes

1   A. Moortgat, *Die Kunst des Alten Mesopotamien*, I. *Sumer und Akkad*, Cologne 1982, pls 72–77.

2   H. Liebowitz, *Terra-cotta Figurines and Model Vehicles*, Bibliotheca Mesopotamica 22, Malibu 1988, pls I–XXI.

3   E. Strommenger & P.A. Miglus with contributions from K. Kohlmeyer, J.-W. Meyer, D. Rittig & F. M. Stępniowski, *Tall Biʿa/Tuttul*, V, *Altorientalische Kleinfunde,* Wissenschaftliche Veröffentlichungen der Deutschen Orient-Gesellschaft, 126, Wiesbaden: Harrassowitz, 2010, pls 2–20.

4   A. Moortgat, *op. cit.* (n. 1), pls 86, 88.

5   A. Otto, Das Oberhaupt des westsemitischen Pantheons ohne Abbild? Überlegungen zur Darstellung des Gottes Dagan, *Zeitschrift für Assyriologie* 96 (2006), pp. 242–268. This type, well attested at Tell Biʿa, is understood by E. Strommenger (in E. Strommenger & P.A. Miglus, *op. cit.* (n. 3), p. 19) as portraying the god Dagan or his consort.

6   A. Petty, *Bronze Age Anthropomorphic Figurines from Umm el-Marra, Syria: Chronology, Visual Analysis and Function,* BAR International Series 1575, Oxford 2006, p. 55.

7   J.-W. Meyer & A. Pruss, *Kleinfunde von Tell Halawa A*, Schriften zur voderasiatischen Archäologie 6, Ausgrabungen in Halawa 2, ed. W. Orthmann, Saarbrücken 1994, p. 58.

e. A temple on a high podium[26]

About 40 m east of the Hypogeum and about 15 m east of the street, on the south-eastern slope of the tell, a large building was found during the renewed excavations. The plan of the building as well as the complex system of platforms set against its north wall indicate that the building was a temple (*Fig. 53*).

The temple, with an approximately north–south orientation, was rectangular in shape, 9.50 m wide and at least 11.50 m long on the outside. The interior width of the building was c. 6.30 m. The southern end was lost, taken away by the large trench in which the Thureau-Dangin expedition collected the Chalcolithic sherds mentioned above. The walls were made of mud-bricks, almost entirely lost, resting on a stone base.

The position of the temple, on the slope of the tell, must have required some terracing work. The tell was probably cut into to prepare a surface on which to erect the temple. Towards the east, it stood on top of a wall of limestone blocks, which could be recognized down to a depth of about 4 m in the large sounding opened in the slope of the tell (*Fig. 54*). The top of this supporting wall, which still bore traces of white plaster, formed a kind of bench, about 60 cm wide, also coated with white plaster, which extended alongside the outer face of the eastern wall of the building. The temple was thus standing on a sort of high podium visible from afar to anyone going up the Euphrates valley.

A unique feature of the building was the system of benches and platforms erected in its northern part (*Figs 53*

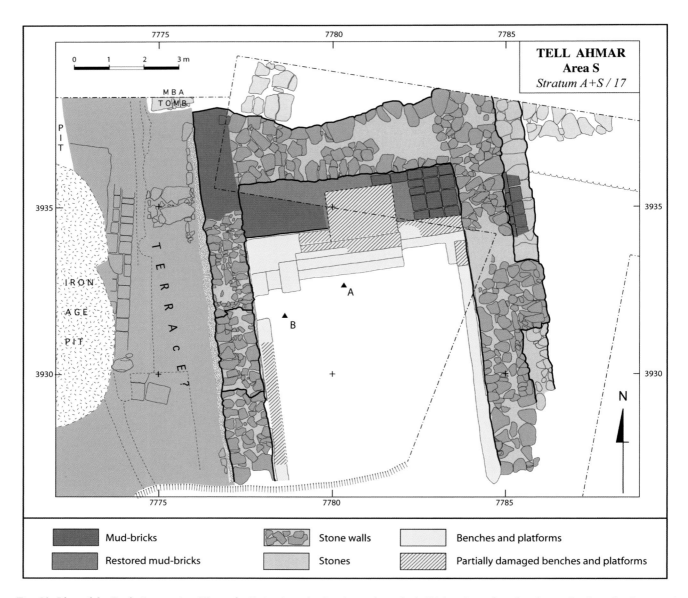

Fig. 53. Plan of the Early Bronze Age IV temple. Point A marks the place where the bull's head was found and point B where the decorated vase and the eyes of a small wooden sculpture were found.

and 55). Such a system was not uncommon in Mesopotamian and north Syrian temples of the third millennium. What makes the Tell Ahmar temple probably unique is the complexity of these installations. Often, one or two platforms were associated with one or two steps or benches. At Tell Ahmar the situation was more complex. The installations were organized in three groups of uneven width. A high platform was set in the north-western corner of the cella with two lower platforms projecting from it towards the south. In the middle, long benches, extending over about 3 m, formed kinds of steps. White lines visible to the north of these benches were in fact traces of the plaster coating of two more benches and possibly a platform, about 2.80 m wide in the middle of the north wall, which had been almost entirely destroyed by the Middle Bronze Age occupation. Lastly, two benches, slightly lower than the middle ones, extended up to the east wall. Benches also ran along the east and west walls. To the east, the bench joined the installations set against the north wall and, at the junction, it was topped by a kind of platform. To the west, another bench extended

alongside the wall and stopped at about 70 cm from the platform inserted in the north-west corner.

Between this complex of benches and platforms and the north wall, a solid mass of mud-bricks, about 1.30 m wide, did not form a wall strictly speaking, but rather a kind of block which may not have been part of the building's initial phase of use. Underneath these bricks, a pebbled surface covered with white plaster must have represented an earlier floor of the temple. The complex of benches and platforms would thus be an addition to the original layout of the temple.

What was the purpose of this brick mass? The platform that can be hypothesized in the middle of the north wall may provide an answer. If we consider that it is not uncommon to find niches, of varying dimensions, in the middle of one of the smaller sides of the third millennium temples, we may wonder whether the middle platform was not the front part of such a niche and, as it was impossible to push back the north wall, we may surmise the brick mass was intended to give enough space to the niche to extend over a suitable depth (*Fig. 56*). The only function of the brick mass could thus

Fig. 54. EB IV Temple: Stone facing of the temple's podium (looking W). The stones visible on the right were set against the podium and belong to a later period.

Fig. 55. EB IV Temple: Excavated remains of the temple (looking NE). In the foreground are fallen beams and, in the background, the complex system of benches and platforms.

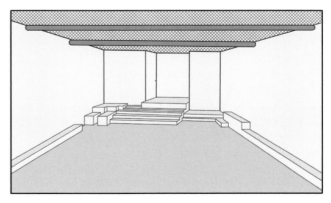

Fig. 56. EB IV Temple: Tentative reconstruction of the rear part of the temple.

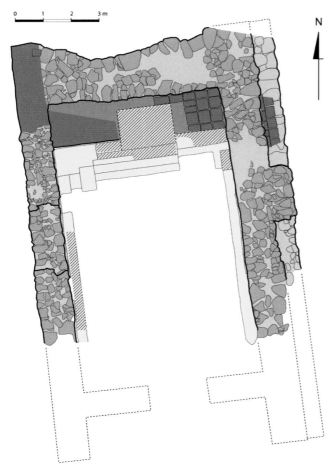

0   1   2   3 m

N

Fig. 57. EB IV Temple: Tentative reconstruction of the original plan of the temple.

have been to make possible the addition of a large niche to the original plan of the building. Assuming that the back of the niche was not the north wall itself, but a one-brick thick facing, the niche could have had a total depth of about 1.30 m.

A difficult problem is to know where the entrance was. No doorway was visible in the excavated remains. A comparison with other Early Bronze Age temples could give some indications. There were long room buildings with an entrance in one of the longer sides and broad room buildings with a doorway in the middle of one of the shorter sides. The first category was generally found in Mesopotamia, both in southern Mesopotamia and in the Habur region. The second was more common in northern Syria and in the Euphrates Valley. Given that benches and platforms were more common in long room temples, the entrance of the Tell Ahmar building should preferably be looked for in the lost end of the east or west walls. However, the restitution of a doorway in the west side is made difficult by the possible presence of a large bricky terrace, which has already been mentioned. On the other hand, the restitution of a doorway in the east wall would also encounter a difficulty, because

the temple was erected on top of a podium and a ramp or a flight of stairs would have been necessary to reach the building from this side. There only remains the possibility of an entrance from the south. This would have been the easiest way of access. A street similar to the possible tombs' alley uncovered at some distance to the west could have led to the temple. If this were the case, the temple of Tell Ahmar would find its place in the long series of temples with a deep cella and an entrance through one of the shorter sides. It would thus combine elements belonging to the more specifically Mesopotamian tradition – the complexity of the arrangements set against the northern wall – with a layout belonging to the north-Syrian tradition: a long room plan with an entrance in one of the shorter sides (*Fig. 57*).

The building collapsed in a violent blaze that caused the superstructures to fall. The entire surface was littered with round blackish beams 14–20 cm in diameter and in some cases at least 4 m long (*Fig. 55*). The core of these beams had completely disappeared, so that the logs looked like wooden pipes. The reason for this, according to a suggestion made by Marie-Agnès Courty, may have been that the wood was only burnt on the surface, which allowed the outside of the logs to be preserved, whereas the inside, by remaining ligneous, underwent the normal process of wood decomposition. The wood of these logs has been identified by Philippe Gerrienne of the University of Liège as Euphrates poplar (*Populus euphratica*). Marie-Agnès Courty, who must be thanked for the information, has obtained a radiocarbon date for the beams of 2469–2279 cal BC,[27] which may be closer to the reality than another date obtained from a piece of charcoal from within or immediately below the plastered floor (2670–2460 cal BC).[28]

It has not been possible to reconstruct the covering system of the temple. The diameter of the beams, which did not exceed 20 cm, and their length, never exceeding 4 m, make it very unlikely that any of them could have covered the entire span between the east and west walls. Two or three rows of beams, supported by columns, must have been needed to support the roof. Remains of these columns might have been found if the entire surface of the room could have been cleared.

Underneath the collapsed beams was a white plaster coating fallen from the ceiling. It made an uneven surface that was often difficult to distinguish from the floor, which was also plastered. The floor, however, was smoother and apparently less distorted by the collapse of the superstructure. It is not clear how this plaster was applied. It appears to have been flat and smooth, but there is no trace of the material, for instance planks, on which it could have been laid.

Notable differences could be observed in the construction technique of the temple walls. The east wall, of which only the stone base remained, was about 1.20 m wide and rested on the stone podium described above. The north wall, also standing on a stone base, was more difficult to identify. It seems to have split open at its eastern end, which made it difficult to study. We can assume that it also consisted of a wall about 1.20 m wide. The west wall consisted of two segments. Throughout most of its length, its stone base was about 1.20 m wide and preserved to a maximum height of almost 2 m. It had a regular facing both inside and outside. At the level of the brickwork behind the benches and platforms, its structure changed. The stone base was lower and two or three layers of brick were preserved above the stones. The essential difference, however, was the irregularity of the outer facing, as if the cohesion of the wall had been less important on this side. In addition to this, a foundation trench was running all along the wall on its west side. It follows therefrom that, in contrast to the north and east walls, the west wall must have been at least partly concealed from view, probably because it was set against the terrace to which reference has already been made several times.

The floor of the temple could only be exposed over a width of about 1.50 m in front of the benches and platforms until circumstances brought research to a sudden end. The material recovered consisted mainly of small cups, sometimes associated with large plates or bowls, and

jars.[29] There must have been several hundreds of ceramic vessels, judging from the abundance of sherds (*Fig. 58*). A few dozen complete specimens could be reconstructed (*Fig. 59*). The cups were probably used to drink or to dedicate the liquid kept in large containers to the god honoured in the temple.

Such a container was found in the north-west corner of the cella at the point marked B on Figure 53. It was a large jar, broken into many fragments, and remarkable for its incized decoration depicting various stylized animals (*Fig. 60*). The neck was surrounded by two snakes. On either side of the spout, two lion heads modelled in the round were applied on the jar. Only the head on the left one has been preserved (*Fig. 61*). The upper part of the vessel was decorated with animal figures such as bird, quadrupeds and fish (*Fig. 62*).

The sherds of this large jar were found mixed with fragments of charred wood with a finer texture than that of the logs. Two eyes made of various materials were still attached to one of these fragments (*Fig. 63*). They must have belonged to a figure seen from the front. It can therefore be assumed that they come from a wooden panel sculpted in low relief and bearing one or more figures. Figures seen from the front are relatively rare in Syro-Mesopotamian art of the third millennium. The most frequent were a lying androcephalous bull and a standing bull-man. Unfortunately the fragments do not allow an exact identification of the figure. The wooden pieces associated with the jar were almost surely the remains of a support, table or chest with a sculpted decoration, on which the jar was placed.

An outstanding discovery was a wooden sculpture with an eye made of stone, which represented a bull's head viewed from the side (*Fig. 64*). It must have been part of a panel sculpted in low relief, the other elements of which have not been found. The state of preservation of the sculpture still allows to appreciate the finesse of its execution and its style typical of Syro-Mesopotamian art

Fig. 58. EB IV Temple: Broken vessels on the floor of the temple.

Fig. 59. EB IV Temple: Selection of pottery vessels found on the floor of the temple.

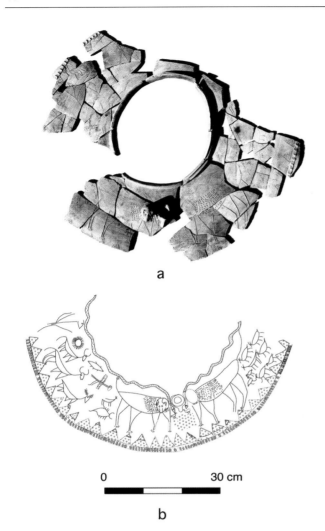

a

b

Fig. 60. EB IV Temple: Fragments of a large decorated jar (S14 PL1055) (drawing: Cristina Baccarin).

Fig. 61. EB IV Temple: One of the two lion heads applied on the upper part of jar S14 PL1055.

Fig. 62. EB IV Temple: Detail of the incised decoration of jar S14 PL1055. Horned quadrupeds, a fish and a stylized sun are recognizable.

Fig. 63. EB IV Temple: Fragments of wooden sculpture (S14 O.303).

in the second half of the third millennium.[30] It is by no means a "provincial" work.

The sculpture, together with the soil it was adhering to, was entrusted to the laboratory of the National Museum of Damascus for consolidation. It then became apparent that only a kind of leaf of a few millimetres thick remained. The object certainly suffered the same fate as the beams of the roof. Only the charred surface was preserved.

Another eye almost identical to that of the bull's head was also discovered, but the sculpture to which it belonged could not be found. Finally, a curious terracotta object in the shape of a domino must be mentioned (*Fig. 65*). A perforation ran through its entire length. Similar objects, but made of alabaster, were found in the third millennium temples of Qara Qozaq and Tell Biʿa.[31] The nature of the cult practised in the temple escapes us completely. We do not even know to which deity, or deities, it was dedicated.

Despite the relatively modest size of the site, which did not exceed two hectares in the Early Bronze Age, a temple, whose proportions and materials show that it was not a provincial chapel, had been erected there to serve the needs

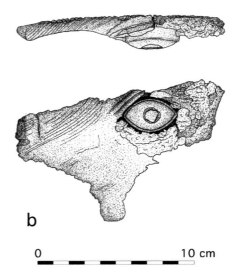

Fig. 64. EB IV Temple: Wooden sculpture figuring a bull's head (S14 O.297); a) the head in situ *at the time of discovery among the pottery scattered on the floor; b) drawing of the bull's head (drawing: Thomas Genty).*

Fig. 65. EB IV Temple: "Domino" in terracotta (S14 O.299) (drawing: Thomas Genty).

Fig. 66. Bricks below the Hypogeum (looking W).

of a population certainly larger than that which inhabited the site. Like the Hypogeum, it occupied a position that made it visible from afar, and like the Hypogeum, it shows that Tell Ahmar must have had a function of prestige at the regional level.

f. A monumental terrace?

Immediately to the west of the temple appeared a combination of mud-bricks, terre pisée and packed soil which was very different from the debris whose accumulation usually make a tell. This conglomerate seemed to be connected to a brick mass observed further north-west, under a Late Bronze Age house (House A14). The temple, which stood on a high podium overlooking the valley, would thus have been associated, towards the west, with a fairly large artificial terrace. Actually, the association of a temple with a high terrace was not without parallels in the Syro-Mesopotamian world.

However, it should be noted that brick masses associated with packed soil have been recognized in other parts of the tell. Immediately to the west of the small House A12, which was located at the north end of the street section exposed between the Hypogeum and the temple, another mixture of bricks and packed soil came to light. Similarly, in the area of the Hypogeum, the North Room and the eastern wall of the tomb rested on a thick layer of bricks that was recognized to a depth of one metre (*Fig. 66*). Finally, Building M10, a little further west, was also built on a mixture of bricks and packed soil, which was recognized over a distance of about 5 m towards the south.

It is tempting to combine these observations and to wonder whether all these features were not connected to each other and whether the entire southern flank of the tell could not have been consolidated by the construction of a vast artificial terrace (*Fig. 67*).

The hypothesis does not go without difficulties, particularly in the Hypogeum area. While it is true that the terrace was recognized on the west, north and east sides of the funerary complex, its presence towards the south was more problematic. A series of horizontal accumulations could be observed on this side and bricks only appeared about three metres below the base of the southern wall of the Hypogeum. On the other hand, the terrace could be seen at a higher level towards the west near Building M10, creating a surprisingly uneven terrain. As for the street to the east of the Hypogeum, it was clear that it meandered along the southern flank of the tell – which must have been narrower at that time than in later periods – and therefore must have covered the terrace, which was nevertheless visible near House A12 to the north. Lastly, in the temple area, the terrace would have made difficult the access to the temple.

These difficulties could only be resolved by a large-scale excavation carried out down to the terrace level throughout its entire surface. However, the similarities in composition together with the difficulty to recognize any regular shape give some credence to the hypothesis that these compact masses of building materials were the remains of a gigantic effort to consolidate and regularize the southern flank of the tell. Was it a fortification system? It is impossible to say. However, the thickness of the system is more likely to suggest a terrace than a rampart.

It would not be the only example of a large Early Bronze Age terrace. Suffice it to recall Tell Gre Virike[32] and Halawa[33] on the Euphrates, and Tilbeshar on the Sajur.[34]

The date of construction of this terrace cannot be determined. It necessarily pre-dates the Early Bronze Age IV buildings. Could it have been built to accommodate them? This is doubtful given that Building M10, the Hypogeum and the temple have all cut into it. The terrace, if it really was a terrace, must have already existed for some time when these constructions were erected.

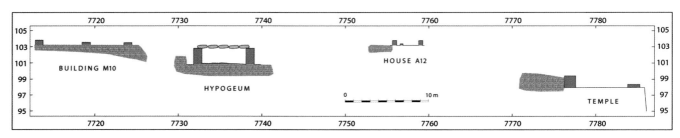

Fig. 67. Schematic section through the SE sector of the tell. The beige areas show the different sectors where parts of the hypothetical Early Bronze Age monumental terrace have been observed.

Early Bronze Age Pottery (Cristina Baccarin)

The ceramic corpus of Tell Ahmar in the third millennium finds its place within the context of the second urban period and, more specifically, the so-called Early Bronze Age IV period in the second half of the third millennium.

Pottery comes from clearly differentiated contexts, especially funerary and sacred contexts. The most homogeneous material comes from the Hypogeum, which provided a particularly remarkable assemblage. The temple also yielded a significant corpus. However, pottery coming from the Hypogeum's North Room(s) and from the modest installations lining the street that was winding up on the southern slope of the tell – the possible tombs' alley – looks more domestic in nature, in the sense that it includes pottery intended for food preparation.

This ceramic corpus has common technical characteristics. The typology, however, differs according to the context of use.

Ware types

Third millennium pottery at Tell Ahmar is generally of high quality and made with carefully purified clay. It contains a few inclusions which are of a size smaller than a millimetre. A large part of the production is made using a potter's wheel. However, a few examples are made using clay coils to form the walls of the vase and finished on the wheel without that the joints between the various clay circles are completely erased.

Pottery is fired at high temperature and homogeneously, with only very rare traces of reductive or oxidizing firing. The inner and outer surfaces are smoothed, sometimes burnished, both internally and externally. In some cases burnishing is carried out horizontally, more rarely vertically or in both directions. Decoration is not common. The most frequent is the so-called comb decoration, *i.e.* an incised decoration consisting of parallel, often undulating lines. Rarer are incised geometric patterns, often potter's marks. Finally, painted decoration is very rare and mainly restricted to the Euphrates Banded Ware. Some examples are made with coarser clay and must have been used as Cooking Pots.

If we take into account major factors such as quality of the clay, colour, surface treatment, decoration and firing, we can group the corpus of Tell Ahmar into five main types which can be found in all the ceramics analysed:

(1) *Plain Simple Ware (PSW)* is the most common and widespread type, made of carefully purified clay that can be designated as fine or medium depending on the frequency and size of the inclusions.

(2) *Fine Ware (FW)* is perfectly homogeneous and fired at high temperature with very little inclusions.

(3) *Euphrates Banded Ware (EBW)* is charcaterized by horizontal painted red or brown bands. Its carefully smoothed surface gives it a particularly shiny appearance. At Tell Ahmar, two types of Euphrates Banded Ware can be recognized. The first, EBW1, is characterized by dark red bands painted on the upper part of the body and on the neck of the vessel (*Fig. f1*). The second, EBW2, also known as Dark Euphrates Banded Ware (DEBW), is characterized by a firing process that makes it crumbly and gives it a lamellar texture. It is dark grey in colour with greenish highlights. The outer surface is burnished in a spiral.

(4) *Syrian Metallic Ware (SMW)* is an imitation of the Metallic Ware that is found in regions further east and so-called because of its dark grey colour and the metallic sound it makes when it is struck (*Fig. e1*). It is a fine ceramic, made of purified clay, fired at very high temperature. The SMW differs from the Metallic Ware by its paste that is not as fine and contains inclusions visible to the naked eye.

(5) *Cooking Pot Ware (CPW)* (*Fig. h1*) is a coarser ceramic that is fired at low to medium temperature. It contains relatively large inclusions, usually mineral, of up to 2 mm.

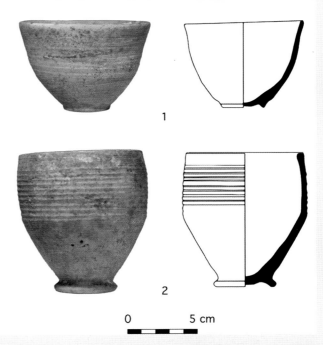

Fig. a. Cups and Goblets: 1) cup (Aleppo M9425); 2) goblet (Aleppo M9724).

Shapes and use

Irrespective of the context of their discovery, the pottery forms found at Tell Ahmar can be subsumed into a few broad categories.

Cups have profiles that vary from slightly flared (*Fig. a1*) to straight. They may have been used for drinking.

Goblets are made in the shape of a truncated cone or with more vertical walls. The outer surface can be smooth or corrugated (*Fig. a2*). They too were most likely used for drinking.

Bowls show a certain diversity (*Fig. b*), mainly in the shape of the rims. Some bowls, known as Tripod Bowls, rest on three cylindrical legs (*Fig. b2*).

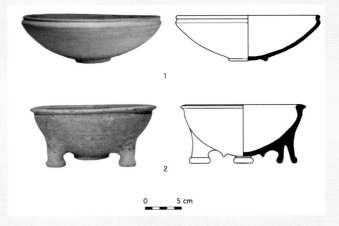

Fig. b. Bowls: 1) bowl (Aleppo M9418); 2) tripod bowl (Aleppo M9802).

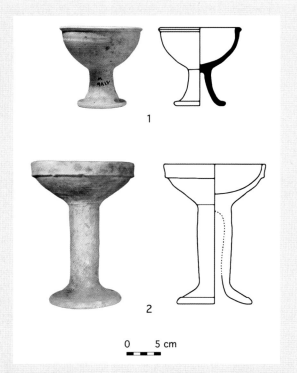

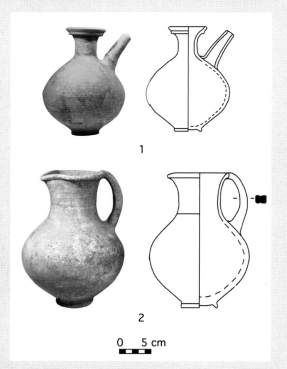

Fig. c. Pedestal bowls: 1) Fruit cup (Aleppo M9817); 2) Champagne cup (Aleppo M9817).

Fig. d. Jugs: 1) with a spout (Aleppo M9815); 2) with a handle (Aleppo M9422).

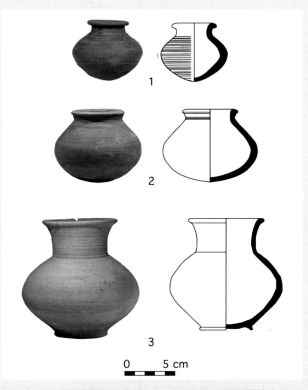

Fig. e. Small jars: 1) with a short neck (Aleppo M9786); 2) with a short neck (Aleppo M9820); 3) with a high neck (A19 PL238).

It can be assumed that the bowls were used to present food, either solid or liquid, from which the guests could help themselves.

Pedestal bowls can have a straight or slightly flared profile. Very characteristic are the Fruit Cups (*Fig. c1*) and the Champagne Cups (*Fig. c2*). Like the bowls, they were used to present food.

Jugs can have a handle (*Fig. d2*), a spout (*Fig. d1*) or simply a pinch of the lip which gives the rim a trilobed shape (*Fig. d2*). Their opening can be wide (*Fig. d2*) or restricted with a high neck (*Fig. d1*). Obviously, they were used to serve liquids.

Small jars are rounded containers which may have a short neck (*Fig. e1–2*) or a high neck (*Fig. e3*). Their function is unclear. They can probably have been used either for storing or serving certain foodstuffs.

Footed jars are high neck jars resting on a single (*Fig. f1–2*) or triple foot (Tripod Jars) (*Fig. f3*). Some of them are made in the typical Euphrates Banded Ware (*Fig. f1*). Such jars were probably used for a variety of purposes, including storage, food preparation and presentation at the place of consumption.

Medium jars are larger than the previous types (*Fig. g*), sometimes with small handles (*Fig. g1*). They were

Fig. f. Footed jars: 1) Euphrates Banded Ware (A19 PL111); 2) with a single foot (Aleppo M9448); 3) tripod jar (Aleppo M9416).

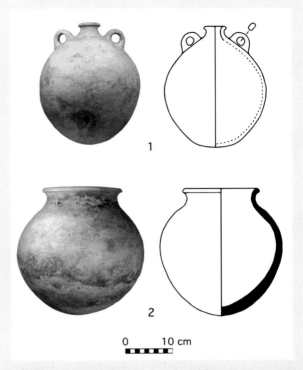

Fig. g. Medium jars: 1) with a small handle (Aleppo M9446); 2) with a wider opening (Aleppo M9447).

used to store certain foodstuffs for periods ranging from a few days to a few months. The large storage jars, in which wine and oil, among others, were stored, are not attested.

Cooking pots, which are made of a distinct type of ware, are low-necked jars in which food was cooked (*Fig. h*). Sometimes they have a triangular handle attached to the rim. Some specimens show a combed decoration, either vertical or forming horizontal wavy lines, on the upper part of the body.

Context of use

If we now consider the context in which these ceramics are found, we find significant differences.

Pottery found in burials

Jars, Bowls and Goblets form the largest category, followed by Fruit Cups, Champagne Cups and Jugs. The Euphrates Banded Ware is found almost exclusively in funerary contexts. The tombs essentially contained vessels for the consumption of food. In addition, the Hypogeum included unusually shaped vases, such as double or triple bowls, "saucepans", strainers and pots with applied anthropomorphic or theriomorphic motifs as well as incised decoration (*Figs 34–37*), certainly luxury items.

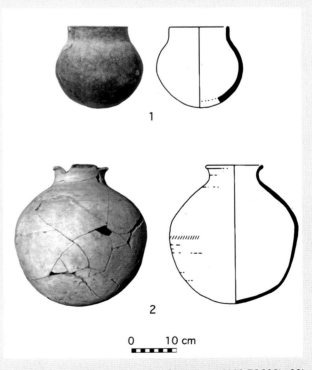

Fig. h. Cooking pots: 1) with a wide opening (A10 PL228); 22) with a restricted opening (A9 PL229).

This material was intended to be used during the funeral meal or to enable the deceased to take part in banquets organized in their honour.

Pottery from the temple

Small Goblets and Cups are the most characteristic and abundant pottery shapes found in the temple. Jars and Bowls are less frequent in the temple than in domestic and funerary contexts. Some of the jars are characterized by a short neck and a thick, rounded rim or by a globular body and a neck. One open jar, with a spout and without a neck, a high carination and a rounded and modelled rim, is decorated with an incised scene associating animals with geometric motifs (*Fig. 59*). The assemblage also includes three small pottery stands.

The pottery from the temple thus seems to have been used to offer or consume small quantities of a liquid which was probably kept in jars such as the large decorated jar.[1]

Pottery from domestic contexts

Bowls and Jars are the most common vessels, found in roughly equal quantities. Goblets are less common. As may be expected, Cooking pots are also present.

Regional context

The Early Bronze IV pottery from Tell Ahmar shows close analogies with finds made at other sites in the Euphrates Valley in the same period, from Kurban Höyük on the Anatolian Upper Euphrates to Tell Bi'a on the Syrian Middle Euphrates. Towards the west, in northern Syria, the analogies are also significant with Ebla (Mardikh IIB1), Hama (Period J) and the Amuq Plain (Phase J). Small goblets and cups are well known in the so-called "chaliciform" pottery, which is typical of inner Syria. They are found in both domestic and funerary contexts.

Further east, in Upper Mesopotamia, comparisons are more difficult to find. There are, however, analogies with Tell Chuera (*Kleiner Antentempel, Steinbau I*) situated between the Balih and the Euphrates. The study of pottery emphasizes the originality of the Euphrates Valley in the third millennium. It also shows that, as is the case in the second millennium, its cultural affinities associate it more with the Syrian plateau than with Mesopotamia.

Note

1   C. BACCARIN, Consumption in a temple? An interpretation of the ceramic repertoire of the Early Bronze Age temple at Tell Ahmar (north Syria), *Proceedings of the 9th International Congress on the Archaeology of the Ancient Near East* 3, *Reports*, ed. O. KAELIN & H.-P. MATHYS, Wiesbaden 2016, pp. 163–175.

***

Seen in the long run, the development of Tell Ahmar from the late sixth millennium to the second half of the third brought it from the status of a village to that of a settlement housing at least two prestigious buildings.

The original village was associated with the Mesopotamian culture of Ubaid and may have experienced the first signs of social differentiation if it is correct to assume that it included at least one tripartite house. It then lived the life of a small village community, staying away from the great Mesopotamian expansion of the Uruk period. Only at the beginning of the second half of the third millennium did Tell Ahmar rise above the status of an agricultural settlement. It is the time when the tell seems to have been reinforced, at least on its southern flank, by a large artificial terrace before prestigious monuments– a monumental funerary complex and a temple – were both erected in a dominant position which made them visible from afar in the valley. In addition, a small street might have been lined with funerary structures. All these constructions required resources well beyond the capabilities of a modest rural settlement.

Various attempts have been made to include the sites of the Middle Euphrates Valley, and thus Tell Ahmar, in socio-political systems based on kinship[35] and including small unstable units in permanent conflict with each other.[36] The affirmation of their identity, notably through the construction of monumental tombs, would have enabled these groups to ensure and perpetuate their cohesion. It must be acknowledged, however, that neither the archaeological reality nor the written records – essentially the Ebla texts – allow for a clear-cut conclusion. Admittedly, Tell Ahmar possessed a monumental funerary complex whose symbolic role, perhaps linked to the veneration of a common ancestor, is difficult to deny, but the site cannot be reduced to this complex. It also possessed a temple whose size and high position, dominating the valley, shows that its influence must have gone beyond the local level. On the other hand, no evidence of fortification could be found for the period when these monuments were in use. To the east the temple, resting on a high podium, was not protected by any defensive structure and, to the south, the street coming up from the valley made it impossible that any defensive structure could have been erected there. The large terrace that seems to have consolidated the tell was not very likely to have had a military role. Material evidence points to a ceremonial rather residential or defensive function for the site.

The image drawn by the written documentation – essentially the Ebla archives, which date from the twenty-fourth century – leaves little room for small, mobile, autonomous communities roaming in the region and competing for the control of the territory. On the contrary, it reveals a system in which large urban centres such as Ebla, Nagar (Tell Brak), Mari, Kish or, a little later, Agade exercized authority over a series of smaller settlements organized in a hierarchy that facilitated their control.[37] Northern Syria and Mesopotamia had adopted an urban lifestyle and were interacting, sometimes violently, in the context of a hierarchical society dominated by regional powers. The individual autonomy of the local communities must have been rather slim in such a system. Mobile pastoralists such as those of Ibal and Martu operated further south.

On the contrary the existence of local ceremonial sites assuming a symbolic function within an urban context is well illustrated by the Ebla texts.[38] In the ritual of the royal wedding, the king and the queen went on a long procession, which lasted for several days, and stopped in various places to make offerings and perform some rites. Of special importance was NEnaš, described as "house of death" which means something like "mausoleum". The exact location of NEnaš is unknown, but it was not at Ebla. Another focus of the dynastic cult was Darib, assumed to be modern Atareb on the road to the Amuq plain. Other places were the cult centre of a specific deity, to whom prayers were addressed and offerings dedicated on particular occasions. Some of these places were politically and economically insignificant. Their importance stemmed from the presence of a particular temple or of the tomb of one or more royal ancestors. Tell Ahmar may have been such a symbolic place even though the institutional-ideological framework in which it was inserted is unknown.

This role would be clearer if the political geography of the Tell Ahmar region were better known. Only two sites have been identified with certainty, namely Carchemish upstream from Tell Ahmar and Emar downstream. The identification of a third site, Tell Bazi with Armi,[39] remains problematic. A treaty concluded by Ebla with Abarsal[40] – perhaps to be identified with Tell Chuera in Upper Mesopotamia[41] or Roman Barsalium on the Euphrates much further upstream from Tell Ahmar[42] – tends to show that most of the left bank of the Euphrates between Carchemish and Emar could

have been under Abarsal's control.[43] Further east, Harran, with which Ebla had intense relations,[44] was the seat of a local power. Coincidentally, it is interesting to note that the shortest road from Ebla to Harran went through Tell Ahmar.

Tell Ahmar had become part of a system in which Northern Syria and Mesopotamia interacted and adopted an urban lifestyle in a hierarchical society dominated by regional powers. Its exact place in this system still eludes us, but reducing the site to the role of a fortress[45] – a role that is not confirmed by archaeology – or seeing it only as a tomb raised to the rank of a unifying symbol for a mobile population[46] does not account for the diversity of the remains that have been uncovered. At the present stage of research, Tell Ahmar in the second half of the third millennium looks like a ceremonial centre – both cultic and funerary – serving a community that was not necessarily located in its close proximity.

Notes

1   *Til-Barsib*, pp. 120–124 (M. Dunand).

2   Sample TAH 99 A15 F15.109 = UtC-9924: 6185±45 BP, 68.2% 5260–5050 cal BC (1.00), 95.4% 5300–4990 cal BC (1.00) (analysis made at the Belgian Royal Institute for Cultural Heritage).

3   H. HAMMADE & Y. YAMAZAKI, *Tell al-'Abr (Syria): Ubaid and Uruk periods*, Mémoires de l'Association pour le progrès de l'histoire et de l'archéologie orientales 4, Leuven-Paris-Dudley (MA), 2006.

4   Y. NISHIAKI & T. MATSUTANI (ed.), *Tell Kosak Shamali: The archaeological investigations on the Upper Euphrates, Syria*, 1, *Chalcolithic architecture and the earlier prehistoric remains*, UMUT Monograph 1, Oxford 2001. The possibility that one of the excavated houses was a tripartite house is raised by the authors but dismissed as not very likely (pp. 92–93).

5   Y. YAMAZAKI, The terminal Ubaid assemblage of Tell al-'Abr and its identity, *After the Ubaid: Interpreting change from the Caucasus to Mesopotamia at the dawn of urban civilization (4500–3500)*, ed. C. MARRO, Varia Anatolica XXVII, Paris 2012, p. 186 (I thank D. Giannessi for this reference).

6   Preliminary reports on the Habuba excavations were published in *Mitteilungen der Deutschen Orientgesellschaft* 101 (1969) to 108 (1976). For Tell Kannas, see provisionally A. FINET (ed.), *Lorsque la royauté descendit du ciel...: Les fouilles belges du Tell Kannâs sur l'Euphrate en Syrie*, Mariemont-Louvain-la-Neuve 1983.

7   G. van DRIEL & C. van DRIEL-MURRAY, Jebel Aruda 1977–1978, *Akkadica* 12 (1979), pp. 2–28; EID., Jebel Aruda, the 1982 season of excavation, interim report, *Akkadica* 33 (1983), pp. 1–26.

8   E. PELTENBURG, E.J.H. EASTAUGH, M. HEWSON, A. JACKSON, A. McCARTHY & T. RYMER, Jerablus-Tahtani, Syria, 1998–9: Preliminary report, *Levant* 32 (2000), pp. 53–75; F. STEPHEN & E. PELTENBURG, Scientific analysis of Uruk ceramics from Jerablus Tahtani and other Middle–Upper Euphrates sites, *Artefacts of Complexity: Tracking the Uruk in the Near East*, ed. N. POSTGATE, London 2002, pp. 173–190.

9   See the web site <http://aushariye.hum.ku.dk/english/earliest_remains/>.

10 H. HAMMADE & Y. YAMAZAKI, *op. cit.* (n. 3).

11 *Associated Regional Chronologies for the Ancient Near East and the Eastern Mediterranean*, IV, *Middle Euphrates*, ed. U. FINKBEINER, M. NOVÁK, F. SAKAL & P. SCONZO, Turnhout 2015.

12 Strata A15/1, A15/2 and A15/3 correspond to Strata A, B and C of the excavation report published in *Tell Ahmar, 1988 Season*, Abr-Nahrain Supplement Series 2, Leuven 1990, pp. 11–24.

13 *Til-Barsib*, pp. 96–119 (M. Dunand).

14 Her preliminary observations have been published in C. BACCARIN, Burial practices in the middle Euphrates area during the early Bronze Age: The contribution of the hypogeum of Tell Ahmar (north Syria), *Broadening Horizons 3. Conference of Young Researchers Working in the Ancient Near East*, ed. F. BORRELL TENA, Bellaterra (Barcelone) 2012, pp. 137–149; EAD., The Hypogeum of Tell Ahmar: An analysis of the monumental burial complex in the context of the Early Bronze Age funerary practice, *Ancient Near Eastern Studies* 51 (2014), pp. 213–225.

15 Sample A19.40 S19.20 = UtC-7244: 3855±40 BP; 68.3%: 2399–2375 cal BC (0.15), 2358–2274 cal BC (0.59), 2251–2205 cal BC (0.25); 95.4%: 2455–2196 cal BC (1.00) (analysis made at the Belgian Royal Institute for Cultural Heritage).

16 Sample A19.40 S19.21 = IRPA-1240: 3785±30 BP; 68.3%: 2275–2236 cal BC (0.33), 2206–2171 cal BC (0.35), 2169–2141 cal BC (0.32); 95.4%: 2290–2131 cal BC (0.94), 2077–2047 cal BC (0.06) (analysis made at the Belgian Royal Institute for Cultural Heritage).

17 Sample A19.39 S19.19 = UtC-7243: 3880±30 BP; 68.3%: 2451–2429 cal BC (0.18); 2403–2308 cal BC (0.82); 95.4%: 2459–2276 cal BC (0.97), 2226–2207 cal BC (0.03) (analysis made at the Belgian Royal Institute for Cultural Heritage).

18 C.L. WOOLLEY, *The Royal Cemetery*, Ur Excavations II, London-Philadelphia 1934, pp. 78, 556 and pl. 166.

19 L. DUGAY, Early Bronze Age burials from Tell Ahmar, *Si un homme ... Textes offerts en hommage à André Finet*, ed. P. TALON & V. VAN DER STEDE, Subartu, XVI, Turnhout 2005, pp. 37–49.

20 *Til-Barsib*, plan C.

21 G. BUNNENS, Unfinished work at Tell Ahmar: Early and Middle Bronze Age finds, *Archaeological Explorations in Syria 2000–2011* (Proceedings of ISCACH-Beirut 2015), ed. J. ABDUL MASSIH, Sh. NISHIYAMA, H. CHARAF & A. DEB, Oxford, p. 31.

22 *Til-Barsib*, pp. 108–110 (M. Dunand).

23 A. PORTER, The dynamics of death: Ancestors, pastoralism, and the origins of a third-millenniun city in Syria, *Bulletin of the American Schools of Oriental Research* 325 (Feb. 2002), pp. 11–16; EAD., Communities in conflict: Death and the contest for social order in the Euphrates river valley, *Near Eastern Archaeology* 65 (2002), pp. 160–161.

24 E. PELTENBURG (ed.), *Mortuary Practices at an Early Bronze Age Fort on the Euphrates River*, Tell Jerablus Tahtani, Syria, 1, Levant Supplement Series 17, Oxford 2015, pp. 45–67.

25 A. ARCHI, Cult of the ancestors and funerary practices at Ebla, *(Re-)Constructing Funerary Rituals in the Ancient Near East* (Proceedings of the First International Symposium of the Tübingen Post-Graduate School "Symbols of the Dead" in May 2009), ed. P. PFÄLZNER, H. NIEHR, E. PERNICKA, & A. WISSING, Wiesbaden 2012, pp. 7–9; ID., Remarks on ethnoarchaeology and death in the ancient Near East, *How to Cope with Death: Mourning and funerary practices in the Ancient Near East* (Proceedings of the International Workshop – Firenze, 5th–6th December), ed. C. FELLI, Ricerche di Archeologia del Vicino Oriente 5, Pisa 2017, pp. 32–34.

26 G. BUNNENS, A third millennium temple at Tell Ahmar (Syria), *Proceedings of the 9th International Congress on the Archaeology of the Ancient Near East* 3, *Reports*, ed. O. KAELIN & H.-P. MATHYS, Wiesbaden 2016, pp. 187–198; ID., *art. cit.* (n. 21), pp. 32–35.

27 Sample TAH 2010–331 Poz-64514 3879±35 BP.

28 Sample S10.35 S01 = UtC-9242: 4030±40 BP; 68.2 %: 2620–2610 cal BC (0.05), 2580–2470 cal BC (0.95); 95.4 %: 2840–2810 cal BC (0.02), 2670–2460 cal BC (0.98) (analysis made at the Belgian Royal Institute for Cultural Heritage).

29 C. BACCARIN, Consumption in a temple? An interpretation of the ceramic repertoire of the Early Bronze Age temple at Tell Ahmar (north Syria), *Proceedings of the 9th International Congress on the Archaeology of the Ancient Near East* 3, *Reports*, ed. O. KAELIN & H.-P. MATHYS, Wiesbaden 2016, pp. 163–175.

30 A. ROOBAERT, Fragments de sculptures en bois retrouvés dans un temple du IIIᵉ millénaire av. J.-C. à Tell Ahmar (Syrie), (forthcoming).

31 G. MATILLA SÉIQUER *et al.*, *Tell Qara Qûzâq – III: Campañas VII–XI (1995–1999)*, Aula Orientalis, Supplementa 29, Sabadell (Barcelona) 2012, pp. 78–86, fig. 18–27 and pl. 4/11–18; P. MIGLUS & E. STROMMENGER, *Tall Biʾa–Tuttul*, VIII, *Stadtbefestigungen, Häuser und Tempel*, Saarbrücken 2001, pls 129/10 and 130/6.

32 A. T. ÖKSE, A 'high' terrace at Gre Virike to the north of Carchemish: power of local rulers as founders?, *Euphrates Valley Settlement: The Carchemish sector in the third millennium BC*, ed. E. PELTENBURG, Levant Supplement Series 5, Oxford 2007, pp. 94–104.

33 F. LÜTH, Tell Halawa B, *Halawa 1977 bis 1979: Vorläufiger Bericht über die 1. bis 3. Grabungskampagne*, ed. W. ORTHMANN, Saarbrücker Beiträge zur Altertumskunde 31, Bonn 1981, pp. 91–92, 97, 98, 99, 109, Beilagen 12–16.

34 C. KEPINSKI-LECOMTE & R. ERGEÇ, Tilbeshar 1998, *Anatolia Antiqua* 7 (1999), pp. 245–247.

35 A. PORTER, The dynamics of death: Ancestors, pastoralism, and the origins of a third-millennium city in Syria, *Bulletin of the American Schools of Oriental Research* 325 (Feb. 2002), pp. 1–36.

36 E. PELTENBURG, Conflict and exclusivity in Early Bronze Age societies of the Middelle Euphrates Valley, *Journal of Near Eastern Studies* 72 (2013), pp. 233–252.

37 See for instance A. ARCHI, Polity interaction in the age of Ebla, in *Proceedings of the International Symposium on Syria and the Ancient Near East*, ed. F. ISMAIL, Aleppo 1995, pp. 13–17; C. CASTELLE & E. PELTENBURG, Urbanism on the margins: Third millennium BC Al-Rawda in the arid zone of Syria,

Antiquity 81/313 (2007), pp. 601–616; M.G. BIGA, Au-delà des frontières: guerre et diplomatie à Ébla, *Orientalia* NS 77 (2008), pp. 289–334.

38 A. ARCHI, Cult of the ancestors and funerary practices at Ebla, *(Re-)Constructing Funerary Rituals in the Ancient Near East* (Proceedings of the First International Symposium of the Tübingen Post-Graduate School "Symbols of the Dead" in May 2009), ed. P. PFÄLZNER, H. NIEHR, E. PERNICKA & A. WISSING, Wiesbaden 2012, pp. 5–31; ID., Religious duties for a royal family: Basing the ideology of social power at Ebla, *Journal of Near Eastern Studies* 76 (2017), pp. 293–306.

39 A. OTTO, Archaeological perspectives on the localization of Naram-Sin's Armanum, *Journal of Cuneiform Studies* 58 (2006), pp. 1–26; EAD & M.G. BIGA, Thoughts about the identification of Tall Bazi with Armi of the Ebla texts, *Proceedings of the 6th International Congress on the Archaeology of the Ancient Near East* I, ed. P. MATTHIAE, F. PINNOCK, L. NIGRO & N. MARCHETTI, Wiesbaden 2010, pp. 481–494.

40 P. FRONZAROLI, *Testi di cancelleria: I rapporti con le città (archivio L. 2769)*, Archivi Reali di Ebla, Testi XIII, Rome 2003, No 5, pp. 43–76.

41 A. ARCHI, P. PIACENTINI & F. POMPONIO, *I nomi di luogo dei testi di Ebla (ARET I–IV, VII–X e altri documenti editi e inediti)*, Archivi Reali di Ebla, Studi II, Rome 1993, pp. 89–91.

42 G. BUNNENS, Site hierarchy in the Tishrin Dam area and third millennium geopolitics in northern Syria, *Euphrates Valley Settlement: The Carchemish sector in the third millennium BC,* ed. E. PELTENBURG, Levant Supplement Series 5, Oxford 2007, pp. 49–50.

43 A. ARCHI, La ville d'Abarsal, *Reflets des deux Fleuves: Mélanges André Finet*, ed. M. LEBEAU & P. TALON, Leuven 1989, pp. 15–19.

44 A. ARCHI, Ḫarran in the III millennium B.C., *Ugarit-Forschungen* 20 (1988), pp. 1–8.

45 E. PELTENBURG, *art. cit.* (n. 36), p. 238.

46 A. PORTER, *Mobile Pastoralism and the Formation of Near Eastern Civilizations: Weaving together society*, Cambridge 2012, p. 197.

2

Tell Ahmar in the second millennium

None of the remains excavated during the French excavations could be dated, at least formally, to the Middle or Late Bronze Age. The renewed excavations have been more fortunate. Exploration of the south-eastern sector of the tell, at the junction of Area A with Area S, has made it possible to recognize a stratigraphic sequence that shows how the third millennium ruins were progressively covered by the second millennium occupation.

1. Independent Syria (c. 2000–1600)

a. The beginnings of the second millennium (c. 2000–1800)

The second millennium opens with a period of instability marked by movements of populations, among which are the Amorites who rose to power in most urban centres.

At Tell Ahmar, the third millennium temple was never rebuilt, which should be taken as a sign of radical break in the development of the site. It was a frequent occurrence for places of worship to survive the jolts of history, either because the cult was perpetuated in the very place where it was practised, or because a new cult tried to annihilate the old one by taking its place. Nothing of the kind happened here. Clear evidence of the rupture was shown by the construction of four large ovens of the *tannur* type directly on top of the ruins of the temple (*Figs 68* and *69*). These ovens, which measured about 1 m in diameter, were much larger than most *tannur*s and probably represented a sporadic re-occupation of the site (Stratum A+S/16).

This brief re-occupation seems to have been followed by a period of abandonment, because, if no significant accumulation had yet occurred at the time of the *tannurs'* construction, the re-occupation of Stratum A+S/15 was cut into the tell's flank when the remains of the temple were no longer visible, *i.e.* after they had disappeared under the accumulation resulting from natural erosion. This is revealed by a peculiarity of the west and north walls of the rooms marked 4 and 5 on *Figure 70*. The extreme irregularity of

their outer surface contrasted sharply, especially in Room 4, with the regularity of their inner surface. Walls built in this way must have been fragile and can only be understood if Rooms 4 and 5 were built by cutting into the tell so that the west and north walls were leaning directly against the artificial face of the mound. As the floor of the group of Rooms 4–5–6 is higher by about 80–90 cm than that of the

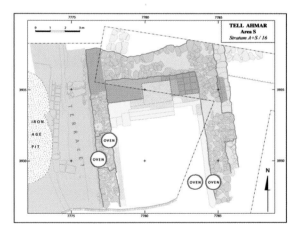

Fig. 68. Plan of Stratum A+S/16.

Fig. 69. Ovens of Stratum A+S/16 (looking SE). Two of the four excavated ovens, one (S14 F27) on top of the stone base of the east wall of the temple, the other (S14 F28) dug into the floor.

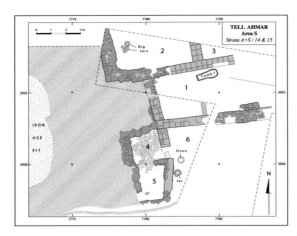

Fig. 70. Plan of Strata A+S/14 and 15. The tell, represented by the hatched area on the plan, has been cut into to make room for the structures.

Fig. 71. Strata A+S/14 and 15: Rooms 4 and 5 (looking SW).

temple, one can conclude that a period of abandonment followed the destruction of the third millennium sanctuary and the brief re-occupation of Stratum A+S/16. This allowed the process of tell formation to continue until a new occupation – Stratum A+S/15 – was established in the Middle Bronze Age on a flat area obtained by cutting into the flank of the tell.

The constructions of Stratum A+S/15 comprised six separate rooms or spaces (*Fig. 70*) and might represent two phases of occupation. Some floors were found at an elevation of approximately 99.00 – Rooms 2 (western part), 4 and 5 – and other floors at an elevation of 98.70/98.50 – Rooms 2 (eastern part), 3 and 6. No floor was recognized in Room 1. The unity of the stratum, however, is made likely by the continuity of the walls, in particular the south wall of Rooms 2 and 3, and the west wall of Room 1 but, in order to keep the possibility of two independent strata, the lower floors are considered to belong to Stratum A+S/15 and the higher floors to Stratum A+S/14.

This architectural ensemble can be subdivided into two units, the most coherent of which was organized around the small room marked 4 on the plan (*Figs 70* and *71*). This room communicated, to the south, with a trapezoid-shaped room – Room 5 – and, to the east, it opened onto Room 6, which may have been a courtyard.

Fig. 72. Stratum A+S/14: large pedestal jar from Room 2 (S2 PL458) (drawing: Andrew S. Jamieson).

The organization of the northern part was less clear. Rooms 2 and 3 seemed to have been two rooms of one construction, which extended northwards beyond the excavated area. The wall that delimited these rooms to the south rested directly on the north wall of the third millennium temple, whose ruins were preserved on a higher level here. Room 1 could have been only an open space separating the southern ensemble (Rooms 4, 5 and 6) from the northern one (Rooms 2 and 3). The western wall of Room 1 would have had the sole function of retaining the land on this side.

Two large vessels lay on the upper floor of Room 2. One stands out not only because it is almost completely preserved but also because its shape, with a foot, is poorly attested (*Fig. 72*). A similar specimen was found at Halawa, in the region of the Great Bend of the Euphrates, where the excavators dated it to the beginning of the second millennium, *i.e.* to the Middle Bronze Age I.[1]

In Room 1 an enigmatic feature was uncovered against the north wall. It was a pit whose walls were consolidated by the application of a thick layer of mud plaster. The shape of the pit, which was wider towards the east than towards the west, and its dimensions – about 1.50 m long and 60 cm wide – suggested that it could have been a tomb, although it was only about 30 cm deep and no bones were found in it. The problem is to know whether it was dug from Stratum A+S/15 or from higher.

The solution came from a few sherds found around the pit as well as in the pit itself. These sherds could be assembled to form the neck and rim of a jug of the so-called *Syro-Cilician Ware* and, more specifically, of the so-called Eye-Vase type, which has a neck decorated with two eyes (*Fig 73*)[2] The area of greatest frequency of this type of ceramic corresponds to the region of Tarsus in Cilicia and the Amuq plain in the lower Orontes valley, hence its name Syro-Cilician. However, some examples have been found outside this area, particularly at Ebla. This pottery is generally dated to around 1800 (Middle Bronze Age II). Such a date is hardly compatible with the date suggested by the pedestal vase, but it is understandable if the pit with which the ceramic fragments were associated was dug from a later stratum, which unfortunately cannot be identified.

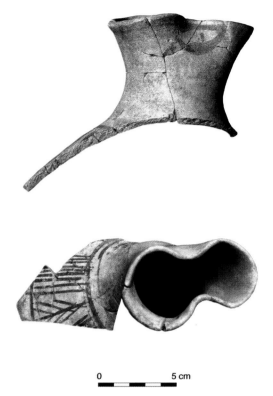

Fig. 73. Stratum A+S/14: Fragment of a Syro-Cilician jug (S3 PL473+478).

The period to which Strata A+S/14 and 15 belonged would therefore be around the beginning of the Middle Bronze Age (Middle Bronze I), when the Amorite dynasties were taking control of the urban centres of northern Syria. Judging by the admittedly small surface that could be explored and by the nature of its architecture, Tell Ahmar was probably a modest rural settlement at that time.

A series of occupation surfaces, belonging to Strata A+S/13 and A+S/12, covered the remains just described. They consisted of stone walls and wall foundations which, although they did not form complete plans, provided enough evidence to show that the establishment as a whole was gaining in importance.

b. The apogee of independent Syrian states (c. 1800–1600)

The Near East, around 1800, entered a new period of prosperity (Middle Bronze Age II), about which the Mari archives shed a vivid light. Rulers, whose names belonged to the Amorite group of West Semitic languages, reigned over the main kingdoms of the time and maintained relations between them, sometimes peaceful, sometimes violent, in a diplomatic game where the reversal of alliances was constant. From Ugarit to Babylon, from Carchemish to Hazor, messengers, merchandise – armies as well – moved, met or fought each other. Such an intensity of exchange was

unknown since the second half of the third millennium, when the Ebla archives shed light on a similar game of alternately friendly and conflictual relations. Two Hittite military campaigns, one led by Hattushili I and the other by Murshili I, put an end to this period towards the end of the seventeenth century.

Tell Ahmar, whose name is not known at that time, was on the border of various areas of influence. The Mari archives show that the short-lived kingdom of Upper Mesopotamia, during the time of Shamshi-Addu (eighteenth century), maintained trade relations with Asia Minor. It must therefore have been interested in the Upper Euphrates valley and in the Tell Ahmar region. The same archive shows the importance of the kingdom of Yamhad, whose capital was Aleppo. Zimri-Lim of Mari married a daughter of the king of Aleppo. The archives of Shehna (Tell Leilan), a little later, suggest that Yamhad also had interests in Northern Mesopotamia, and Tell Ahmar was on the most direct road leading from Aleppo to Upper Mesopotamia. Closer to the site, Carchemish gained power and may have extended its domination over Tell Ahmar. To the south, Emar, the great river port on the road linking southern Mesopotamia to the Mediterranean coast, dominated a portion of the Euphrates.

The renaissance that marked the Middle Bronze Age II period also affected Tell Ahmar.

House S3

On the south-eastern slope of the tell, the remains of a house, House S3 formed the bulk of Stratum A+S/11 (*Fig. 74*).[3] Its walls were made of mud-brick on a stone base. The plan appeared to be almost complete (*Fig. 75*). It consisted of four rooms and an open space.

Room 1 contained many pottery sherds and several complete vessels as well as basalt implements, among them a tripod bowl and grinding stones in the shape of clothing irons (*Fig. 76*).

Room 1 connected with Room 2 through a doorway with a stone threshold. The floor of Room 2 was laid at a lower level. A large jar was buried in the north-east corner of the room and a fragment of clay strip with the impression of a seal was found near the jar (*Fig. 77*). Three figures bearing a spear and walking to the right could be recognized on this impression. These figures had been carved perpendicularly to the axis of rotation of the cylinder, so that they looked as if they were lying down when the seal was unrolled horizontally. Above the three spear-bearers was a scorpion flanked by two birds which had been carved in the direction of the axis of rotation. This clay strip must have served as a tag, perhaps to identify the jar or its owner.

The south wall of Room 2 was destroyed, eroded away together with the south flank of the tell. It may not have been in line with the south wall of the neighbouring room (Room 3), as the floor of Room 2, as well as the wall separating the two rooms, extended beyond the southern boundary of Room 3.

The threshold of the door that connected Room 2 to Room 3 was slightly higher than the floor of the two rooms. A door in the south wall gave access to a paved space, marked 4 on the plan, which must have been a small courtyard protected from the east wind by a low

Fig. 74. Stratum A+S/11: House S3 (looking S). In the foreground on the left is the excavation trench from the late 1990s, in which part of the building had already been explored.

wall. Room 3 was a kitchen subdivided into three parts. Room 3a formed a kind of corridor linking Rooms 2, 3 and Courtyard 4. Room 3b included a cylindrical oven of the *tannur* type and a flat basalt grinding stone. A kind of recess, Room 3c, seems to have been built in the south-east corner. It was delimited by a few stones to the west and a brick mass to the north that is more likely to have been a bench then the base of a wall.

A partition wall subdivided Room 5 into two parts, Room 5a to the west and Room 5b to the east. In Room 5b a paved surface was covered by a plastered floor. In Room 5a there was a solid mass of bricks whose function might have been to support stairs leading to a possible storey. If this were the case, one might think that the storey only covered part of the house – above Rooms 1 and 5 – thus adopting a layout illustrated by terracotta house models, well known in the Euphrates valley, which represent houses of which the rear half was covered by a storey. However, the explanation is not without difficulties. It should be noted, for example, that the wall that separated Room 5a from Room 5b and the mass of bricks in Room 5a rested on the floor. They must therefore have been a later addition to the building. This

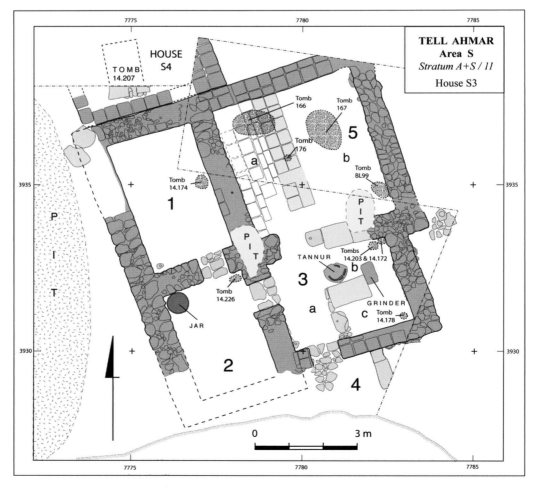

Fig. 75. Stratum A+S/11: Plan of House S3.

implies either that the upper storey was also an addition or that in the first state of construction the upper storey was accessed by another means, perhaps a wooden staircase. It should also be noted that no debris fallen from the upper storey was found during the excavation, which further reduces the possibility of the presence of one.

The location of the main door of the building deserves some clarification. The plan published in a preliminary

Fig. 76. House S3: Basalt implements found on the floor of Room 1. Three grinding stones in the shape of a clothing iron (a: S14 BsL33; b: S14 BsL30; d: S14 BsL31) and a tripod bowl (c: S14 BsL32).

report shows a door in the west wall of Room 1.[4] Its presence had been suggested by the existence of flat stones, which, extending across the outer wall of the building, looked like the slabs of a threshold. As the wall was almost completely destroyed at this point, the hypothesis of a doorway seemed more than plausible. In the course of further excavation, however, it became apparent that the slabs were in fact large stones which rested on top of other large stones. This called into question the hypothesis of a threshold. Doubts were further confirmed when it was noted that a plaster coating ran on a height of about 10 cm along the base of the destroyed wall and of the assumed threshold. It thus became clear that the plaster coating was all that was preserved of a vanished wall. The entrance to the house had therefore to be looked for elsewhere. The only other known access was the doorway connecting Courtyard 4 with the kitchen (Room 3). However, considering that it is not very likely that the main entrance was through the kitchen, there only remains the possibility that the main access was through the now vanished south wall of Room 2.

Several tombs appeared under House S3, in accordance with a widespread custom in ancient Western Asia. Burials, especially of children, were often dug in the houses that the living continued to occupy. Of the nine tombs identified, only two (Tombs S2+3 F166 and S2+3 F167), perhaps three (Tomb S2+3 BL99), were adult graves, all under Room 5. The others contained the bodies of infants or young children.

0   5 cm

Fig. 77. House S3: Fragment of a clay tag found in Room 2 (S14 O.12).

A first child's grave was under Room 1, against the east wall, about halfway between its extremities (Tomb S14 F174). The body rested on half a jar and was not accompanied by any offerings. A similar tomb was found in the north-eastern corner of Room 2 (Tomb S14 F226). The child had also been laid on half a jar and without offerings. In addition, this tomb had been covered with a quadrangular stone, which, over time, had crushed the tomb's contents. A third tomb was uncovered in the south-east corner of Room 3 (Tomb S14 F178). It is not certain, however, whether the body, as in the previous cases, rested on half a jar. Sherds covered the body and, although they could not be assembled to reconstruct a complete jar, it is not impossible that the burial took place in a damaged jar which was more than half preserved and whose upper part would have been broken by soil compaction. Two burials were dug in the north-east corner of Room 3, practically one above the other (*Fig. 78b*). The upper burial, another young child, was dug in open ground and covered with pottery sherds. It contained a small carinated bowl and a bronze earring near the left ear. The lower burial, still that of a child, was noteworthy by both its layout – two fragments of a large jar that had been laid flat – and the quality of its offerings, which consisted of a carinated bowl, a small bottle, as well as a necklace made of red jasper and a bronze pin (*Fig. 78a*).

The adult graves found under Room 5 were dug into Stratum A+S/12a, immediately below the level of House S3 (A+S/11). Tomb S2+3 BL99 in the south-east corner of Room 5b, was heavily damaged. Only fragments of a skull and arm bones, possibly of an adult, were found, together with a small carinated bowl (PL 02.391). Another tomb, Tomb S2+3 F176 under the partitioning wall, must have been a small jar burial judging by the sherds associated with it. It contained bones of a child. A third tomb, Tomb S2+3 F166, extended both under the partitioning wall and under Room 5a. It was a pit burial, which had partly destroyed one of the walls of Stratum A+S/12a. An adult had been laid down in bent position, lying on his right side with his head to the east. According to Jean-Marie Cordy of Liège University, the tomb also contained the remains of a child. It is possible that this was a double burial, an adult having been buried with a child, but it is more likely that the adult's grave had damaged a child's grave when it was dug.

Finally, in the northern part of Room 5b, a large jar burial, Tomb S2+3 F167, turned out to be the richest of the tombs excavated under House S3 (*Fig. 79*).[5] It was oriented approximately north–south and contained a body in a flexed position, lying on its left side with its head to the north. According to Jean-Marie Cordy, the tomb also contained the remains of a child and the bones of a young sheep. These animal bones can be understood as a funerary offering but the remains of a child are more difficult to explain. In the southern half were burnt bones and charcoal fragments. The tomb also contained two carinated bowls and a plate

(*Fig. 79b*) as well as a bronze toggle pin (*Fig. 79a*) and a haematite cylinder seal (*Fig. 79c*). The seal was probably attached by a cord to the eye of the pin, following a known practice. The scene carved on the seal showed a male figure – a prince or a king – facing right and raising his right hand in a gesture of respect to a female deity standing on a bull. The deity was identified with the rain goddess by Adelheid Otto. Behind the deity, to the right, another deity in a long robe also raises both hands. A secondary scene comprised two registers separated by a guilloche: in the upper register a couple was sitting on either side of a vase with flowing water and the lower register was entirely occupied by a sphinx. Again according to Adelheid Otto, the style and motifs had affinities with the seals of Yamhad and the neighbouring kingdom of Carchemish. The seal could date from around 1750–1725. The C[14] analysis of a charcoal fragment from Tomb S2+3 F167 does not help to clarify the chronology. It suggests a date between 1940 and 1690.[6]

House S3 disappeared in an intense fire. It also seems to have been violently shaken. The wall separating Rooms 1 and 5 was leaning eastwards in the direction of the slope of the tell. At the same time, the threshold of the door connecting Room 1 to Room 2 had subsided to the east (*Fig. 80*) and a crack was created along the wall between Room 1 and Room 5 (*Fig. 81*). This crack was filled with a large quantity of pottery and debris from the destruction of the building, which rules out post-disaster ground movements.

Fig. 78. House S3: Child burials in the NE corner of Room 3 a) offerings from Burial S14 F203: jasper necklace (S14 O.215), bronze toggle pin (S14 O.214), carinated bowl (S14 PL728), small bottle (S14 PL729); b) the upper burial (S14 F172) is visible in the corner above the lower jar burial (S14 F203).

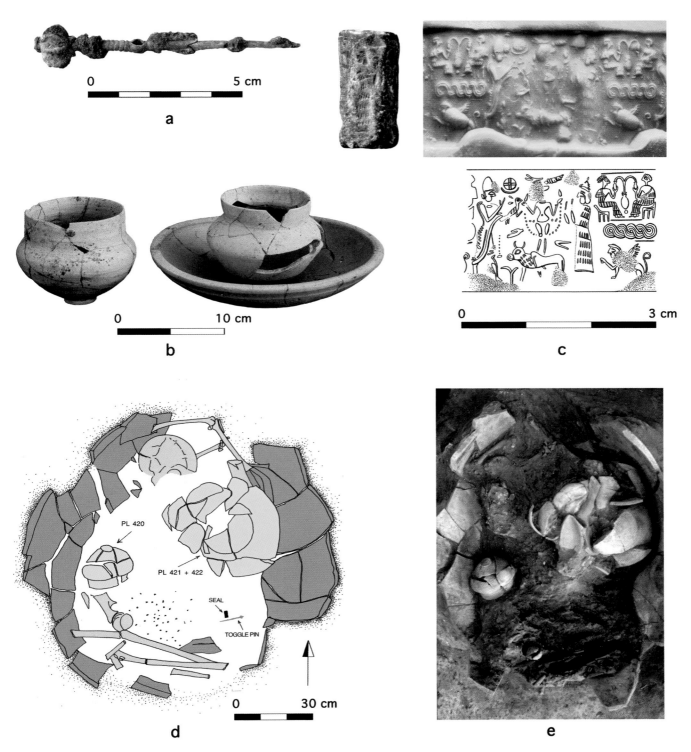

Fig. 79. Jar burial S2+3 F167: a) bronze toggle pin (S2+3 O.180); b) two carinated bowls (S2+3 PL420, S2+3 PL422) and shallow bowl (S2+3 PL421); c) seal S2+3 O.179 (drawing: Adelheid Otto); d) drawing (Andrew S. Jamieson); e) photo of the burial.

The most likely explanation is that House S3 was affected by lateral movements of the kind earthquakes can produce. House S3 may therefore have been destroyed by a natural cause and not as a result of human intervention.

A sample of charcoal from the kitchen (Room 3) gave a date around 1760/1630.[7] The destruction of the building must therefore have occurred at the turn of the eighteenth and seventeenth century.

A burial vault

To the north of House S3, and adjoining it, was another construction, most of which extended northwards into the unexcavated area (House S4) (see plan in *Fig. 75*). Under this building, behind Room 1, a tomb – Tomb S14 F207 – had been built. It was more monumental than the tombs

usually found underneath the floor of houses (*Fig. 82*)[8]. Oriented north–south, it was built of stones and about 1.60 m wide on the outside (1 m on the inside) and 1.70 m long on the inside. The floor was paved with stones (*Fig. 85*) and the roof was made up of six limestone slabs, inclined at about 45°, arranged in groups of three on either side of the chamber so as to form a pitched roof (*Fig. 83*). Long stones were placed at the top of this structure to form a kind of rudimentary keystone. The entrance, probably

Fig. 80. House S3: Doorway between Rooms 1 and 2 (looking N).

Fig. 81. House S3: South-east corner of Room 1 (looking SE).

Fig. 82. Tomb S14 F207: South wall before opening the tomb.

Fig. 83. Tomb S14 F207: Roof of the tomb. The photo was taken at the beginning of the excavation before the floor was reached.

Fig. 84. Tomb F14.207: Disjointed bones of at least three skeletons.

Fig. 85. Tomb S14 F207: Pavement of the tomb.

located to the north, was closed by a large triangular slab. Towards the south, the tomb was closed by several irregular stones. The total height of the ensemble was about 1 m (*Fig. 82*).

The grave, which could not be entirely excavated due to the outbreak of war, contained a large bowl and a surprisingly large number of disjointed bones, including skulls of young adolescents (*Figs 84* and *85*). It must have been a family vault, in which the bodies already laid to rest were pushed back to make room for a new burial. Also surprising was the number of sheep bones mixed with human bones. The burials were probably accompanied by meat offerings.

Administrative Building Complex

In the Middle Bronze Age II, an unusual group of constructions stood on top of the tell, in Area M (*Fig. 86* and *87*).[9] Five architectural units, each consisting of a series of rooms, were built side by side with a slight change in orientation

Fig. 86. Middle Bronze Age Administrative Complex (Area M) (looking E). A fragment of the Iron Age pebble mosaic (see p. 88) is visible in the bottom left corner.

so that the whole complex formed an arc. Access to each of these units was from the south. The buildings were closed on the north side. The three central units – referred to, from west to east, as Blocks 1, 2 and 3 – were the most impressive.

Block 1 consisted of three rooms, with access via the central room (*Fig. 88*). From there, a door led to Room 3 to the west. The access to Room 1 to the east was blocked by carefully laid bricks. It is probable that in the final state of the building, the entrance to the room was from above. Wooden debris was found in the room, which may have belonged to a ladder or staircase. The walls of Block 1 were very thick: 1.60 m for the south wall and 1 m for the north wall, which at some point was increased to 1.40 m. The outer face of this wall, before it was enlarged, was coated with white plaster. Finally, it should be noted that the south wall of this block was leaning inwards (*Fig. 89*). Block 1 contained several large jars with a high neck incised with wavy lines and a thick out-turned rim with a grooved decoration (*Fig. f*, p. 72). It also contained small vessels and basalt grinding stones. A bronze pin with a human figure on its head was retrieved from Room 3 (*Fig. 90*). Block 1 thus had the appearance of a small warehouse where goods such as oil, grain or flour, possibly also beer or wine, were stored.

Block 2 appears to have been built after Blocks 1 and 3 (*Fig. 91*). Its west and east walls formed an acute angle with its north wall and an obtuse angle with its south wall, as if they had had to follow the orientation of walls already existing on either sides. This block, whose north and south walls were 1.40 m wide, consisted of five rooms. Three of them – Rooms 1–3 to the west – were completely empty. No material or accumulation resulting from occupation has been identified. The small Rooms 2 and 3 (*Fig. 92*), separated by a wall 1.40 m thick, could have served as a

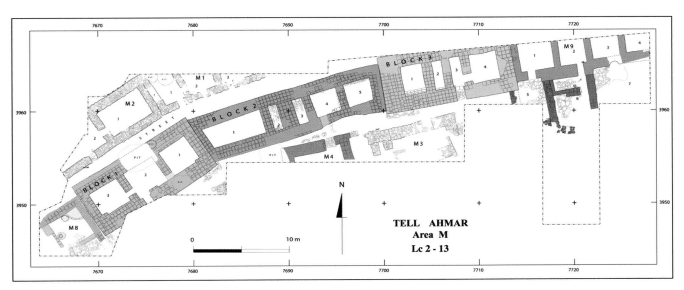

Fig. 87. Plan of the MBA Administrative Complex and later structures.

Fig. 88. Administrative Complex: Block 1 (looking NE).

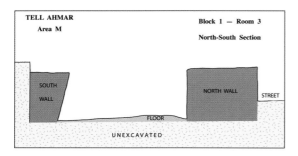

Fig. 89. Administrative Complex: Section across Room 3 of Block 1.

staircase, although it is not clear where the starting point of this staircase would have been. Rooms 4 and 5, on the other hand, were filled with a regular accumulation of ashy deposit containing pottery sherds. It is not impossible that Rooms 4 and 5 originally formed one room, as the wall separating them was not bonded into the outer walls of the building. A door at the western end of the south wall of Room 4 had been blocked and Room 5 had no door altogether. As with the south wall of Block 1, the south wall of Rooms 4 and 5 in Block 2 was leaning towards the inside of the building. The function of Block 2 remains unclear.

Block 3 consisted of four rooms (*Fig. 93*). Room 1, to the west, had no door and was sunk in the ground. Its floor was much lower than, for instance, the floor of Room 4. The difference in level was about 2 m. Room 2, which was very narrow like Rooms 2 and 3 in Block 2, was "empty" like them. Room 3, also very narrow, served as a vestibule to Room 4, which was the largest room in the block. A jar burial had been dug under the floor of Room 4, in the north-east corner (Tomb M11 F48). The bones were quite disturbed, but the body seemed to have been lying in a bent

Fig. 91. Administrative Complex: Block 2 (looking E).

Fig. 90. Administrative Complex: Bronze pin decorated with a human figure (M6 O.19).

Fig. 92. Administrative Complex: Rooms 2 and 3 of Block 2 (looking N).

position on its left side with its head to the east. It could be the body of a girl of about 12 years of age. No material, except for a knucklebone, appears to have accompanied her.

The finds in Rooms 1 and 4 were of particular interest. Room 1 was filled with blackish soil containing a large number of grains, apparently wheat. On the floor were a few mud-bricks, probably used to wedge the grain sacks stored in the room, and fragments of a large jar with a high neck, of the same kind as those found in Block 1 (*Fig. 94*). Mixed with the blackish fill were small vessels and a bronze sickle blade (*Fig. 95*). One might think that this room was used as a silo. However, considering that it was the only room in this building complex that contained grain, it is doubtful whether the quantities stored could have fed a large number of people. Rather, it must have been grain intended for sowing as has been suggested to the author by François Barbo. Most surprising, however, was the discovery of around fifteen lumps of clay with impressions of cylinder seals, as well as an actual cylinder seal made of baked clay (*Fig. 96*). Some of these clay lumps bore the imprint of a coarse cloth, probably from sackcloth, or of a basket (*Fig. d*, p. 66). The grains

found in the room must therefore have been kept in sealed bags. More interestingly, six of the seal impressions were obtained with the same seal, which had women as its central figures (*Fig. g*, p. 67). There is therefore a strong probability that the grain stored in Room 1 was stored there by an administration in charge of managing these reserves. It was not the personal property of a family.

A clay tag was lying on the threshold of the door between the entrance hall (Room 3) and Room 4 (*Fig. 97a–b*). It had been impressed with the seal figuring women, that had been used to produce six of the impressions found in Room 1. The profile of this tag was sinuous in shape and appeared to correspond to the profile of a large jar at the junction of the neck and the shoulder (*Fig. 97c*). It could therefore have been applied to a jar in order to identify, for example, its provenance or owner. As we saw above, a fragment of another tag was found in House S3. Tags of this kind were found at Tell Bi'a[10], among other places.

Room 4 yielded a dozen of clay lumps with cylinder seal impressions, some of which appear to have been used to seal bags. Most of them bore impressions made either with a seal involving the figure of the Storm-God (*Fig. f*, p. 67) or a seated figure holding a tree branch. The repeated use of the same seals would tend to confirm that an administration, holder of these seals, was operating in this building.

The three central blocks, although structurally independent, formed an architectural unit. Their dimensions and construction technique as well as the layout of the rooms show this clearly. At both ends were constructions of lesser

Fig. 93. Administrative Complex: Block 3 (looking E).

Fig. 95. Administrative Complex: Bronze sickle blade from Room 1 of Block 3 (M10 O.36).

Fig. 94. Administrative Complex: Artefacts scattered on the floor of Room 1 in Block 3 (looking SE).

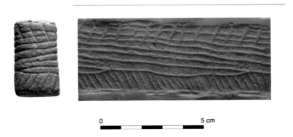

Fig. 96. Administrative Complex: Clay cylinder seal from Room 1 of Block 3 (M10 O.10.5).

architectural quality, which seem to have extended the central unit in eastern and western direction.

To the west of Block 1, a small, approximately square structure served as a kitchen (Building M8) (*Fig. 98*). An oven, a large jar, basalt millstones and two types of permanently installed earthen basins were found there, one semi-circular in the north-east corner and the other, smaller and elongated in shape, in the south-west corner. Its walls were thinner than those of the three central blocks and their bricks were much more crumbly. Towards the west, there was no wall in the strict sense of the word, but a block of masonry extended by a small partition wall. The north wall, however, the thickest of this building, extended westwards outside the excavated area. There may therefore have been at least one other room beyond the masonry block. The wall that closed off the kitchen to the south did not belong to the original plan. In the first design of the building the kitchen was open on this side and was accessed via a paved surface sloping towards the interior of the room. The paving probably belonged to a courtyard and the east wall extended southwards, probably to close off the courtyard. The kitchen was covered, whatever the presence of the oven might suggest, as many roof fragments were found in the debris accumulated in the room. A young

Fig. 98. Building M8 (looking N).

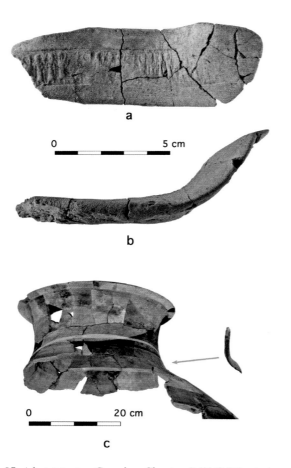

Fig. 97. Administrative Complex: Clay tag (M11 O.25): a) obverse with the seal impression; b) profile showing the curving shape of the tag; c) high neck jar similar to the one on which the tag might have been applied.

Fig. 99. Building M8: Child Burial M5 F60: a) bronze pin (M5 O.25); b) bowl (M5 PL60); c) view of the tomb (north to top).

child had been buried under the floor in the north-west corner of the room (Tomb M5 F60) (*Fig. 99*). The grave, which was an in-ground burial, contained two carinated bowls, one of which was intact, and a bronze pin found on the skeleton's ribs.

To the east of Block 3, four rooms of a building were exposed (Building M9), whose northern part extended into the unexcavated area (*Fig. 100*). Its construction technique was not without analogy to that of Building M8. Its walls were also thinner than those of the central blocks and they were also built with lower-quality bricks. Walls made of even more crumbly bricks defined spaces towards the south. These walls formed an addition to the original construction: they butted up against the south wall of the building and rested on the paved surface of a courtyard which sloped from south to north like the courtyard to the south of Building M8.

A pit grave was excavated in the north-east corner of Room 2, partly entering the north baulk (Tomb M12 F38) (*Fig. 101*). The body of a 6- or 7-year-old child was lying on its right side, in flexed position with the head to the north. Several objects had been deposited with the body, including three carinated bowls, nine knucklebones, a bronze pin and a few beads found near the neck.

Among the material recovered from Building M9, in addition to pottery, a collection of seven seal impressions from Room 1 is worth mentioning. Several of these impressions were made on door sealings and six of them bore the impression of the same seal showing two giants (*Fig. e*, p. 66). The role of Room 1 in the management of the administrative system was thus important enough to justify that its access was controlled. Building M9, despite its different architecture, must have been under the same authority as Block 3 and probably all the buildings of Area M.

The great differences in construction between Buildings M8 and M9, on the one hand, and the three central blocks, on the other, make it impossible to see in M8 and M9 parts of blocks comparable to the other three. However, it is

clear that they all formed a functional unit. Their curving disposition, the massive appearance of the three central blocks and the presence of "empty" rooms are reminiscent of a casemate wall. The impression is reinforced by the fact that, in addition to the curve defined by the buildings, access was apparently exclusively from the south, *i.e.* from within the curve. They may therefore have formed the northern part of a fortification system which would have been complemented to the south by symmetrically disposed buildings, now destroyed and perhaps washed away by the erosion of the southern part of the tell. Be that as it may,

Fig. 101. Building M9: Child Burial M12 F38 under the floor of Room 2: a) Knucklebones (M12 O.61); b) beads found near the body's neck (M12 O.61); c) bronze pin (M12 O.63); d) small bowls (from left to right: M12 PL79, PL78, PL80); e) view of the tomb (north to top).

Fig. 100. Building M9 (looking NE). The floor of the courtyard, on the right, slopes steeply down to the north.

this complex formed a structure whose security had to be ensured by thick walls and effective access control. The use of seals and the presence of storage facilities suggest that it was an official building in which goods, including foodstuff, were stored. Domestic functions were not absent, however, probably to serve the needs of the building's management staff. Building M8, as well as the courtyards, were used for food preparation and Building M9 could have been used as a residential structure. The co-existence of a domestic as well as administrative function of this architectural complex would explain why burials were associated with them.

The authority under which this building complex operated is unknown. It is unlikely to be a local authority. The cultural affinities of the material found – mainly pottery and seal impressions – presents more similarities with the western regions than with Upper Mesopotamia. Assuming that culture and political influence were going hand in hand, Tell Ahmar may have been dependent on his neighbour Carchemish, but it may also have been a border post of the kingdom of Yamhad, which is known to have sought to extend eastwards beyond the Euphrates. In either case, the geographical position of the site, close to the crossing point formed by the confluence of the Sajur and the Euphrates, placed it in an ideal position to play the role of a trading station at the crossroads of two of the main communication routes of the ancient Near East.

The Administrative Complex and House S3 both disappeared in a violent fire which, judging by the great similarities observed in the material from both architectural ensembles, must have occurred at the same time towards the end of the Middle Bronze Age. Two radiocarbon analyses give dates corresponding to the periods 1780–1600 and 1750–1530,[11] which are not fundamentally different from the date obtained, as we saw above, from House S3 (1760–1630). However vague they may be, these dates do not preclude the simultaneous destruction of the two architectural ensembles some time during the Middle Bronze Age II. What was the cause? A great earthquake that would have shaken Tell Ahmar, causing a fire and the destruction of the buildings, is a plausible possibility.

A cuneiform tablet from the eighteenth/seventeenth century

A definite proof of the practice of writing at Middle Bronze Tell Ahmar was given by the discovery of a cuneiform tablet that had been thrown away in a pit to the south of Building M9. Unfortunately, it was badly damaged (*Fig. 102*). Its right side was broken off and its back, which was probably inscribed, was worn out. It was clear, however, that the tablet was written in the Middle Bronze Age II, at the time of the Mari archives or shortly afterwards. It is also clear that it was a letter, although it is impossible to be

more precise at this point. The tablet came to light during the 2010 campaign and was deposited in the Aleppo Museum. The political situation has prevented it from receiving the study it deserves.

There results from this discovery that archives, perhaps of an official nature, must have been kept somewhere on the tell. As no tablets were found in the excavated buildings – although a sudden and violent destruction was favourable to the preservation of written documents – the archives must have been located elsewhere.

Finally, it should be noted that the place where the tablet was discovered, a pit, illustrates the way in which the ancients managed their records. Only those texts that were of practical interest to the archive holder were preserved. Unnecessary documents were destroyed or thrown away. They were therefore often found in pits, as is the case here, or re-used, for example to chock a jar or to level a floor. Large collections of tablets, such as those from Mari or Ashurbanipal's library, come from levels of destruction and were only preserved because there was no one to come and retrieve them.

0   3 cm

Fig. 102. Cuneiform tablet (M13 T24).

The Middle Bronze Age seal impressions
(Adelheid Otto)[1]

The Middle Bronze Age seal impressions that were found at Tell Ahmar during the renewed excavations are important for several reasons. Firstly almost all of them come from a well-defined archaeological context: that of buildings – referred to as the Administrative Complex – of the Middle Bronze Age II, part of which probably served as storerooms. This means that the way the seals were used provides information on the sealing practices in use in the administration of these buildings. Secondly, the iconographic and stylistic characteristics of these impressions place them in a period for which very few dated seals are available, making them a valuable point of reference in the history of Old Syrian glyptic. Thirdly, the iconography of the seals is particularly interesting because the figures and deities depicted on them reflect the north Syrian pantheon at a time when it is poorly attested. And last but not least, they indicate a "Tell Ahmar Seal Style" with very distinctive motifs, composition and style, which fills a regional void, since Middle Bronze Age seals of this region have been lacking secure benchmarks.

Sealings as evidence of administrative practices

A total of 34 fragments of clay objects bearing one or several seal impressions each have been found in the ruins of the Administrative Complex of Area M. These fragments take various forms. Some are lumps of clay with a seal impression on one side, slightly convex, and on the other, slightly concave, marks of cords, wood, wickerwork, sticks or cloth. We have tried to reconstruct from these marks the object which was closed or sealed and obtained some information on the operations that took place in the rooms. For instance, several of these artefacts were door sealings (*Fig. a*) impressed with the same seal decorated with the unusual figure of two bearded giants. Their supernatural nature and size were emphasized by engraving them horizontally around the cylinder (*Fig. e*). This seal must have belonged to one of the persons in charge of the storerooms.

More than a third of the sealings are in the form of clay strips, also called *languette*. These fine, elongated strips of pure clay – on which the seal was rolled – were originally embedded in a large lump of crude clay with heavy temper which covered the mouth of a jar (*Figs c* and *77*). This was the most common method for sealing jars in the Middle and Late Bronze Age.[2] However, in many cases the fine clay strip has chipped off from the crude clay lump and is found separately in excavation. The curved shape of several clay strips helps to reconstruct the type of jar which had been sealed (*Fig. 97*).

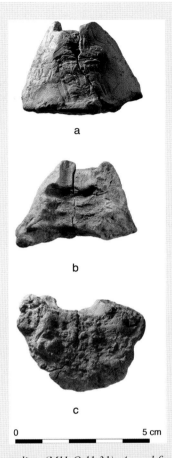

a

b

c

0   5 cm

Fig. a. Door sealing (MI1 O.11.31). A cord fixed to a door's leaf was wrapped around a stick stuck in the wall next to the door and a lump of clay was applied on the base of the stick; a) obverse: the lump took the shape of a truncated cone; b) reverse: imprint of the cord around the stick; c) base: marks left by the irregular surface of the mud plaster covering the wall.

Fig. b. Modern "bolt" in a house of Tell Ahmar. A device similar to the ancient locking system is still in use in some houses of the village.

Other sealings served as closures of bags and baskets (*Fig. d*). In general, they could either have been made on site or have arrived with the sealed objects and therefore have come from outside. However, the number of occurrences and the similarity of the clay are good indicators of the local or foreign origin of these sealings. In Tell Ahmar it can be observed that several of the people working in the buildings of Area M appear to have sealed objects of different kinds. For example, the owner of a very peculiar seal showing four female figures (*Fig. g*) was responsible for sealing baskets (M10 O.4) (*Fig. d*) as well as jars (M11 O.31) (*Fig. 97*).

The iconography of the seals

The impressions of fourteen different cylinder seals could be identified. Five of them show surprisingly similar scenes with more-or-less the same protagonists, which are exemplified here with Seal 1 (*Fig. f*). First comes the Storm-God in the posture of the "smiting god", *i.e.* a god brandishing a weapon with his right arm as if he was about to smite a foe. He is dressed in a short tunic and wears a pointed tiara decorated with horns, from which a long lock of hair runs down his back. He holds a weapon in each hand. Next comes a winged and armed figure, wearing a cylindrical headdress with two horns. The identification of this deity – due to the hairdress clearly characterised as female – is challenging for lack of contemporary Syrian religious texts; the most convincing interpretation is that of the goddess Anat, Ba'al's companion.[3] Opposite the Storm-God is standing another deity with long hair, wearing a horned helmet topped by a crescent. So far, it is impossible to recognize the sex of this figure, since the long hair can be worn by male and female deities. But it is tempting to interpret this deity either as the Moon-God himself or as Ningal, his female companion, who played an important role in the Mesopotamian pantheon from the third to the first millennium BC.[4] The close association of the Storm-God and the Moon-God (of Harran) in this area in the first millennium BC has often been emphasized.[5] This seal is a further hint that this close connection goes back to at least the second millennium.

An incense burner placed between these two deities illustrates the veneration of both and their status on a par. Other elements in the field are the Egyptian *ankh* sign, a scorpion and a star – so-called filling motifs which are found on every example of this seal group from Tell Ahmar. The iconography, style and composition of these five seals are so homogeneous that they must have been produced by the same workshop. Dozens of seals from the art market are so similar that they can be tentatively attributed to the same workshop.[6] It is therefore reasonable

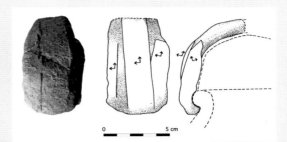

Fig. c. Languette used to seal a jar (M11 O.47) (drawing: Adelheid Otto). Fine clay strips are shown in white, with arrows indicating the orientation of the seal impressions. Dotted areas indicate the crude clay lump in which the strips were embedded.

Fig. d. Bag or basket sealing (M10 O.10.4); a) obverse: the seal has been rolled at least three times on the fresh clay; b) reverse: marks left by the canvas of a bag and by the cord that was used to fasten the bag.

Fig. e. Impression of a seal engraved with the figure of two giants (M11 O.11.31) (drawing: Adelheid Otto).

to assume that the workshop was active at Tell Ahmar itself or in its vicinity.

A completely different scene was depicted on a small seal which was only 1.5 cm high (*Fig. g*). Two pairs of two figures each are depicted. The main scene shows a female person in adoration standing in front of an enthroned woman who is holding a branch in her right hand. Both women are covering their heads with peculiar veils. A crescent moon and the *ankh* sign are depicted between them. The secondary scene shows two figures in long garments with long hair opposite a pole with a three-pronged top. Especially remarkable are the two women of the main scene, since they are dressed in a typical Syrian fashion. Due to the fact that Syrian deities do not necessarily wear a horned crown, it is difficult to know if two mortal women or two goddesses are depicted in an adoration scene. What is certain, however, is that this type of female person is frequent only on Syrian seals, which can be attributed to the Middle Bronze Age II period on stylistic grounds, but most of which are without provenence unfortunately, except for one example from Ugarit.[7] Although this seal seems very different from the seals of the "Storm-God Group" from Tell Ahmar at first sight, a seal from the art market bridges the gap between these seals: it depicts both – the Storm-God opposite the winged armed goddess, and the 'veiled woman'.[8] Therefore it may be assumed that both seals (*Figs f* and *g*) originated in Tell Ahmar. We can even go a step further and attribute the majority of the impressed seals to a distinctive "Tell Ahmar Seal Style".

Completely different in motif and style and probably not of local origin are the impressions of three "Common Style" seals showing stylized figures with raised spade-shaped hands. The type of sealing and the kind of clay indicate that these pieces had entered the buildings with imported goods. Seals of this kind are known in northern Syria and Anatolia in the Assyrian merchant colonies from around 1800 to the seventeenth century.[9] A rather coarse seal made of clay, decorated only with incised lines, may come from the same region (*Fig. 96*).[10]

Dating of the seals

The seals are undoubtedly Old Syrian. However, their precise place in the Old Syrian glyptic is not easy to determine, as there are few Syrian seals that are accurately dated to the period after 1760 (in middle chronology). The best point of reference is still Alalakh VII, from which two comparable seals originate.[11] Furthermore, the evolution of the style as well as the motifs of the Tell Ahmar seals, especially the thickened fringe of the garments, show that these seals are later than 1760, but must pre-date the last phase of Alalakh VII.[12] They must therefore date to the

Fig. f. Impression of a seal engraved with a religious scene involving the Storm-God (M11 O.11.56) (drawing: Adelheid Otto).

Fig. g. Impression of a seal engraved with female figures (M10 O.10.4) (drawing: Adelheid Otto).

period from around 1760 to 1700, a period that is difficult to pinpoint due to the lack of dated examples. The Middle Bronze II context of the Tell Ahmar sealings thus offer a most precious new point of reference for numerous seals which have so far not been attributed to any region or period.

In short, the seal impressions show that Tell Ahmar was a place where goods could be stored and processed in permanent storehouses. In addition, they also bear witness to contacts with Anatolia. It should be remembered that many impressions of Karahöyük, Acemhöyük and *Kārum* Kanish Ib also come from the Carchemish region. As one of the main Old Assyrian trade routes crossed the Euphrates in this region, these seal impressions are a testimony to the importance of the role played by Tell Ahmar as a stage on the trade route linking Assyria with Anatolia and Syria in the second half of the eighteenth century.

Notes

1   Although I was never present at Tell Ahmar during the excavations, I was able to study the sealings in the National Museum of Aleppo in 2008. The final publication of the sealings is in preparation by the author.

2   A. OTTO, *Tall Bi'a/Tuttul* IV, *Siegel und Siegelabrollungen*, WVDOG 104, Saarbrücken 2004, pp. 53–56, 111–113, pls 58–63, 111–114, 118–119. Around 363 jar sealings with embedded sealed strips (or *languettes*) were found in the palace of king Yasmah-Adad at Tuttul, 350 of which had been sealed by a servant of his father, Shamshi-Adad.

3   W. ORTHMANN, *Untersuchungen zur späthethitischen Kunst*, Saarbrücker Beiträge zur Altertumskunde 8, Bonn 1971, p. 273; D. COLLON, A cylinder seal with a camel in the Walters Art Gallery. *The Journal of the Walters Art Gallery 36, Essays in Honor of Dorothy Kent Hill*, 1977, p. 2.

4   A. ZGOLL, Ningal A. I. In Mesopotamien, *RlA* 9 (2001), pp. 352–356.

5   G. BUNNENS, *A New Luwian Stele and the Cult of the Storm-God at Til Barsib–Masuwari*. TELL AHMAR II, Leuven-Paris-Dudley (MA) 2006, pp. 70–73 with relevant literature.

6   See for example a nearly identical seal: B. TEISSIER, *Ancient Near Eastern Seals from the Marcopoli Collection*, Berkeley-London 1984, No 475.

7   The seal R.S. 7.181 (according to the excavator, found not far from the stele of the *Baal au Foudre*) depicts a similar woman in adoration and a similar storm god. See C.F.-A. SCHAEFFER-FORRER, *Corpus des cylindres-sceaux de Ras Shamra – Ugarit et d'Enkomi Alasia*, Paris 1983, pp. 25–26.

8   B. TEISSIER, *op. cit.* (n. 6), No 483.

9   S. MAZZONI, Continuity and development in the Syrian and Cypriote Common Glyptic styles, *Insight through Images: Studies in honor of Edith Porada*, ed. M. KELLY-BUCCELLATI, Bibliotheca Mesopotamica 21, Malibu 1986, pp. 171–182; S. ALP, *Zylinder- und Stempelsiegel aus Karahöyük bei Konya*, Ankara 1968, pls 12–14.

10   S. ALP, *op. cit.* (n. 9), pls 15.34.

11   D. COLLON, *The Seal Impressions from Tell Atchana/Alalakh*, Alter Orient und Altes Testament 27, Kevelaer-Neukirchen-Vluyn 1975, Nos 20, 21.

12   For the development of Syrian glyptic in the eighteenth century and the change around 1760 see A. OTTO, *Die Entstehung und Entwicklung der Klassisch-Syrischen Glyptik. Untersuchungen zur Assyriologie und Vorderasiatischen Archäologie* 8, Berlin–New York 2000, pp. 279–281.

c. The end of the Middle Bronze Age

A comparison between the plan of the Administrative Complex of the renewed excavations and the plan of the so-called Aramaean level of the French excavations suggests that the Administrative Complex did not completely disappear after the fire (*Fig. 103*). If the two plans are superimposed, they reveal a great similarity between the north-western part of the buildings, which the early excavators considered to be Aramaean, and the eastern part of the Administrative Complex. Room 49 of the French plan corresponds to Room 5 of Block 2, Rooms 46 to 48 correspond to the entire Block 3, and Rooms 56 and 57 correspond to Rooms 1 and 2 of Building M9. The only missing feature is the dividing wall between Rooms 2 and 3 in Block 3. The similarities are too strong to be due to

chance. The plan of the French expedition shows remains similar to the more recently excavated buildings. It should be noted, however, that the differences are also significant. In particular, the constructions corresponding to Block 2 extend to the north and to the south, whereas no trace of corresponding walls extending to the north have been found during the renewed excavations. It must therefore be concluded that the buildings have been redesigned and that the remains found during the French excavations do not correspond to the upper part of the walls uncovered during the recent excavations, but rather to a rearrangement of these buildings after a violent fire had ravaged them. All the buildings that formed the Administrative Complex would then have been extended, or at least some of them, to the north and south.

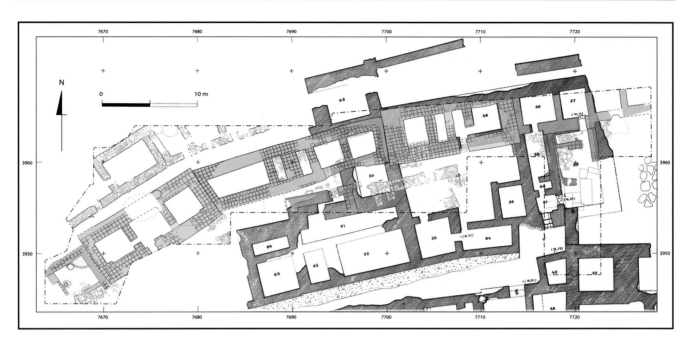

Fig. 103. Superimposition of the plans of the niveau araméen *of the French excavations (in grey) and of the Administrative Complex of Area M.*

Confirmation of this reorganization can be found in the remains excavated immediately above the walls of Block 2, which have been flattened by the French excavations. Several basalt grinding stones, mixed with blackish soil, were found on top of the preserved remains of Room 5 (*Fig. 104*). These must have been debris lying on a floor excavated by the French and to a large extent removed by them.

So, the Administrative Complex did not completely disappear in the great fire that set it ablaze. The buildings still existed when, towards the end of the Middle Bronze Age or the beginning of the Late Bronze Age, small houses (M1–M4 on *Fig. 87*) with a stone footing were built on either side of the complex from which they were separated by narrow streets.

Actually, other discoveries, dating from the Middle Bronze Age, seem to come from a higher, and thus later, level than the administrative buildings exposed during the renewed excavations. Four polished haematite stones in the shape of small axes were found in the fill immediately to the south of Room 4 of Block 3 (*Fig. 105*). These were associated with a small trapezoidal stone object with a large central perforation (*Fig. 106*). Such a stone must have been one of the components of a bivalve mould for casting metal objects. A curious feature of this stone was the rather rough motif incised on one of its narrow sides, which depicted a nude female supporting her breasts. The engraving, carved in hollow, seems to indicate that the motif was intended to be impressed like a seal on soft material.

Fig. 104. Debris on a later floor of Room 5 of Block 2 (looking NE).

Against the exterior face of the south wall of Room 1 of Block 2, excavation encountered a jar burial whose top was only a few centimetres lower than the preserved top of the wall (Tomb M9 F20) (*Fig. 107*). Without ruling out the possibility that this tomb may have belonged to the same level as the Administrative Complex, it seems more likely that it was dug from a later level, possibly but not necessarily the one revealed by the French excavations. It contained the body of an adult laid in a bent position, lying on its left side with its head to the north. The grave included two small carinated bowls, a small, rounded bottle and a plate (*Fig. 107c*).

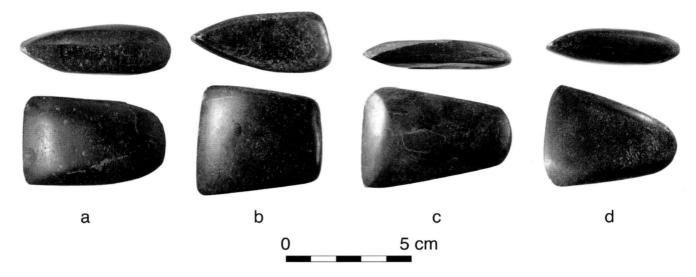

Fig. 105. Polished haematite stones in the shape of small axes (from left to right: M11 O.1, O.2, O.3, O.8).

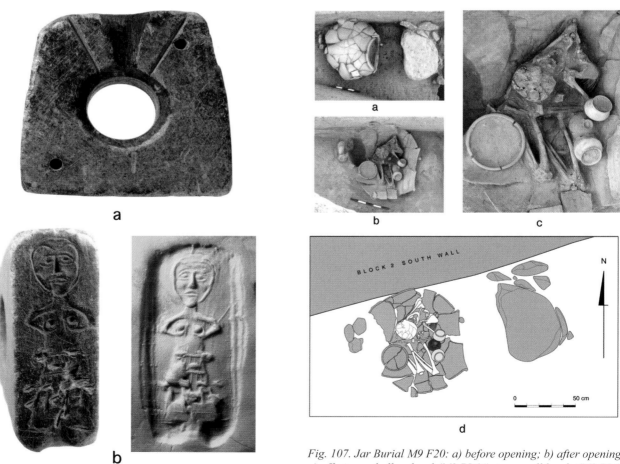

Fig. 106. One of the two components of a bivalve mould. (M10 O.10): a) interior side; b) figure carved on one of the narrow sides.

Fig. 107. Jar Burial M9 F20: a) before opening; b) after opening; c) offerings: shallow bowl (M9 PL64), two small bowls (M9 PL61 and PL62), jug (M9 PL63); d) drawing of the tomb by Virginia Verardi; the stones shown to the west of the tomb were probably used to wedge the burial jar, but the relationship between the tomb and the large stone to the east is uncertain.

Middle Bronze Age pottery (Silvia Perini)

Most of the Middle Bronze Age pottery come from two architectural structures: the Administrative Complex on top of the tell and House S3 on the south-eastern slope of the tell.[1] These two structures are roughly contemporary and can be dated to the Middle Bronze Age II (c. 1750–1600).

Typology

The classification of the pottery is based on the study of 3659 so-called "diagnostic" sherds, *i.e.* sherds bearing an element of form or decoration, and 48 complete vessels. A first distinction is made between closed shapes and open shapes, *i.e.* vessels whose opening diameter is either smaller (*e.g.* a bottle) or larger (*e.g.* a bowl) than the largest diameter of the body. Secondly, a number of technical characteristics are taken into consideration, such as type of paste, method of manufacture, surface treatment and decoration. This has led to the recognition of fourteen closed shapes, designated as CS 01–14, and nine open shapes, designated as OS 01–09. The dimensions of the vessels allow to define three categories – small, medium and large – according to the criteria listed in Table 1.

Shape and function

Functions have been inferred from an analysis based upon a multi-disciplinary approach, which includes investigation of vessel techno-morphological analysis, context of recovery, as well as comparative analysis. Residual features were also analysed to identify calcium oxalate, which is a salt of oxalic acid (an organic compound) and the principal component of beerstone, and tartaric acid, which is a white crystalline acid that occurs naturally in many plants and particularly in grapes (and thus wine).

Here follows a summary of the conclusions.

Closed shapes

FOOD PREPARATION AND CONSUMPTION

CS01:   Bottles (*Fig. a*), small or medium sized, often with a smooth surface or painted decoration. The aesthetic aspect of these bottles seems to be important. They must have contained a less common liquid than water, although analysis of the residues showed no trace of beer or wine.

CS02:   Medium to large jars that can be linked to short-term liquid storage activities (*Fig. b*). Red-slipped surface treatments, which would have aided the jars' permeability, were applied to the interior and exterior surfaces in six examples. In addition, the thick walls of those examples would have kept the content fresh for longer. The wide opening suggests that a tool (*i.e.* a ladle or a small bowl) was used to extract the content from the vessel rather than the vessel being tipped for this purpose.

CS05:   Medium, slightly carinated vessels (*Fig. c*), which may have been used for the temporary storage of foodstuffs and for transporting them over short distances.

Table 1

Vessel shape	Diameter (cm)	Height (cm)	Vessel size
CS	3–11	<15	Small
	12–30	15–40	Medium
	>30	> 40	Large
OS	10–11	<10	Small
	12–38	<10	Medium
	>38	>10	Large

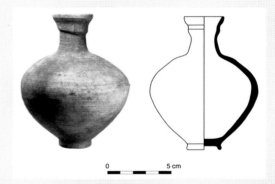

Fig. a. Bottle (CS01) (M10 PL49) (drawing: Silvia Perini).

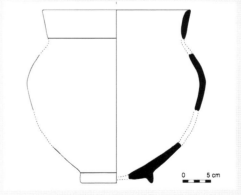

Fig. b. Middle size jar (CS02) (S14 PL583) (drawing: Silvia Perini).

CS13:   Pots without neck. The restricted shape suggests CS13 would have been used for cooking, possibly in boiling activities (*Fig. d*). The high presence of medium to large inclusions makes CS13 vessels suitable for thermal shock resistance.

STORAGE AND TRANSPORT

CS08 and CS09: Jars with high/medium neck that were used in activities involving long-term storage and long-distance transport (*Fig. e*). The narrow medium/high restricted neck and the small rim diameter lead to the hypothesis that this shape was used for storing liquid (*e.g.* wine, beer) or dry food such as seeds. Considering the high presence of these types of vessel, it is reasonable to suggest that they were also used in the short-distance transportation of water. Two CS08 samples showed positive results for oxalic acid (possibly beer), whilst a third (found in a domestic context) provided a negative result, but did exhibit a +/– reaction to tartaric acid (possibly wine). Both CS08 and CS09 have a standardized shape that is characterized by a rim diameter normally between 10 cm and 14 cm.

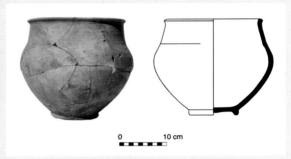

Fig. c. Middle size carinated bowl (CS05) (M6 PL55) (drawing: Silvia Perini).

CS04:   Medium to large jars (*Fig. f*). Residue analysis undertaken on three samples shows a positive

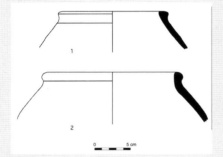

Fig. d. Cooking Pots (CS13) (1: S14 PL657 ; 2: M12 PL7) (drawing: Silvia Perini).

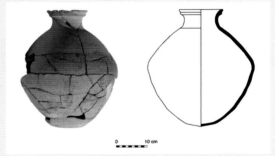

Fig. e. Middle size jar (CS08) (M6 PL121) (drawing: Silvia Perini).

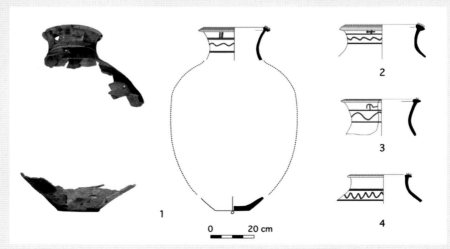

Fig. f. Large storage jars (CS04) (1: M2 PL120; 2: M5 PL49; 3: M5 PL53; 4: M8 PL47) (drawing: Silvia Perini).

reaction to calcium oxalate, suggesting that these vessels were used as a container or for processing beer. Some of the CS04 are also characterized by a base with a small perforation in the middle suggesting that they were involved in some filtering activities. The small hole served to leak the content of the vessel. Similar vessels would have rested on some sort of pedestal or another vessel placed underneath that would be used to allow the content to ooze out. According to the dimension, CS04 would have been used for long-term storage, probably of grain (large dimension vessels), and long-distance transport (medium dimension).

CS11:   Flasks, known as "pilgrim flasks", with an average capacity of about 3.7 litres (*Fig. g*). Relatively rare in the Euphrates region and of a shape that makes them difficult to handle for serving a drink, they appear to have been used to carry a liquid over a fairly long distance.

Open shapes

FOOD SERVICE AND CONSUMPTION

Open shapes are, by their very nature, related to the serving and consumption of food, solid or liquid, and beverages.

OS01 (*Fig. h*) and OS02: Deep bowls, made of common or cooking ware. They are probably multi-purpose, used for the preparation (cooking ware) or consumption (common ware) of dry or semi-liquid food.

OS03:   Deep bowls (*Fig. i*). They are among the most frequently encountered types. They may have been used to transport food over a short distance, for example to serve and consume food. It is also possible that OS03 bowls were used as lids. These bowls, as well as the OS08 bowls, are also found in funerary contexts. They may have been used at funerary banquets or as containers for food offerings.

OS08:   Small carinated bowls easy to hold and transport (*Fig. j*). Moreover, the rim profile would have been advantageous for direct drinking. These bowls must therefore have been associated with the consumption of liquid or semi-liquid food rather than with dry content. In burial contexts, they were probably used for libations and offerings. Four jar stoppers have been found associated with these shapes.

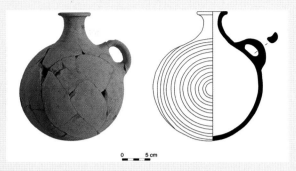

Fig. g. "Pilgrim Flask" (CS11) (M6 PL129) (drawing: Silvia Perini).

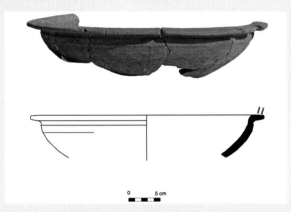

Fig. h. Medium bowl (OS01) (M5 PL123) (drawing: Silvia Perini).

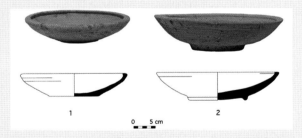

Fig. i. Deep bowls (OS03) (1: S14 PL668 ; 2: M12 PL28) (drawing: Silvia Perini).

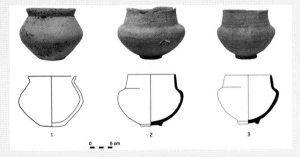

Fig. j. Small carinated bowls (OS08) (1: M9 PL61; 2: S14 PL351; 3: S14 PL426) (drawing: Silvia Perini).

Decoration

Middle Bronze Age pottery is rarely decorated, except for jars with a wavy line decoration made with a comb on the neck or shoulder (*Fig. f*) and cords applied to the surface.

The regional context

Although often in conflict, the political powers also maintained diplomatic and commercial relations. The kings of Mari, Aleppo, Shubat-Enlil, Qatna and Ebla not only traded with each other, but also entered into marriage alliances or negotiated use-rights of pastureland. The archives of the time provide information on the size and capacity of the ships that transported goods on the Euphrates. The intensity of these relations is reflected in the similarities between the ceramic production of Syria and northern Mesopotamia.

The ceramic forms as well as the decoration made of incised lines, applied cords and smoothed surfaces are commonly found at the neighbouring sites of Tell Ahmar, *e.g.* Şaraga Höyük and Zeytinli Bahçe on the Anatolian Euphrates; Tell Aushariye, Tell Qara Qozaq, Tell Shiyukh Tahtani in the Tishrin Dam area; Tell Hadidi, Tell Munbaqa in the Tabqa Dam area and as far as Baghouz and Haradum on the border between modern Syria and Iraq. They are also found in north Mesopotamia, for example at Chagar Bazaar and Tell Leilan in the Habur basin.

The CS04 jars are particularly representative of the Euphrates sites. They can be found, with similar marks, for example at Şaraǧa Höyük, Tell Aushariye and Haradum. As the CS08 and CS09 high neck jars could probably be used for long distance transport, it will come as no surprise to find them not only in the Euphrates region, but also in Northern Mesopotamia and in the Habur basin. Finally, although the OS03 and OS08 bowls are not intended for use in long-distance transport, they show morphological similarities with pottery from other regions. Their joint use in funerary contexts, observed at Tell Ahmar, is found elsewhere on the Euphrates, notably at Zeytinli Bahçe, Tell Shiyukh Tahtani, Tell Aushariye, Tell Hadidi and Baghouz. The similarities in shape, decoration, potters' marks and funerary customs underline the intensity of economic relations and the community of culture that characterized the Amorite society of Syria and North Mesopotamia in the Middle Bronze Age.

Note

1 S. Perini, *Ceramic Vessel Production, Use and Distribution in Northern Mesopotamia and Syria during the Middle Bronze Age II (c. 1800–1600 BC): A functional analysis of vessels from Tell Ahmar, north Syria*, unpublished PhD thesis, Edinburgh University, 2014; ead., Frequency and distribution of ceramic functional categories at Tell Ahmar (Syria) during the Middle Bronze Age II (c. 1800–1600 BC), *Proceedings of the 7th International Congress on the Archaeology of the Ancient Near East* 3, ed. R. Matthews & J. Curtis, Wiesbaden 2012, pp. 235–248.

2. Syria under foreign domination (c. 1600–1200)

Be they the cause or only the symptom of the change, the Hittite incursions into northern Syria marked a turning point in the political history of the region at the beginning of the Late Bronze Age. The powerful kingdom of Yamhad disappeared forever. No local power replaced it. A period of uncertainty began in the sixteenth century, during which outside powers sought to gain a foothold in Syria. Egypt extended its domination over Palestine and, around 1500, Thutmosis I, according to his grandson Thutmosis III, would have erected a monument on the right bank of the Euphrates, probably in the region of Carchemish. The fifteenth century saw the Hurrians of Mittani extend their power from Upper Mesopotamia to the Mediterranean. Tell Bazi, downstream from Tell Ahmar, yielded two tablets showing that the region was subjected to Mittani.[12] It is more than likely that Tell Ahmar was under the same authority. In the fourteenth century Suppiluliuma I, King of Hatti, subdued northern Syria and installed his son Piyashili/Sharru-kushuh on the throne of Carchemish with authority over all northern

Syria. Tell Ahmar, close to Carchemish, was probably under Carchemish's direct control. Hittite rule lasted until the end of the twelfth century, which is also the date usually assigned to the end of the Bronze Age.

J.D. Hawkins has assumed that the name of the site, in the Mittanian/Hittite period, could have been Mazuwati, a city mentioned in the treaty concluded by Suppiluliuma with Mattiwaza of Mittani.[13] Mazuwati must indeed have been located between Carchemish and Emar. It could be the ancient form of Masuwari, one of the names of Tell Ahmar in the first millennium. However, the shift from "t" to "r" in Mazuwati/Masuwari makes the identification problematic. In the absence of corroborating evidence, it is better to leave the question open.

The stratigraphic sequence of Areas A and S shows a decline of the occupation in this part of the site after the destruction of House S3. It was covered by a few floors and poor walls that formed Stratum A+S/10. These remains could represent the beginning of the Late Bronze Age. A few sherds of the so-called Nuzi ware (*Fig. 108*), which

Fig. 108. Sherds of the so-called Nuzi Ware (S14 PL397 and PL442).

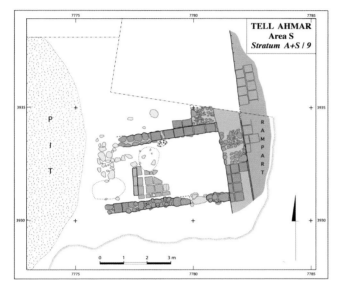

Fig. 109. Stratum A+S/9: Plan of House S2. The buiding is set against a massive block of bricks which must be part of the fortification system of the acropolis during the Bronze Age.

was characteristic of the period of the Mittanian domination (Late Bronze Age I), were found in levels of this period.

a. House S2

Immediately above these remains a house, House S2 (*Fig. 109*), had been erected, which belonged to Stratum A+S/9. It was not very well preserved either, so that it is impossible to say whether the building consisted of the only room that was exposed or whether it was larger. A bronze adze (*Fig. 110*) and a coarse clay cylinder seal (*Fig. 111*) were recovered from the debris filling House S2. The decoration of the seal consisted of carelessly incised quadrupeds, possibly caprids, drawn in such a way that the seal had to be unrolled vertically to see the motifs correctly.

b. House A14

Outstanding among the remains of the second half of the second millennium was another house, House A14 (Stratum A+S/8), located to the north-west of House S2, in Trenches

Fig. 110. Bronze adze (S14 O.146) (drawing: Antonietta Catanzariti).

Fig. 111. Clay cylinder seal (S14 O.125).

A28/29 (*Figs 112* and *113*).[14] The plan was almost complete (*Fig. 112*). Only the eastern corner of the house had disappeared. The mud-brick walls rested on a stone footing that was narrower than the upper part of the wall. A half-brick facing concealed the stones from view both inside and outside the building. A few slabs – three on the outside of the north-western wall and one near the western corner – completed this facing by forming kinds of orthostates.

The building consisted of three long parallel rooms – Rooms 1–3 – which were perpendicular to a fourth room, Room 4. The entrance was through a door in the west wall of Room 2 (*Fig. 114*). Two upright stones, sorts of orthostats, framed the door and three steps led down to the interior of the house. It is likely that another entrance was located in the east wall of Room 4 because the base of the wall was

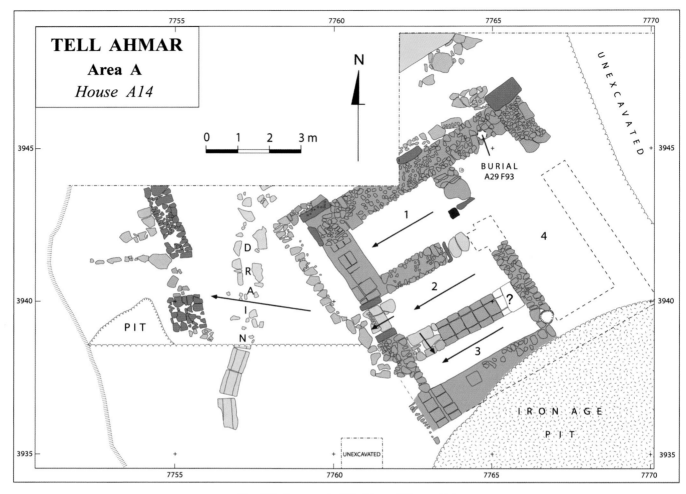

Fig. 112. Stratum A+S/8: Plan of House A14.

Fig. 113. Stratum A+S/8: House A14 (looking W). The bricks in the foreground, under the range pole, could belong to the possible third millennium terrace mentioned in Chapter 1.

abruptly interrupted, some distance from the north-east corner, by two large stones which probably corresponded to the doorframe. Beyond this the wall was destroyed.

Room 2 was connected to Room 1 and probably to Room 3. There was no direct access from either Room 2 or Room 3 to Room 4.

The house had a peculiarity that is difficult to explain. The three parallel rooms 1–3 were built on a sloping surface, which dropped down about 1 m over a distance of more-or-less 4 m from west to east. Only Room 4 stood on a flat ground. There was no step to compensate for the difference in level. Both the carefully plastered floors and the stone bases of the walls followed this slope. It is hard to imagine that ordinary domestic activities could have taken place in such an inconvenient environment. The rooms had been subsequently filled in with bricks, probably to level the ground and allow the building to be re-occupied. This re-occupation was only documented in the north-west corner of Room 1, where an oven of the *tannur* type stood on a horizontal floor.

There was another peculiarity. On the right, for those entering the house through the doorway of Room 2, two long

Fig. 114. Stratum A+S/8: House A14, doorway in the SW wall (looking NE).

stones had been stacked up, with the upper stone slightly out of line with the lower one. This assemblage, which rested on a stone base, probably formed the first steps of a staircase that, after a landing and a turn, would have been extended by wooden stairs above Room 3, which, in this case, would have been a staircase. However, a carefully smoothed floor was found under the hypothetical stairs, suggesting that this space was used as a true room. Could there have been stairs and, at the same time, domestic occupation underneath. In such a case, the access could have been from the other end of the room, where the extremity of its north wall was destroyed.

The house stood on a brick mass, which is clearly visible on the photograph of *Figure 113* as well as on the side of a large pit immediately to the south. This mass is assumed to have been part of the terrace, which, as we saw above, possibly flanked the Early Bronze Age Temple to the west.

A child's grave found on the stone base of the north wall of Room 4 raises a problem (Tomb A29 F93) (*Fig. 115*). It is possible that it was dug from a higher level, but the grave may have been set there during the construction of the house. In the preliminary report, the second solution was accepted as the most likely. However, the very position of the grave itself, close to the edge of the wall, would rather indicate a burial dug from a higher level.

Two seals belong to the same level as the house. One was a grey stone cylinder seal depicting highly schematic spear bearers, which, by its motif and technique, recalls the so-called Common Style of Mittanian glyptics (*Fig. 116*). The other was a rudimentary stamp seal carved from a hard, whitish stone, a kind of marble, with the figure of an animal, probably a quadruped in the so-called "flying gallop" position (*Fig. 117*). It comes from the open space to the west of the house.

The historical context of this house is given by a comparison with the buildings that have been excavated, notably at Tell Bazi, a few dozen kilometres downstream from

a

b

Fig. 115. House A14: Child burial A29 F93 dug in the NW wall of Room 4: a) the tomb included a medium (A29 PL293) and a small jar (A29 PL308); b) N corner of the house; the tomb is to the left of the white arrow.

0   3 cm

Fig. 116. Stone cylinder seal (A29 O.157).

Tell Ahmar,[15] and at Emar even further downstream on the Euphrates.[16] The houses were designed on a similar model according to which a long room was flanked on one side by two or more smaller perpendicular rooms. These houses could also have had a staircase, which gives more weight to the possible presence of stairs in Room 3.

Fig. 117. Stone stamp seal (A28 O.4).

It appears from these observations that both House S2 and House A14 may have been in use during the Mittanian period. The time of their abandonment is unclear.

3. Possible second millennium fortifications

The French expedition excavated a puzzling structure consisting of a large mass of bricks that they called *pilier de soutènement*.[17] Maurice Dunand considered it to be the substructure of a platform supporting the Assyrian palace (*Fig. 118*). The actual function of this *pilier* ("pillar"), however, appears to be anything but clear. The published

a

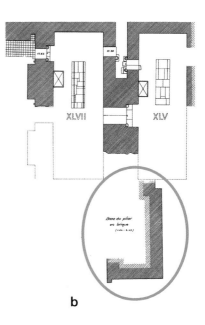

b

c

Fig. 118. The so-called pilier de soutènement *of the Assyrian palace: a) at the time of the French excavations (after* Til-Barsib, *pl. xxxviii/1); b) plan drawn by the French archaeologists suggesting the relationship between the* pilier *(circled in red) and the palace (after* Til-Barsib, *Plan D); (c) as it was found during the renewed excavations (looking W).*

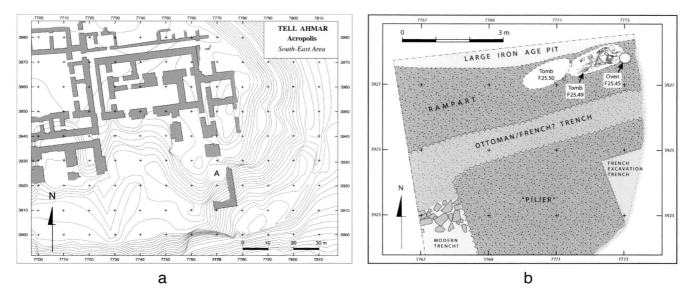

Fig. 119. Plan of the SE sector of the Acropolis showing the respective positions of the Assyrian palace and the pilier *de soutènement (after Wolfe's topographic survey): a) the area marked A shows the location of the excavations conducted on the top of the* pilier; *b) plan of the excavations; the dotted area marks the place where the characteristic bricks of the* pilier *were recognized.*

plan shows that the palace, before its southern part had been carried away by erosion, extended on either side of the so-called pillar without that any other supporting structure could be observed (cf. *Fig. 119a*). The renewed excavations have shown that the pillar was connected to a wall with an approximately east–west orientation (*Fig. 119b*), which extended further inside the tell and behind the place where the southernmost rooms of the palace must have been. The texture of the bricks – a fine, yellowish clay – and their dimensions – c. 35 × 37 × 10 cm –[18] makes it likely that they both belonged to the same construction. The pillar is therefore more likely to have been a tower strengthening a fortification wall.

On top of the preserved part of this wall, two burials had been dug. One of them (Tomb A25 F49) contained two bodies facing each another (*Fig. 120*). Next to it and at the same absolute elevation was a *tannur* oven, which in turn partly covered a bowl made of blackish ware probably dating from the Middle or Late Bronze Age.

The obvious conclusion is that at least two, possibly three, archaeological levels existed between the so-called pillar and the palace. The tomb must have been excavated from a level that was higher than that of the oven, and the oven probably covered the level of the plate. It would thus appear that the so-called pillar lacked any connection with the palace. It must have belonged to a defence system, probably a tower built to consolidate a rampart dating back to long before the construction of the palace. Unfortunately, this rampart could not be exposed over a long distance. It was cut towards the west by the digging operation that also damaged the buildings that lined the third millennium

Fig. 120. Tomb A25 F49 with two bodies facing each other (north to top). The tomb has damaged an oven, the bottom of which can be seen on the right above the rim of a bowl.

street and, towards the east, it was taken away by the deep sounding of the French expedition. Towards the north, a large early Iron Age pit had destroyed it.

A few sherds used to level the stone base of the pillar show that the construction may date back to the Middle Bronze Age. The fortifications to which the pillar belonged would therefore have been erected in the second millennium.

***

It is a whole section of Tell Ahmar's history that the renewed excavations brought back to light. Particularly well represented is the so-called "Middle Bronze Age II" period, around 1800–1600. A series of occupations include carefully constructed buildings and tombs, among which was a burial vault. A group of buildings apparently served both as storerooms and as an administrative centre. Tell Ahmar, perhaps located at the border between the kingdoms of Yamhad, centred on Aleppo, and Carchemish, seems to have been a trading station on the routes linking Mesopotamia with regions further west. The Administrative Complex disappeared in a violent fire and was re-occupied and enlarged, possibly at the turn of the Middle and Late Bronze Age. Was the fire caused by one of the Hittite raids that ravaged Syria and Mesopotamia in the late Middle Bronze Age? The excavation of House S3 destroyed by a fire probably at the same time as the Administrative Complex suggests another possibility. The remains of the house were found in such a state that the destruction by an earthquake is likely. This earthquake could have caused the fire that also ravaged the Administrative Complex. The disaster could therefore have been the result not of a war but of a natural cause.

The early times of Late Bronze Age I (c. 1600–1400) are represented in particular by a house astonishingly built on a sloping surface. The house, which consisted of three parallel rooms flanking a long transverse room, illustrates an architectural design known in the valley of the north Syrian Euphrates in the Mittanian and Hittite periods. Sherds of the typical Nuzi Ware point to an occupation during the Mittanian period. Hittite occupation is more elusive.

Notes

1   J.-W. Meyer *in* W. Orthmann, *Halawa 1977–1979*, Saarbrücker Beiträge zur Altertumskunde 31, Bonn 1981, pl. 49.2 and pp. 29–30.

2   A.S. Jamieson, A painted Eye-Vase from Tell Ahmar and the Syro-Cilician painted ceramic tradition, *Si un homme ... Textes offerts en hommage à André Finet*, ed. P. Talon & V. Van Der Stede, Subartu XVI, Turnhout 2005, pp. 79–83.

3   G. Bunnens, Tell Ahmar in the Middle and Late Bronze Age, *Proceedings of the 6th International Congress on the Archaeology of the Ancient Near East* II, ed. P. Matthiae, F. Pinnock, L. Nigro & N. Marchetti, Rome 2010, pp. 116–117.

4   G. Bunnens, *art. cit.* (n. 3), fig. 5, p. 121.

5   The tomb was published by A. Roobaert, A. Otto, & A.S. Jamieson, Middle Bronze Age evidence from Tell Ahmar, *Abr-Nahrain* 35 (1998), pp. 95–134.

6   Sample TAH S02.167 S13 = UtC-9243: 3510±40 BP; 68.2%: 1890–1750 cal BC (1.00), 95.4%: 1940–1730 cal BC (0.98), 1710–1690 cal BC (0.02) (analysis made at the Belgian Royal Institute for Cultural Heritage).

7   Sample TAH S14.136 S07 = KIA-36445: 3410±20 BP; 68.2%: 1740–1685 cal BC; 95.4%: 1760–1630 cal BC (analysis made at the Belgian Royal Institute for Cultural Heritage).

8   G. Bunnens, Unfinished work at Tell Ahmar: Early and Middle Bronze Age finds, *Archaeological Explorations in Syria 2000–2011* (Proceedings of ISCACH–Beirut 2015), ed. J. Abdulmassih, Sh. Nishiyama, H. Charaf & A. Deb, Oxford 2018, pp. 35–37.

9   G. Bunnens, *art. cit.* (n. 3), pp. 111–115.

10 A. Otto, A newly discovered link in the chain of ancient oriental administration: On the interpretation of sealed Langetten, *Damascener Mitteilungen* 8 (1995), pp. 85–93; ead., *Tall Bi'a Tuttul*, IV, *Siegel und Abrollungen*, Wissenschaftliche Veröffentlichung der Deutschen Orient-Gesellschaft 104, Saarbrücken 2004, p. 163.

11 Room 2 of Block 1: sample TAH M06.51 S16 = KIA-28274: 3390±35 BP; 68.2%: 1740–1630 cal BC; 95.4% 1780–1600 cal BC. Room 1 of Block 3: sample TAH M10.17 S01 = KIA-36444: 3360±40 BP, 68.2%: 1740–1710 cal BC (9.2%), 1700–1600 cal BC (59.0%); 95.4%: 1750–1530 cal BC (analyses made at the Belgian Royal Institute for Cultural Heritage).

12 W. Sallaberger, B. Einwag & A. Otto, Schenkungen von Mittani-Königen an die Einwohner von Baṣīru: Die zwei Urkunden aus Tall Bazi am Mittleren Euphrat, *Zeitschrift für Assyriologie* 96 (2006), pp. 69–104.

13 J.D. Hawkins, The Hittite name of Til Barsip: Evidence from a new hieroglyphic fragment from Tell Ahmar, *Anatolian Studies* 33 (1983), pp. 131–136.

14 G. Bunnens, *art. cit.* (n. 3), pp. 117–118.

15 A. Otto, *Alltag und Gesellschaft zur Spätbronzezeit: Eine Fallstudie aus Tell Bazi (Syrien)*, Subartu XIX, Turnhout 2006, pp. 14–16.

16 J.-C. Margueron, Emar: un exemple d'implantation hittite en terre syrienne, *Le Moyen Euphrate*, ed. J.-C. Margueron, Strasbourg 1980, pp. 291–301.

17 M. Dunand in *Til-Barsib*, p. 42, plan D and pl. xxxviii/1.

18 M. Dunand noted 38 × 38 × 13 cm for the bricks' dimensions (*Til-Barsib*, p. 42).

Part Two

Tell Ahmar between Luwians, Aramaeans and Assyrians: Birth of a regional capital

The Early Iron Age, from around 1200 to the Assyrian conquest of Tell Ahmar in 856 (roughly Iron I and II), marked a new turning point in the history of Western Asia. The great powers that dominated the history of the region in the second half of the second millennium were either wiped off the map or considerably weakened. The disappearance of Hittite domination in northern Syria left a vacuum in which several groups infiltrated and clashed. Most prominent among them were Luwians, Aramaeans as well as Assyrians who, from the reign of Tiglath-pileser I (1114–1076) onwards, were trying to impose themselves on the Euphrates region. Carchemish, which had ruled northern Syria on behalf of the Hittite ruler in the second millennium, survived by maintaining a fiction of continuity with the defunct empire and once again became a regional power. The Assyrians implicitly recognized its status by avoiding direct confrontation with the city and by calling *Hatti* the regions west of the Euphrates. No matter the role of Carchemish, for the first time since the fall of the kingdom of Yamhad independent polities emerged. Tell Ahmar, then called Masuwari and possibly integrated into the Aramaean tribal state of Bit Adini, seems to have enjoyed full autonomy despite its proximity to Carchemish. In the ninth and eighth centuries Assyria progressively absorbed the multiple and diverse world of northern Syria, mixing brutal conquest and more or less voluntary submission according to a method that calls to mind the policy of the British Empire towards India.

For the first time in its history, Tell Ahmar found an opportunity to exert an influence that went beyond the local level.

The word *Luwian* will be used to refer to the people and its language, and *Syro-Hittite* to refer to the material culture of northern Syria.

3

Tell Ahmar/Masuwari/Til Barsib and the Aramaean tribe of Adini (c. 1200–856)

The most striking feature of the early first millennium at Tell Ahmar is the extension of the settlement. It began to spread west of the tell, on a natural eminence, the "Middle Town", now occupied by the modern village. The tell itself became an acropolis.

The evolution, however, was progressive. The early stages of this evolution are best illustrated in the eastern part of the tell, at the junction of Areas A and S. Three strata – respectively, from the oldest to the most recent, Strata A+S/7, A+S/6 and A+S/5 – are relevant to the problem.

1. Assyrians and Aramaeans

The two earliest strata, A+S/7 and A+S/6 were contemporaneous with the struggles that opposed the declining power of the Middle Assyrians to the rapidly expanding Aramaean groups. Architecture consisted of modest buildings, small houses with mud-brick walls resting on a stone base. No complete plan could be recognized. It seems that the houses were often rebuilt. Tell Ahmar must have become a village again at that time, at least judging by the small area that could be excavated.

Pottery was essentially of local manufacture, with the rather coarse burnished ceramic typical of Iron II gradually appearing. Remarkable was the presence of a large proportion of Middle Assyrian pottery, especially the carinated bowls (*Fig. 121*), which could be the sign of an Assyrian presence at Tell Ahmar at that time.

There was more than pottery to indicate a possible Assyrian presence. A grey stone cylinder seal typical of the Middle-Assyrian style was found in Stratum A+S/6 (*Fig. 122*). The main motifs were a two-headed eagle, which raised its wings as if they were arms, a bull-man and a deer.

On the other hand, local culture did not seem to be as poor as pottery and the excavated remains would suggest. A bone sculpture depicting a feline's paw, whose style can

be compared with that of some of the Carchemish reliefs that are usually dated to the eleventh century, was found in Stratum A+S/7 (*Fig. 123*).

If all these factors are taken together, the historical context seems to be that of the last Middle Assyrian attempts to control the western regions during the reigns of Tiglath-pileser I and Ashur-bel-kala in the eleventh century, when the Aramaeans were taking possession of the Euphrates valley. It should also be noted that Shalmaneser III specifically referred to the nearby cities Pitru and Mutkinu as foundations of Tiglath-pileser I:

Fig. 121. Middle Assyrian bowl (A27 PL155).

Fig. 122. Stratum A+S/6: Middle Assyrian cylinder seal (A29 O.29.80).

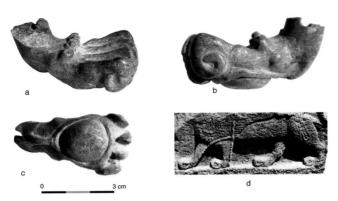

Fig. 123. Stratum A+S/7: Bone carved in the shape of a lion's paw (A29 O.29.115): a–c) the paw seen from various angles; d) relief with a sphinx, from the "Water Gate" at Carchemish (detail of Carchemish, II, pl. B28b).

> The town of Ana-Ashur-uter-asbat, which the people of Hatti call Pitru, which is on the Saju[r, on the other bank] of the Euphrates, and the town of Mutkinu, which is on this bank of the Euphrates, which Tiglath-pileser (I), my ancestor, a prince who preceded me, had seized, (and that) in the time of Ashur-rabi (II), king of Ashur, the Aramaeans had taken by force, these cities I have restored them.[1]

Tiglath-pileser's conquests did not last long, as Pitru and Mutkinu fell into the hands of the Aramaeans during the reign of Ashur-rabi II, between 1012 and 972. The brutal destruction of Stratum A+S/6 is perhaps related to these struggles between the Middle Assyrian kings and the Aramaeans and even, more precisely, to the Aramaean conquest at the time of Ashur-rabi II.

2. Luwians and Aramaeans

Before turning to Stratum A+S/5, we need to consider epigraphic material consisting of Luwian inscriptions, most of which were found at or near Tell Ahmar but, for most of them, out of archaeological context, and Assyrian royal inscriptions, mainly the inscriptions of Shalmaneser III.

a. Luwian inscriptions: Masuwari

The Luwian inscriptions from the Tell Ahmar region can be dated, according to J. David Hawkins, to the late tenth and early ninth centuries,[2] let us say to c. 920–880. The same author could also recognize that the toponym *Masuwari* used in these inscriptions was the Luwian name of Tell Ahmar.[3] We saw above (p. 74) that he further hypothesized that *Masuwari* derived from *Mazuwati* known to have been in the region of Carchemish in the second millennium, although it is not impossible, as Martin Makinson has suggested, that *Masuwari* was the Luwian form of *Muṣur* which might have designated a region in northern Syria already during the Middle Assyrian period.[4]

Most informative, as far as political history is concerned, is the inscription TELL AHMAR 1 also known as the *Autobiography of Ariyahina's Son*.[5] It is carved on the large stele of the Storm-God – Storm-God Stele B – known since Hogarth's visit to Tell Ahmar and preserved in the Aleppo Museum (*Fig. 135*). David Hawkins' translation and interpretation of this text will be followed here.[6] The name of the author of the inscription is lost in a gap. We only know that he was the son of a certain Ariyahina. He traces the story of his family back to one Hapatila who seems to have died violently and, therefore, could hardly have had a full reign. He was succeeded by his grandson Ariyahina who was still a child and does not seem to have been able to reign for very long either because he was ousted by Hamiyata's father. Hamiyata's father may have reached a certain age when he dispossessed the legitimate ruler, hence he too is not likely to have had a long reign. Hamiyata succeeded his father and is probably the only ruler on the list to have had a full reign. When he died, his son did not stay in power for long because the legitimate heir could manage to claim back his throne. There results from this that, from the chronological point of view, only three of these rulers must be taken into consideration – Hapatila, Hamiyata's father and Hamiyata – of whom only Hamiyata is likely to have had a full reign. A duration of about 50 or 60 years for the three of them would therefore be a reasonable guess. Hapatila could therefore have got into power at Masuwari c. 60 years before the approximate date of the Luwian inscriptions (920–880), that is any time around 980–940, and Ariyahina's son must have recovered his throne towards the end of the time range assigned to the Luwian inscriptions, that is c. 880.

The extent of the territory placed under Masuwari's control is not known but if – as is always perilous – we transfer to the tenth century information contained in the eighth century inscriptions of Inurta-belu-usur, Assyrian governor of Kar-Shalmaneser, discovered at Arslan-Tash (on which see below pp. 104–105), we see that it may have included Arslan Tash/Hadatu and possibly also Serrin to the southeast of Tell Ahmar. Other toponyms mentioned in relation to Masuwari are more difficult to locate.

Masuwari thus formed an independent polity under the authority of a local dynasty that was in power since the second quarter of the tenth century and it controlled a territory that appears to have extended downstream along the Euphrates as well as eastwards at least as far as Arslan Tash/Hadatu. Towards the north its expansion must have been blocked by Carchemish.

b. Assyrian inscriptions: Til Barsib and Bit Adini

Shalmaneser III conquered Tell Ahmar in 856 after two failed attempts in 858 and 857.[7] The Assyrian conquest took place at a slightly more recent time than that of the Luwian inscriptions but no mention was made of any Luwian presence at Tell Ahmar. Shalmaneser III did not know the name Masuwari and used *Til Barsib* instead, a name that was not found before him in the Assyrian inscriptions. Moreover, he described the city as the stronghold of a ruler that he called either *Ahuni of Bit Adini* or *Ahuni, son of Adini*. This meant that Ahuni was a member either of a tribe bearing the name of its ancestor and founder Adini or of a dynasty founded by one Adini. In any case, Ahuni was obviously a Semite as is shown by both his name and that of Adini, which are West Semitic. As for Til Barsib, it might also be a Semitic name. One of its spellings was Til Barsaib,[8] which points to an original form of the name that could have been "Hill (*til*) of the son (*bar*) of the grey/old man (*šayeb*)".

Bit Adini enters historical records at the time of Adadnirari II at the turn of the tenth and ninth centuries. Adadnirari, who was campaigning in the region of Tûr Abdin in 899, says that he received two female monkeys from the country of Bit Adini "which is on the bank of the Euphrates".[9] A few years later, Ashurnasirpal II quelled a revolt in Bit Halupe, on the lower course of the Habur, where a usurper from Bit Adini had seized power.[10] On another occasion, Ashurnasirpal declared that he pursued Azi-ili, ruler of the region of Laqê, downstream from the confluence of the Habur and the Euphrates, as far as Dummetu and Azmu, "cities of Bit Adini".[11] Dummetu and Azmu are usually identified with Halabiye and Zalabiye upstream from Deir ez-Zor. Lastly, at some stage between 876 and 868, Ashurnasirpal campaigned directly against Bit Adini and seized one of its border cities named Kaprabu,[12] probably in the region of Ras el-Ain.[13] It is on this occasion that we hear for the first time of Ahuni,[14] who, together with Habinu of Til Abni, paid tribute to Ashurnasirpal. Ahuni's submission probably explains why the king could subsequently go through Bit Adini and cross the Euphrates.[15] During this march he "conquered" several of Bit Adini's cities such as Marina (in which some propose to recognize Bur Marina, the modern Shiyukh Foqani north of Tell Ahmar)[16] Rugulitu, of unknown location, and Yalligu (or Alligu) which one hypothesis places at Tell Beddayeh, also called Hledjak,[17] some distance north of Tell Ahmar. Ashurnasirpal seems thus to have campaigned in the region of Tell Ahmar as Tiglath-pileser I before him. Til Barsib/Masuwari, however, is not mentioned.

Assyrian records thus know Tell Ahmar under the possibly Semitic name Til Barsib, attested from 858 onwards.

It was the stronghold of a ruler bearing the Semitic name Ahuni, mentioned for the first time in c. 876–868, and member of a larger polity called Bit Adini – another Semitic name – which is attested from 899. This is in sharp contrast to the Luwian evidence, dating from c. 920–880, which calls Tell Ahmar Masuwari and implies that Tell Ahmar was under Luwian influence.

There is thus an apparent inconsistency in the evidence available to us and much ink has been spilled trying to resolve it.[18] However, the inconsistency might be more apparent than real if we realize that the two categories of documents take different points of view. The Luwian inscriptions, which were written on behalf of local rulers, see things from the inside. The Assyrian sources, which reflect the view of conquerors coming from the east, see them from the outside.

c. Towards a reconstruction of Tell Ahmar's history c. 1100–856[19]

The chronological sequence drawn from the Assyrian inscriptions – which includes three key moments (the conquests of Tiglath-pileser I, the Aramaean conquest, the conquest by Shalmaneser III) – is put into parallel with the chronological sequence from the Luwian inscriptions in Table 2.

There are striking coincidences between the two sequences. The Aramaeans occupied sites of the Tell Ahmar region a few decades before Hapatila is likely to have ascended the throne of Masuwari. Bit Adini entered the historical stage at more-or-less the same time as Hamiyata was active at Masuwari and Ariyahina's son recovered his dynastic heritage at more or less the same time as Ahuni of Bit Adini was mentioned for the first time.

This leaves two possibilities. Either the rulers known from Luwian inscriptions represent a local political development in the broader framework of Bit Adini or each of the sequences reflect a different aspect of the same reality. There are indications that the latter possibility is closer to the historical truth.

An analysis of the personal names occurring in the Luwian inscriptions of Tell Ahmar shows that some of them might be explained as Semitic. For instance, in the *Autobiography of Ariyahina's Son*, the name Hapatila,

Table 2. Chronological sequences drawn from Assyrian and Luwian evidence.

(1)	c. 1100	Conquest of Pitru and Mutkinu by Tiglath-pileser I (1114–1076)		
(2)	c. 1000	Conquest of Pitru and Mutkinu by the Aramaeans (Ashur-rabi II 1012–972)	c. 980/940	Hapatila becomes ruler of Masuwari
	899	First mention of Bit Adini (Adad-nirari II 911–891)	c. 920/880	Luwian inscriptions centring on Hamiyata
	c. 876/868	First mention of Ahuni (Ashurnasirpal II 883–859)	c. 880	Ariyahina's son recovers his throne
(3)	856	Conquest of Pitru, Mutkinu and Til Barsib by Shalmaneser III		

rather than a Hurrian name as sometimes assumed, could be the Luwian transcription of the name *'Abd-'ila*, a distant ancestor of Arabic Abdallah, and meaning "Servant-of-God" or "Servant of El". Similarly, Hamiyata could transcribe a name like *'Ammî-yada'* meaning something like "My-(Divine-)Parent-Knows-(Me)". A third name, for which a Semitic interpretation seems possible, appears in an unprovenanced inscription known as ALEPPO 2.[20] Its author was one Arpa, a name that E. Lipiński explains as "Born-on-the Fourth-Day".[21]

If the possibility of a Semitic etymology is accepted, it becomes possible to consider the rulers of Masuwari, and first and foremost Hamiyata, as Semites and, most probably, Aramaeans. Masuwari's socio-political structures, to the extent we know them, point in the same direction. They belong to a system based on kinship, either tribal or by lineage. The word "brother" appears in contexts where it seems to imply some kind of consanguinity between members of the ruling elite, although it cannot be entirely ruled out that the word is to be taken literally. For instance, Arpa, in the already mentioned inscription ALEPPO 2 speaks of his "lord and brother" (§ 3), his "brother Hamiyata" (§ 9), and also refers to "(what) I shall present to my brother in goodness" (§ 17). Hamiyata himself, in a broken context, speaks of "the brother or the brother's son" in the inscription carved on Storm-God Stele A (§ 18).[22] Lastly, Ariyahina's son says of Hamiyata that "me he made great(er) than his (own) brothers" (§ 16). Members of the ruling class might have considered themselves brothers because they belonged to the same lineage or to the same tribal group. All this is compatible with an Aramaean rulership over the city.

How can we reconcile the Luwian and Assyrian perspectives? There are two notable differences between them. The first concerns the protagonists of local history. The Luwian inscriptions ignore Ahuni and the Assyrian texts do not mention any of the two dynasties known through the *Autobiography of Ariyahina's Son*. The second difference concerns the very name of Tell Ahmar, Masuwari in one case, Til Barsib in the other.

As far as Ahuni is concerned, it is generally considered that Til Barsib was its main residence and, therefore, the capital of Bit Adini. Shalmaneser III most often referred to Til Barsib as the "stronghold" of Ahuni. Only very exceptionally did he call it the "royal city" of the Aramaean ruler. In fact, as Hélène Sader noted, the real capital, or at least the main residence, of Ahuni seems rather to have been Shitamrat where he led his last resistance.[23] This would leave room for a local government different from that of Ahuni, but dependent on him. From this point of view, one may wonder whether this local power is not precisely the one represented by the local "Luwian" rulers who would have been "brothers" of Ahuni and therefore members of the "House of Adini" (literal meaning of "Bit Adini").

The Aramaean takeover might have happened in two stages. First, at the turn of the eleventh and tenth century, Aramaeans belonging to an unspecified group settled in the region of Pitru and Mutkinu. At the same time Hapatila founded a dynasty at Masuwari. Then, a century later, Bit Adini entered the stage and a usurper (Hamiyata's father) seized power in Masuwari. Such a reconstruction, however hypothetical it may be, is the most plausible in the present stage of knowledge.

In such a context, the adoption of the Syro-Hittite art style and of the Luwian language might have been due to reasons of prestige. Both art style and language were very much alive in neighbouring Carchemish, only 20 km away. Anxious to revive the urban traditions of the second millennium and lacking their own traditions in this field, the members of the House of Adini would have adopted means of propaganda which derived directly from the old urban culture and which were easily accessible at a short distance from Tell Ahmar. This would be a good example of what anthropologists call "acculturation".

Similar reasons might explain the use of the two names Til Barsib and Masuwari. As we saw above, Til Barsib seems to be an Aramaic name and could thus be the name given to the town by the Aramaeans when they settled in the region. On the other hand, the name Masuwari associated with the Luwian language would have had the prestige of its origin and would have been considered the only designation worthy of use in monumental inscriptions.

The contradiction between Luwian and Assyrian sources can therefore be resolved by considering the differences in intention and genesis of the two categories of evidence. The Assyrians described what they saw when they encountered an Aramaean tribe or lineage exerting control over an urban centre, whereas the Luwian inscriptions would have given the idealized vision that the rulers of Masuwari wanted to publicize: the image of rulers conforming to the practices of an urban culture rooted in the second millennium. In both cases, the central issue was the control that the House of Adini exerted over an urban centre in the upper Syrian Euphrates.

It is not impossible, moreover, that the process of "Luwianization" of Tell Ahmar was limited to the reign of Hamiyata. All the Luwian inscriptions from the region of Tell Ahmar, when they are sufficiently well preserved to allow the identification of their author, are either written on behalf of Hamiyata (five inscriptions) or linked in some way to his person (inscription of his "brother" Arpa and *Autobiography of Ariyahina's Son* who defeated Hamiyata's heir). It would therefore not be surprising that the adoption of the Luwian language for the writing of monumental inscriptions was the work of Hamiyata himself. And would it be too adventurous to consider that the adoption of the Syro-Hittite style for large stelae and decorative reliefs was also due to Hamiyata?

3. Where was the palace of the rulers of Masuwari?

The existence of a local ruler implies the existence of at least one palace in Masuwari. The most likely place to look for it is, of course, the Acropolis. In fact, Stratum A+S/5 marks a complete re-organization of the eastern sector of the tell. A large building, of which only the foundations were preserved, replaced the houses of the underlying strata. Three walls, up to 1.60–1.70 m wide and oriented east–west, delimited spaces that were filled with a combination of soil and horizontally laid bricks (*Fig. 124*). The cohesion of the walls and the filling material was ensured by layers of reeds placed at regular intervals (*Fig. 125a*). At the time of excavation, the reeds had turned into a pinkish-white powder. The dismantling of one of the two walls showed that it also included layers of branches, which had also been reduced to a pinkish-white powder (*Fig. 125b*).

When superimposed the plan of the so-called *niveau araméen* excavated by the Thureau-Dangin expedition and the plan of the renewed excavations show a great correspondence between the *bâtiment est* of the *niveau araméen* of the French excavations and the foundation walls exposed in the renewed excavations (*Fig. 126*). The orientation and thickness of the walls is the same. The *bâtiment est* also has deep foundations, and the elevation of its floors which fluctuates between 105.45 and 105.64 after conversion into the system adopted by the renewed excavations, corresponds to the level of the top of the northernmost foundation wall (c. 105.60). It is probably one and the same building, which must have been set against a pre-Assyrian rampart whose remains were recognized further down the slope of the tell. Placed stratigraphically above a stratum containing Iron II pottery and immediately below the Neo-Assyrian palace, which dates from Iron III, the *bâtiment est* must date from the end of the Iron II period. These remains most probably belonged to the settlement that Shalmaneser III conquered in 856.

Other remains found on the Acropolis may have belonged to the same period. M. Dunand had already noted that the north-eastern sector of the Neo-Assyrian palace was lower than the rest of the palace in absolute elevation and that it may have belonged to an earlier construction.[24] In fact,

a

b

Fig. 125. Stratum A+S/5: Plant remains found in the walls of the early first millennium (Iron Age II): a) reed layer discovered when dismantling the wall in the foreground of Fig. 124; b) marks left by branches in the wall visible in the background of Fig. 124.

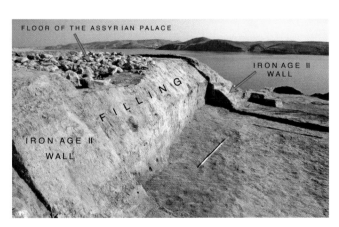

Fig. 124. Stratum A+S/5: Remains of walls probably associated with the bâtiment est *of the French excavations (looking SE).*

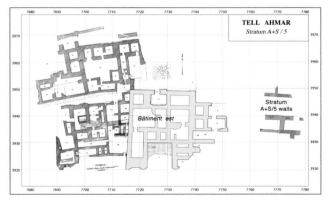

Fig. 126. Combined plan of the niveau araméen *of the French excavations and the Stratum A+S/5 walls of the renewed excavation (adapted from* Til-Barsib, *Plan C).*

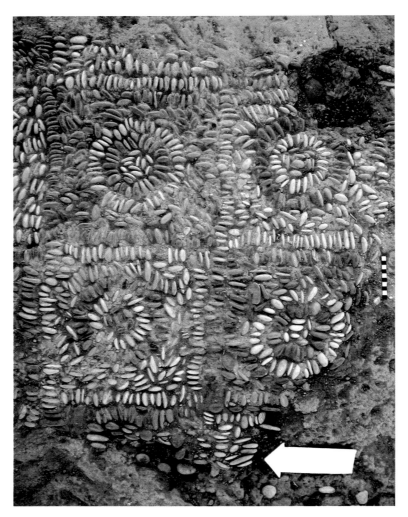

Fig. 127. Assyrian palace: Pebble mosaic floor of Courtyard XLIII.

this sector of the palace was at an altitude close to that of the *bâtiment est*. Courtyard XLIII, at the eastern end of the sector, had a mosaic of pebbles arranged in a checkerboard pattern. Four of its squares were re-exposed during the renewed excavations and transferred to the Aleppo Museum. They revealed a great skill in execution (*Fig. 127*). Black and white concentric circles formed rosettes within the squares. The colours alternated from one square to the next, with a black or white background and a black or white centre. It is not certain, however, that Corridor XLIX, which was also decorated with a pebble mosaic, belonged to the same ensemble. It could have provided the transition between Apartment I and the old building integrated into the palace.

More architectural vestiges were found in the western sector of the Acropolis during the renewed excavations. Another mosaic pavement combining black and white pebbles in a checkerboard pattern appeared immediately below the Assyrian palace (*Figs 128–130*). Only part of the original surface was preserved. This pavement was crossed by at

least two paths of terracotta slabs of north-west to south-east and north-east to south-west orientation respectively. The mosaic squares were irregular in shape and uneven in size (*Fig. 129*). In at least three of them, the pebbles were forming a rosette (*Fig. 130*). The play of colour was greatly simplified here, compared with the other mosaic rosettes. Uniformly black squares were alternating with uniformly white squares.

Apart from the possible existence of a wall to the south-west of the mosaic, no architecture associated with this pavement could be identified. It is likely that the earthworks required for the construction of the Assyrian palace almost entirely destroyed the remains of this level of occupation. However, given its extreme fragility, a mosaic pavement was not very suitable for decorating a square or public space. It is more likely that it belonged to a high standard building with restricted access.

Pebble mosaics will subsequently be adopted in large parts of the Assyrian empire, including Assyrian Tell Ahmar

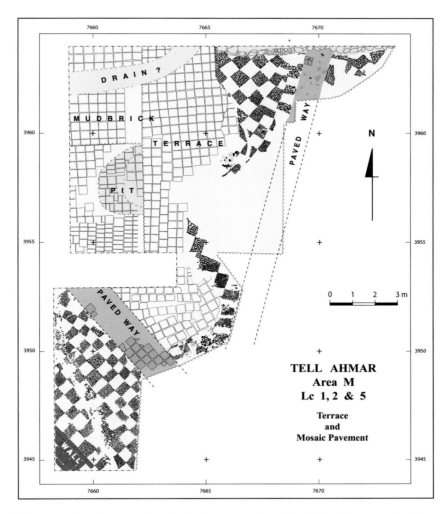

Fig. 128. Plan of the pebble mosaic floor discovered under the Assyrian palace. The bricks that appear in the upper left corner belong to the massive structure that consolidated the flanks of the Acropolis. A curving depression in the upper left corner corresponds to a drain visible in the outer courtyard of the Assyrian palace on the plan drawn by the French expedition (Fig. 161).

(below, pp. 119, 145, 152, 154).[25] Their origin, however, is to be looked for in the Hittite world. The earliest example so far is a pavement uncovered at Uşaklı Höyük in central Asia Minor, dating from the Late Bronze Age.[26]

The Acropolis of Masuwari may thus have had, like other cities of this period – such as Hama, Tell Halaf or Zincirli – several official buildings. At least three of them have left traces. To the west, a high standard building with a courtyard decorated with a pebble mosaic, to the east, the *bâtiment est* with its probable extension towards the eastern edge of the tell, and to the north-east, the building that was later integrated into the Assyrian palace.

One of them may have been the palace of the rulers of Masuwari, unless there was no formal palace and all the buildings erected on the Acropolis formed both an administrative and a residential complex where the rulers resided and from where they exerted power.

4. The residential quarter and the temple of the Storm-God

Of the town itself, it can only be said that it stood on the terrace of the Middle Town, west of the tell. Two soundings (K and L) have established that this area was only occupied during the Iron Age. Driven out of the main mound, now occupied by prestige buildings associated with the central power, the inhabitants of Masuwari were forced to settle further west.

Curiously enough, no sacred buildings have been found dating from the Iron Age on the Acropolis. However, a Luwian inscription raises the possibility that the Storm-God of Aleppo was worshipped at Masuwari[27] and a temple of the Storm-God was mentioned by Inurta-belu-usur, a later Assyrian governor of the city already mentioned above. Unfortunately, neither the French nor the renewed excavations have been able to find a trace of this temple. A possible

Fig. 129. Detail of the pebble mosaic found under the Assyrian palace.

Fig. 130. Rosette-shaped mosaic squares.

location would be at the western end of the Middle Town, under the modern cemetery. This cemetery extends over a small mound which could represent a kind of tell covering the debris of a large building. Sculptures found in its vicinity by the French expedition give credibility to the identification of this hypothetical building with a temple, perhaps the temple of the Storm-God. The statue of an Assyrian official discovered in Area C (see below, pp. 130–131) could also come from it. The question remains open.

5. The power of images

The north Syrian principalities developed extensive programmes of narrative reliefs in the Syro-Hittite tradition to proclaim the political and religious ideals of the ruling class. The excavations at Tell Ahmar have brought to light several such reliefs. Unfortunately, apart from the large Storm-God Stele B uncovered outside the West Gate (*Fig. 135*), none has been found in its original context.

The Syro-Hittite reliefs of Tell Ahmar included stelae, generally quadrangular in section, and orthostats intended to decorate the base of the walls of official buildings – mainly palaces, temples and city gates. Most of the stelae had an official character, intended to be works of political

and religious propaganda. Others were made for wealthy individuals.

a. Religion and politics: The large Storm-God stelae

The official stelae were six in number, all carved with a figure of the Storm-God and a Luwian inscription. Four of these were set up by Hamiyata. The fifth was the stele of Arpa, "brother" of Hamiyata, and the sixth was the stele carrying the inscription of Ariyahina's son.

Iconography of the Storm-God

The best preserved and most elaborate of these stelae was retrieved from the Euphrates in 1999, some distance downstream from Tell Ahmar near the village of Qubbah, hence its name Ahmar/Qubbah Stele (*Figs 131, 132*). The front side (A) was decorated with a sculpture in high relief. The upper half of the other three sides (B, C, D) was carved with a Luwian inscription in which Hamiyata commemorated a military victory.[28]

The sculpture on the front side (*Fig. 132*) combines four motifs whose symbolisms complemented each other. At the top is a winged disc encased in a crescent moon. The winged disc was a solar symbol of Egyptian origin which was adopted in Western Asia in the second millennium and became associated with royal power in the Hittite world without, however, losing its solar character. In several instances, the symbol was enriched with the addition of a crescent, probably to accentuate the cosmic significance of the symbol. It was no longer the sun that was conjured, but also the moon and with them, one can believe, the whole celestial world whose wings covered the world.

The second motif, and the main figure, is the image of the Storm-God, which is also laden with symbols. The god wears a helmet decorated with two pairs of horns that mark his divine status. His attire is a mixture of contemporary features and archaisms. The short tunic with the sword at the side belongs to the dress code of the aristocracy at the beginning of the first millennium, but the sandals with upturned toes were common in both the Bronze and Iron Ages. The long hair braid ending in a loop is one of the distinctive features of the Storm-God in second millennium Hittite Syria. The most important symbols, however, are the objects that the god holds in his hands. In his right hand, he holds an axe, a symbol of lightning's destructive power. In his left is a sort of trident, actually a highly stylized form of lightning. However, the god of thunderstorms should not be seen as an entirely negative power. His force could be beneficial. The rain he caused to fall brought fertility to the earth and prosperity to mankind. He was an ambivalent deity, both destructive and fruitful, who played an essential role in the functioning of the universe. Like the winged disc, he came to be associated with royal power already in the second millennium.

The third motif, the young bull on which the Storm-God stands, complements the symbolism of the divine figure. The bull has been associated from very early with the Storm-God. It could shake the earth with its hooves as the god did with lightning and, like the god, it personified strength and impetuosity. Finally, it was a symbol of fertility, a perfect complement to the god whose rain was another provider of fertility. The bull, when it was associated with the Storm-God, was always young and, at least in the Syrian environment, it could be invoked as an autonomous deity.[29] It was therefore more than a mere symbol.

The fourth motif, the guilloche on which rests the whole scene, also has distant origins. It was found as early as the fourth millennium. In some cases it seems that the guilloche was used to imitate the ripples of moving water. Such is probably the symbolism that we must consider in order to understand the stele of the Storm-God. The guilloche might have been intended to represent either the sea, which the Storm-God defeated according to an old tradition, or, more generally, the cosmic ocean on which the earth rested.

The stele not only bears a divine image but it was also a symbolic composition which illustrates both the cosmic role of the Storm-God, an intermediary between the celestial regions and the ocean depths, and the violent force of the god who, if channelled, brought prosperity to the earth, victory in wartime and political power in peacetime. This symbolism can certainly be extended to the other stelae of the Storm-God found at Tell Ahmar and its region. The number

Fig. 132. The Ahmar/Qubbah stele (Aleppo M 11611).

Fig. 131. Find-spot of the Ahmar/Qubbah stele. The stele appears in the foreground just below the surface.

Fig. 133. Storm-God stele A from Tell Ahmar (Louvre AO 11505) (photo: © RMN-Grand Palais [Musée du Louvre]/Mathieu Rabeau).

Fig. 134. Upper part of the stele bearing the inscription ALEPPO 2 (Stele of Arpa, Aleppo M 6528B). The winged disc at the top and the trident-like thunderbolt on the right are clearly distinguishable. Less clear but still visible is the weapon below the left wing of the winged disc.

sculpture and the god are depicted in exactly the same way as on the stele found in the Euphrates. Particularly characteristic are the trident-shaped thunderbolt – although here the points of the trident undulate – and the axe that the god brandishes. The carving of the relief, however, is stiffer, presumably because the stele did not come from the same workshop.

Another stele is kept in the Bible Lands Museum in Jerusalem.[30] It is of unknown provenance but, as it bears an inscription of Hamiyata, it must come from the Tell Ahmar region or even from Tell Ahmar itself. Like the previous one, this stele was broken at the lower part. As for the motifs, they are the same, including the trident with wavy points. The style, on the other hand, is clearly different from that of the other stelae. The relief here is almost flat.

The stele of Arpa, Hamiyata's "brother", certainly bears a figure of the Storm-God but is more difficult to interpret because it has been almost completely erased and covered by the text. One can only recognize faint traces of the trident-shaped thunderbolt the god is holding in his left hand and of the weapon in his right (*Fig. 134*). More visible, because the inscription does not cover it, is the winged disc associated with a crescent, which crowned the stele. A possible explanation for the preservation of the winged disc could be found in the inscription. Arpa says that he erected a monument – assumedly this stele – to the Sun-God. One can imagine that the stele was originally conceived as a monument dedicated to the Storm-God and carved with a figure of the god below a winged sun disc. Then the figure of the god would have been erased, only the winged disc being preserved, and a stele originally dedicated to the Storm-God was turned into a monument to the glory of the Sun-God.[31] There is no indication

of details common to them establishes the homogeneity of thought that presided over their realization.

A stele from Tell Ahmar, Storm-God Stele A, is unfortunately broken at the bottom (*Fig. 133*). It is therefore not known whether the god was standing on the back of a young bull or whether the entire scene was based on a guilloche, but a winged disc associated with a crescent figured in the upper part of the of a pre-existing inscription. It is thus an uninscribed stele portraying the Storm-God that has been reworked by Arpa and carved with his inscription. Was this change a sign of tensions between Arpa and his "brother" Hamiyata?

If this were the case, it is surprising that Ariyahina's son did not hesitate to adopt the iconography of Hamiyata's stelae on a monument celebrating the defeat of his son and the return of a rival dynasty (Storm-God Stele B) (*Fig. 135*). The occasion would have been favourable for an ideological change. Indeed, all the features of the Ahmar/Qubbah stele are found again on the stele of Ariyahina's son. The style itself is close to it without, however, showing the same plasticity. The tradition that Hamiyata seems to have established had therefore survived him.

Character of the Storm-God – Baal Shamem and the god of Aleppo

The combination of motifs shown in the scene carved on the stelae of the Storm-God is original and seems to be specific to the region of Tell Ahmar. Other reliefs found elsewhere in the Syro-Hittite area are comparable but differ in their use of symbols.[32] Taken individually, these motifs can be traced back to the second millennium. Their association, however, confer an original identity to the Storm-God and highlights his role as a cosmic power. The inscriptions accompanying the reliefs refer to the god by the name Tarhunza, which was the Luwian name of the Storm-God. This is probably only an *intrepretatio luwiana* of the god's name, which must have differed according to the language of the person honouring him. His Semitic name must have been *Hadad* or, more generally, *Baal*, *i.e.* "Lord", an epithet that was frequently used since the second millennium to call the Storm-God.

Four of the six stelae dedicated to the Storm-God designate him as *Heavenly Tarhunza*.[33] It so happens that a form of the Storm-God, which began to spread at the beginning of the first millennium, was that of Baal Shamem, the "Lord of Heaven". The coincidence between the expressions "Baal Shamem" and "Heavenly Tarhunza", together with the emphasis put on the cosmic aspect of the Storm-God on the Tell Ahmar stelae, invites to consider the god depicted on these stelae as close to Baal Shamem, or a prefiguration of Baal Shamem, on whose origins the stelae would thus shed light.

It is possible to go a step further in defining the aspect of the Storm-God portrayed at Tell Ahmar. There are reasons to believe that the figure of the god brandishing an axe and a lightning in the shape of a trident may have been that of the Storm-God of Aleppo. Similar divine figures were formally designated as *Tarhunza of Aleppo*. One was on a Syro-Hittite stele discovered in Babylon and another found in Körkün in Turkey. At Tell Ahmar itself, a stele of Hamiyata designated the divine representation carved on its front side – unfortunately lost, but in all likelihood similar to the other known representations – as that of *Tarhunza of Aleppo* (TELL AHMAR 5, §3). Another feature goes in the same direction. Two inscriptions from Tell Ahmar, TELL AHMAR 5 and 6,

Fig. 135. Storm-God stele B discovered outside the West Gate of Tell Ahmar (Aleppo Museum).

Fig. 136. Fragments of a military parade (after Til-Barsib*, pls ix/2 [a], x/10 [b], ix/3 [c], x/9 [d], ix/1 [e]) (fragments a and e are in the Louvre, AO 23013 and AO 21410 respectively). The fragments have been arbitrarily assembled to give an idea of the kind of scene they may have belonged to. Soldiers were coming back from battle carrying severed heads of enemies.*

mention a person speaking on behalf of the Storm-God, *i.e.* a kind of prophet. The relevant passage in TELL AHMAR 5 is tentatively translated by J.D. Hawkins as "to me his *spokesman* said" (§11) and, in TELL AHMAR 6, as "and the god-inspired (one) said to me" (§22). In one of the cases, the god is formally identified as the Storm-God of Aleppo (TELL AHMAR 5). Prophets of the Storm-God of Aleppo were already known through the texts of Mari in the eighteenth century.[34] Unfortunately, a formal confirmation cannot come from Aleppo. The only representation of the Storm-God that comes with certainty from there was found in his temple on the citadel.[35] This relief, first dated to the eleventh century[36] but now attributed to the period of Hittite domination, was still visible in the eleventh century, when King Taita had a relief with his own effigy placed next to it.[37] The god is depicted in a manner similar to his representations on the stelae of Tell Ahmar – helmet with two pairs of horns, long hair braid, short tunic, sword at the side and shoes with upturned toes – but he holds no object in his two clenched fists. The "Smiting God" posture of the god, with his arms raised as if he were about to strike an enemy, nevertheless implies that he was brandishing at least one weapon and probably two, but their nature is left to the imagination of the viewer.

The Storm-God of Aleppo was, together with the Moon-God of Harran, one of the two main deities of Syria at the beginning of the first millennium. It is therefore not surprising that at Tell Ahmar, the great god of Aleppo was reinterpreted in a way that brought him close to a new form of the Storm-God that was emerging, namely that of

Baal Shamem. The reasons for choosing the Storm-God, in preference to the Moon-God of Harran, were probably political, as we shall see now.

Hamiyata's personal role

As we have seen above, the six large stelae dedicated to the Storm-God were either stelae of Hamiyata or stelae linked in one way or another to his person. The combination of motifs – winged disc enhanced by a crescent, figure of the Storm-God reminiscent of that of the god of Aleppo, young bull and guilloche – may therefore have been a personal choice of Hamiyata. On the other hand, as we already saw, an inscription of Inurta-belu-usur, governor of Kar-Shalmaneser at the beginning of the eighth century, attested to the existence of a temple of the Storm-God in Tell Ahmar. It may be to this temple that the inscription TELL AHMAR 5 was referring when it said that Hamiyata's father had placed granaries under the protection of the god of Aleppo. The temple of the Storm-God, in such a case, could have been dedicated to the Storm-God of Aleppo and honoured there in the form illustrated by the reliefs. Hamiyata, or possibly his father, who was a usurper and therefore in search of legitimacy, would thus have obtained the protection of a god who for centuries had protected royal power.

b. The power and the glory of the rulers of Masuwari: The orthostats

The orthostates can be grouped according to their theme, either military, ceremonial or religious. Among the fragments of a military nature were those that, very likely, came from reliefs showing soldiers in short tunics and holding shields and spears, as well as the severed heads of enemies.[38] The unity of style of these fragments suggests that they were parts of an ensemble representing a military parade (*Fig. 136*). A fragment found on surface during the renewed excavations can be added to these reliefs. It shows a hand holding objects that must be a bow and two arrows (*Fig. 137*). David Ussishkin correctly observed that both the style and the theme of these reliefs were close to the carved decoration of the "King's Gate" of Carchemish,[39] usually attributed to the dynasty of Kings Suhi and Katuwa, *i.e.* to the tenth or early ninth centuries. It was also the time of the Luwian inscriptions of Tell Ahmar. It may therefore be asked whether Hamiyata was not inspired by the style of neighbouring Carchemish to have his reliefs executed. Hamiyata was proud of his military exploits as is especially evidenced by the Ahmar/Qubbah inscription.

A complete, although badly damaged, orthostat belongs to the ceremonial category. It is decorated with a figure walking to the right, wearing a long tunic tightened at the waist by a wide belt to which a sword or dagger is attached (*Fig. 138*). He holds his right forearm at waist height and, in his left hand, carries a staff that rests on his shoulder. The person that the relief portrays must have been a member of the ruling elite parading in some form of ceremony.

Fig. 137. Fragment of Syro-Hittite relief with a hand holding a bow and two arrows.

Fig. 139. Fragment of a relief figuring a bull led to the sacrifice (Aleppo Museum) (photo: Anwar Abd al-Ghafur).

Fig. 138. Syro-Hittite orthostate portraying a member of the ruling elite (Aleppo M 9947).

Aleppo M7495

Fig. 140. Syro-Hittite orthostate with two griffins (Aleppo M 7495) (photo: Anwar Abd el-Ghafour).

Several fragments have more religious overtones. One shows a divine tiara with a pair of horns, another the end of the right wing of what must have been a winged disc, and a few show fragments of animal legs.[40] They may have been part of religious, sacrificial or mythological scenes. They may also have belonged to protective figures. These reliefs are very similar in style to the reliefs of the Suhi-Katuwa period in Carchemish. On one of these fragments, Thureau-Dangin recognized a galloping horse (*Fig. 139*),[41] of which only the lower part of one leg can be seen, accompanied by a man on foot, of which one leg is visible. Actually, the scene must have represented a bull being led to the sacrifice. The figure accompanying the animal was probably a priest, as can be seen in better-preserved scenes from

Malatya[42] and Carchemish.[43] A fully preserved but badly damaged orthostat shows two griffins sitting on either side of a stylized tree (*Fig. 140*). The style and composition of the relief is reminiscent of a Tell Halaf orthostat on which two "unicorns" stand on either side of a stylized tree.[44] The lion's hindquarters carved on another orthostat are likely to come from a protective figure that probably decorated a monumental doorway (*Fig. 141*).

These reliefs give a clear indication of the existence, at Masuwari, of decorative programmes aimed at magnifying the power and piety of the ruling class. Similar programmes developed on the walls of city gates in Malatya, Carchemish, Zincirli and Karatepe. Gates of this kind must have existed at Tell Ahmar but none has been identified so far.

Fig. 141. Fragment of Syro-Hittite orthostat with the hindquarters of a lion.

c. Masuwari's aristocracy: The figurative stelae

Some stelae reflect more personal concerns. They were very likely produced for an economic or political elite, as the costs generated by the execution of these stelae must have been high.

One of them presents a scene of obviously religious character. It shows a figure of the Storm-God very similar to the one carved on the large stelae examined above but was smaller in size (Storm-God Stele C) (*Fig. 142*). As on the larger stelae, the god brandishes an axe and a trident-like thunderbolt and the winged disc at the top of the stele is set in a crescent. However, the god is not standing on a bull and a symbol has been added to the scene. A bird perched on a staff was placed in front of the god. The meaning of this symbol – sometimes associated with the god Ninurta – is unknown here but it indicates that the avatar of the Storm-God represented on this stele is different from the one that the larger stelae were intended to honour. This monument may have been used for a domestic cult of the Storm-God, or it may have been placed by a worshipper in a temple of Masuwari.

A stele with a rounded top shows a standing male figure facing to the left (*Fig. 143*). The general appearance of the figure is very similar to that seen on Syro-Hittite reliefs and statues from the tenth and ninth centuries, especially royal figures portrayed on the reliefs of Carchemish and Zincirli as well as the statues of Ain et-Tell, near Aleppo, and Serrin, east of Tell Ahmar. Like these royal figures, the figure on the stele of Tell Ahmar is dressed in a long robe tightened at the waist by a high belt. He is holding a cup in its left hand and, in his right, a staff – a sign of royalty – that unfortunately is almost completely lost in a break. A curved form visible under the beard could be the crescent-shaped pectoral that is seen on some royal portraits. There are thus reasons to believe that the figure depicted on this stele is that of prince of Masuwari. Stylistically, this

Fig. 142. Storm-God stele C (Louvre AO 13091) (photo: © RMN-Grand Palais [Musée du Louvre]/Hervé Lewandowski).

relief must be added to those that present close similarities with the Carchemish reliefs of the Suhi-Katuwa period. The function of the stele is not known but, given the absence of any detail giving the image a meaning other than that of a simple portrait, it is probably a funerary stele intended to perpetuate the memory of the deceased or an image placed in a sanctuary to invite the divinity to remember the portrayed person.

Fig. 144. Syro-Hittite stele depicting a woman and a child (Aleppo M 7496) (photo: Anwar Abd el-Ghafour).

Fig. 143. Syro-Hittite stele portraying a member of the ruling elite (Aleppo M 7494) (photo: Anwar Abd el-Ghafour).

Another stele stands out for its originality. It shows a rather rare example of a child accompanied by a female figure, most probably his mother (*Fig. 144*). The top of the stele is broken but the start of its curving edge is still visible on the left. The female figure is dressed in a long garment covering her head and tightened at the waist, in the same way as female figures represented at Carchemish. Her feet wear shoes with upturned toes. She stretches her arms over the child, possibly in a gesture of supplication, or she is holding an object that is no longer identifiable. The child, dressed in a similar garment but without head cover, is also wearing shoes with upturned toes. His left arm is bent either to make a greeting gesture or to present an object. The function of this stele is no clearer than that of the previous one. It could be another funerary stele on

which a mother would recommend her child to the powers of the Netherworld. It could also be, as F. Thureau-Dangin thought, a scene of consecration, the child being an oblate,[45] or else a scene of presentation to the court of a prince, where the child would receive a special education.

***

Significant changes in the morphology of the site can be related to new developments of the socio-political structures of Syria at the turn of the second and first millennia.

Tell Ahmar's Acropolis which, judging by the small area excavated, was still a rather modest site, revealed a Middle Assyrian presence, probably linked with Tiglath-pileser I and Ashur-bel-kala's struggle with Aramaean groups along the Euphrates. A cylinder seal and Middle Assyrian pottery suggest that the site may have been occupied by the Assyrians in the same way as, according to Shalmaneser III, Tiglath-pileser I occupied the neighbouring sites of Pitru and Mutkinu.

At the turn of the eleventh and tenth centuries, under the reign of the Assyrian king Ashur-rabi II, Pitru and Mutkinu fell into the hands of Aramaeans. It is at about the same time that the site underwent a complete transformation of its organization. Official buildings were erected on the Acropolis and decorated with pebble mosaics, a decorative device that seems to be of Hittite origin. The residential quarter was transferred to the Middle Town, west of the Acropolis. A temple, possibly of the Storm-God, can be hypothesized in the western part of the Middle Town. These changes were probably associated with the constitution of the principality of Masuwari. Tell Ahmar had reached the status of regional centre.

The rulers of Masuwari – and first and foremost Hamiyata, the son of a usurper – took their inspiration from neighbouring Carchemish to develop propaganda programmes using the style and language of the monumental sculpture and inscriptions of the great city of the Euphrates. A series of large stelae, carved in a style very close to that of Carchemish, were erected by Hamiyata to honour the Storm-God, probably the Storm-God of Aleppo, in a form that presented analogies with that of the emerging god Baal Shamêm. The same Hamiyata adopted the Luwian language, also used in Carchemish, to carve inscriptions to commemorate his deeds. Orthostates celebrating the military power and piety of the princes of Masuwari may have decorated monumental doorways or perhaps a palace. Carved stelae reflected the concerns of the economic and political upper class.

It is not impossible that Hamiyata was a Semite and belonged to the tribe of Adini, which controlled part of the Euphrates valley and of the area immediately to the east. Hamiyata would therefore have been subordinate to Bit Adini whose last leader, Ahuni, was defeated by Shalmaneser III after a series of campaigns launched between 858 and 855.

Masuwari/Til Barsib and neighbouring settlements (Guy Bunnens)

Assyrian inscriptions often refer to a city by its name followed by the words *u kaprānišu*, literally "such city and its villages", although the translation "town" might be more appropriate than "city" in many instances. Consequently, Tell Ahmar being the main site of its region, it may be expected that satellite settlements existed in its close vicinity. We already saw the role Pitru and Mutkinu played in the functioning of the local territorial system. Pitru, the only of these sites that can be located with any degree of plausibility, must have been across the river near Aushariye at about 3–4 km to the west of Tell Ahmar. More difficult to localize is Mutkinu, which could be either Qumluq or Tell Aber on the left bank of the river. Chance finds allow to add two more sites. One was on the road to Qubbah, a village about 3 km east of Tell Ahmar.

Gertrude Bell visited it on the 18th and 19th of February 1909 and briefly reported on her trip:[1]

> Half an hour below Tel Ahmar, among some insignificant ruins, I found a small Hittite inscription cut on a bit of basalt, and close to it a block of limestone carved with a much-effaced Hittite relief. A few minutes further to the east a lion's head, roughly worked in basalt, lay upon a mound. The head is carved in the round; we dug into the mound and uncovered a large block on which the legs were represented in relief. We rode on a few minutes further to Kubbah, a village where the inhabitants are Arabic-speaking Kurds, and found in the graveyard the fragment of a Latin inscription in well-cut letters.[2]

A photograph of the lion is available on the website of her archives,[3] but, although the features of the animal are difficult to discern, it looks more like a bull than a lion. Actually, Paul Perdrizet who visited Tell Ahmar in October 1925, wrote in a letter addressed to René Dussaud and communicated to the *Académie des inscriptions et belles lettres* on 16 October, that he could see a life-size bull protome between Tell Ahmar and Qubbah.[4] In the same letter, before mentioning the bull protome, Perdrizet reported the following:

> It should be added that four kilometres downstream from Tell Ahmar, we saw in the village of Qoubé, built in a house, two Hittite reliefs (about 0.90 × 0.95) representing one two figures, a man and a woman, bringing offerings, the other a king (or a god) making a gesture of prayer, conical helmet, curling hair in the Assyrian style, at the belt a sword with Hittite hilt. Those of the figures, whose feet are preserved, wear shoes with upturned toes.[5]

The present location of the relief with two figures is not known[6] but the other relief was published by François Thureau-Dangin and duly identified as the one Perdizet had seen at Qubbah.[7] It is now in the Louvre (AO 11504) (*Fig. a*). The style of the relief is typically Syro-Hittite and, *pace* Perdrizet and others,[8] it does not reveal Assyrian influence, with the possible exception of the gesture of the hand. The figure, which is walking to the left, is wearing a long tunic tightened at the waist by a wide belt to which a sword is attached. In his left hand he carries a curving staff as can be seen on other Syro-Hittite reliefs and, with his right, he makes a greeting gesture. The figure it portrays must have been a member of the ruling class of Masuwari.

Another relief, which might be the "block of limestone carved with a much-effaced Hittite relief" that Gertrude Bell saw between Tell Ahmar and Qubbah was identified by François Thureau-Dangin some 2 km east of Tell Ahmar and included in the publication of his excavations.[9] It shows a horse rider trampling on an enemy lying on his back (*Fig. b*). The rider, who has a dagger or sword attached to his waist, is shooting an arrow at an invisible target. Like the previous relief, its style, especially in the execution of the horse, is close to Syro-Hittite reliefs and should therefore be dated to the time of the principality of Masuwari.

A third relief is said by Thureau-Dangin to have been found 2 km east of Tell Ahmar, thus between Tell Ahmar and Qubbah.[10] It is probably later than the reliefs presented above and might date from the Assyrian period. Only the upper part of the stone is preserved. A figure is carrying above his head a trail with unidentifiable objects. It must have been part of a procession of tribute bearers.

It is thus a total of about six sculptures and inscriptions, including the Ahmar/Qubbah Stele (see above), that have been discovered at or near Qubbah, most of them dating from the time of Masuwari. It is possible that they were transported from Tell Ahmar but such can hardly be the case of the very heavy Ahmar/Qubbah Stele. It is true that the stele may have been erected on the side of a road and not in a village or a town. However, unlike the area to the east, towards Qubbah, no finds that could be considered to have been removed from the site were made to the west or north of Tell Ahmar. The stelae said to be from Zerkotak (below, pp. 109–110), another modern village close to Tell Ahmar, were actually found at some distance to the north of the city wall, in the same way as the Storm-God Stele B was discovered outside the West Gate. All things considered, the most likely explanation is that an Iron Age site existed at some distance from Tell Ahmar towards Qubbah.

The other site that chance discoveries make a possible candidate for a settlement under Masuwari/Til Barsib's authority in the Iron Age is Qasmiye, some 5–6 km to the north of Tell Ahmar. The tell of Qasmiye has been considerably damaged by modern levelling and ploughing. A column with a polygonal section and a spherical base, lying in a private garden, is said to have come from this tell. The most curious find made at Qasmiye is a lion awkwardly imitating an Assyrian portal lion (*Fig. c*).[11] The sculpture, which

Fig. a. Orthostat re-used in a modern wall at Qubbah (Louvre AO 11504) (photo: © RMN-Grand Palais [Musée du Louvre]/ Franck Raux).

Fig. b. Orthostat found near Qubbah (Aleppo M 9950) (photo: Anwar Abd el-Ghafour).

shows the front and right side of the animal, is badly damaged. It has lost its head and hindquarters. By its stocky proportions, stylization of the hair and execution of the shoulder, this sculpture is similar to works made in north

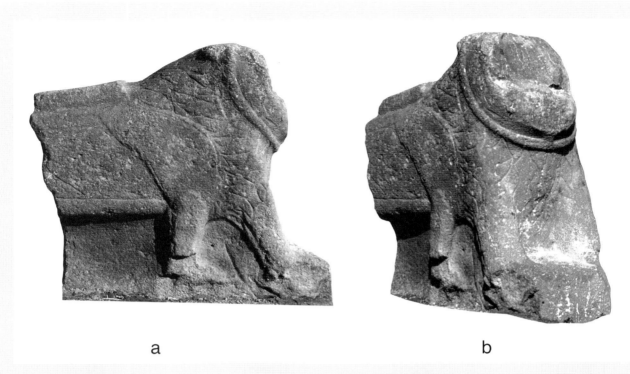

a   b

Fig. c. Portal lion from Qasmiye.

Syria. The sculptor, however, sought to "Assyrianize" his work by duplicating one of the front legs in such a way that, when viewed either from the front or from the side, both front legs would be visible. Unfortunately, he seems to have misunderstood the Assyrian models and, unlike Assyrian lions and bulls, he duplicated the leg that was in the foreground so that the lion gave the impression of having two right front legs, both attached to the same shoulder. The result was a figure that was neither realistic nor justified by a mental and abstract representation of reality.

Notes

1   See her letters dated the same days and her diary (http://gertrudebell.ncl.ac.uk/).

2   G. BELL, The east bank of the Euphrates from Tel Ahmar to Hit, *Geographical Journal* 36 (1910), p. 515; same text in EAD., *Amurath to Amurath*, London 1911, p. 30.

3   Photo J_135 (http://gertrudebell.ncl.ac.uk/photo_details.php?photo_id=2724)

4   'Note de Monsieur Perdrizet', communiquée à l'Académie par M. René Dussaud, *Comptes rendus des séances de l'Académie des Inscriptions et Belles Lettres*, 1925, p. 268 (cf. *Syria* 6 [1925], p. 299).

5   "Il faut ajouter qu'à quatre kilomètres en aval de Tell Ahmar, nous avons vu au village de Qoubbé, maçonnés dans une maison, deux bas-reliefs hittites (0,90 × 0,95 environ) représentant l'un deux personnages, un homme et une femme, apportant des offrandes, l'autre un roi (ou un dieu) faisant le geste de la prière, casque conique, cheveux calamistrés à l'assyrienne, à la ceinture l'épée à poignée hittite. Ceux de ces personnages dont les pieds sont conservés, portent des chaussures à bout recourbé."

6   The relief with two figures that the site of the Perdrizet's archives presents as coming from Qubbah (http://perdrizet.hiscant. univ-lorraine.fr/items/show/1080) was published by F. THUREAU-DANGIN, A. BARROIS, G. DOSSIN & M. DUNAND, *Arslan Tash*, Paris 1931, p. 84 and pl. xiii/3, as found at Meqtele near Arslan Tash.

7   F. THUREAU-DANGIN, Tell Ahmar, *Syria* 10 (1929), p. 202 (no 11) and pl. xxxiv/3; *Til-Barsib*, pp. 160–161 (no 2) and pl. xi/1.

8   For instance V. BLANCHARD in *Royaumes oubliés: De l'empire hittite aux Araméens*, ed. V. BLANCHARD, Paris 2019, no 121, p. 270.

9   F. THUREAU-DANGIN, *art. cit.* (n. 7), pp. 202–203, pl. xxxiv/1; *Til-Barsib*, pp. 137–138 (no 5), pl. x/3.

10 *Til-Barsib*, no 7, pp. 162–163 and pl. xi/5.

11 A. ROOBAERT, Le lion de Qasmiyeh, *Si un homme… Textes offerts en hommage à André Finet*, ed. P. TALON & V. VAN DER STEDE, Subartu XVI, Turnhout 2005, pp. 115–124.

Notes

1 Translation after A.K. GRAYSON in RIMA 3, A.102.2, ii 35–38.

2 CHLI, Part 1, p. 240.

3 J.D. HAWKINS, The Hittite name of Til Barsip: Evidence from a new hieroglyphic fragment from Tell Ahmar, *Anatolian Studies* 33 (1983), pp. 131–136.

4 M. MAKINSON, Muṣru, Maṣuwari and *MṢR*: From Middle-Assyrian frontier to Iron Age city, *State Archives of Assyria Bulletin* 20 (2002–2005), pp. 33–62.

5 CHLI, Tell Ahmar III.6. Tell Ahmar 1, pp. 239–243, pls 99–100.

6 CHLI, Part 1, pp. 239–243.

7 See below, pp. 103–104.

8 The various spellings of Til Barsib can be found in *RGTC* 7/1, s.v. *Til-Barsip*, pp. 253–255 (A.M. Bagg).

9 RIMA 2, A.0.99.2, 48.

10 RIMA 2, A.0.101.1, i 75–99.

11 RIMA 2, A.0.101.1, iii 38–44.

12 RIMA 2, A.0.101.1, iii 50–54.

13 RGTC 7/1, s.v. Kaprabi, pp. 133–134 (A.M. Bagg), with a discussion of all suggested identifications.

14 RIMA 2, A.0.101.1, iii 55.

15 RIMA 2, A.0.101.1, iii 56–77.

16 RGTC 7/1, s.v. Būr-mar'īna, p. 55, and s.v. Marinâ, p. 168 (A.M. Bagg).

17 RGTC 7/1, s.v. Alligu, p. 6 (A.M. Bagg).

18 D. USSISHKIN, Was Bit-Adini a Neo-Hittite or Aramaean state?, *Orientalia* NS 40 (1970), pp. 431–437; Y. IKEDA, Hittites and Aramaeans in the land of Bit-Adini, *Monarchies and Socio-Religious Traditions in the Near East*, ed. T. MIKASA, Wiesbaden 1984, pp. 27–36; G. BUNNENS, Hittites and Aramaeans at Til Barsib: A reappraisal, *Immigration and Emigration within the Ancient Near East: Festschrift for E. Lipiński*, ed. K. van LERBERGHE & A. SCHOORS, Leuven 1995, pp. 19–27; ID., Aramaeans, Hittites and Assyrians in the Upper Euphrates valley, *Archaeology of the Upper Syrian Euphrates: The Tishrin Dam area*, ed. G. del OLMO LETE & G. MONTERO FENOLLOS, Aula Orientalis Supplementa 15, Sabadell (Barcelona) 1999, pp. 605–624; P.-E. DION, *Les Araméens à l'âge du Fer: Histoire politique et structures sociales*, Études bibliques nouvelle série 34, Paris 1997, pp. 86–90; E. LIPIŃSKI, *The Aramaeans: Their ancient history, culture, religion*, Leuven-Paris-Sterling (VA) 2000, pp. 183–193; S. YAMADA, *The Construction of the Assyrian Empire: A historical study of the inscriptions of Shalmaneser III (859–824 BC) relating to his campaigns to the west*, Culture and History of the Ancient Near East 3, Leiden-Boston-Cologne 2000, pp. 139–143; K.L. YOUNGER, Jr., *A Political History of the Aramaeans From Their Origins to the End of Their Polities*, Archaeology and Biblical Studies 13, Atlanta (GA) 2016, pp. 137–143.

19 This problem has already been treated by G. BUNNENS, *A New Luwian Stele and the Cult of the Storm-God at Til Barsib – Masuwari*, Tell Ahmar II, Leuven-Paris-Dudley (MA) 2006, pp. 85–102.

20 CHLI, Part 1, III.5. ALEPPO 2, pp. 235–238.

21 E. LIPIŃSKI, *op. cit.* (n. 18), p. 187.

22 CHLI, Part 1, III.1. TELL AHMAR 2, pp. 227–230.

23 H. SADER, *Les États araméens de Syrie depuis leur fondation jusqu'à leur transformation en provinces assyriennes*, Beiruter Texte und Studien 36, Beirut 1987, p. 92.

24 *Til-Barsib*, pp. 25–26, 41–42 (M. Dunand).

25 G. BUNNENS, Neo-Assyrian pebble mosaics in their architectural context, *The Provincial Archaeology of the Assyrian Empire*, ed. J. MACGINNIS & T. GREENFIELD, Cambridge 2016, pp. 59–70.

26 A. D'AGOSTINO, A mosaic floor from the Late Bronze Age building II of Uşaklı Höyük, central Turkey, *Antiquity*, 93/372 (Dec. 2019), pp. 1–8.

27 TELL AHMAR 5, § 39 (cf. below, p. 94).

28 Published by J.D. HAWKINS *in* G. BUNNENS, *op. cit.* (n. 19), pp. 11–31.

29 G. BUNNENS, *op. cit.* (n. 19), p. 70.

30 I. SINGER, A new stele of Hamiyatas, king of Masuwari, *Tel Aviv* 15–16 (1988–1989), pp. 184–192; CHLI, TELL AHMAR III.2.

31 J.D. HAWKINS observes that the mention of the Sun-God by Arpa probably refers to the winged disc carved at the top of the stele (CHLI, Part 1, p. 238).

32 G. BUNNENS, *op. cit.* (n. 19), pp. 38–42.

33 TELL AHMAR 1, TELL AHMAR 2, BOROWSKI 3, and possibly also TELL AHMAR 5 (all texts published in CHLI).

34 D. CHARPIN, Prophètes et rois dans le Proche-Orient asiatique, *Florilegium Marianum VI, Recueil d'études à la mémoire d'André Parrot*, ed. D. CHARPIN & J.-M. DURAND, Paris 2002, p. 31.

35 J. GONELLA, W. KHAYYATA & K. KOHLMEYER, *Die Zitadelle von Aleppo und der Tempel des Wettergottes: Neue Forschungen und Entdeckungen*, Münster 2005, figs 124 and 126; K. KOHLMEYER, The temple of the Storm God in Aleppo during the Late Bronze and Early Iron Ages, *Near Eastern Archaeology* 72/4 (Dec. 2009), p. 193.

36 J. GONELLA, W. KHAYYATA & K. KOHLMEYER, *op. cit.* (n. 35), p. 92–93.

37 See for instance K. KOHLMEYER, Building activities and architectural decoration in the 11th century BC: The temples of Taita, king of Padasatini/Palistin in Aleppo and ʿAin Dārā, *Empires after the Empire: Anatolia, Syria and Assyria after Suppiluliuma II (ca. 1200–800/700 B.C.)*, ed. K. STROBEL, Florence 2011, pp. 259–262.

38 *Til-Barsib*, pls ix/1–3, x/ 9–10.

39 D. USSISHKIN, On the dating of some groups of reliefs from Carchemish and Til Barsip, *Anatolian Studies* 17 (1967), pp. 181–192.

40 *Til-Barsib*, pl. x/1–2, 5–8.

41 *Til-Barsib*, p. 139.

42 W. ORTHMANN, *Untersuchungen zur Späthethitischen Kunst*, Saarbrücker Beiträge 8, Bonn 1971, pl. 39 (Malatya A/4).

43 W. ORTHMANN, *op. cit.* (n. 42), pl. 20 (Aa/4).

44 M. von OPPENHEIM, *Der Tell Halaf*, Leipzig 1931, Tafel 24/b.

45 *Til-Barsib*, p. 137.

From Til Barsib to Kar-Shalmaneser:
The beginnings of Assyrian domination (c. 856–750)

The Assyrian occupation at Tell Ahmar can be divided into two main periods. The first ran from the conquest in 856 to the consolidation of the empire in the eighth century. The second witnessed the apogee and fall of the empire from the middle of the eighth to the end of the seventh century. The first of these periods will be the subject of this chapter, leaving the other for the last four chapters.

1. Shalmaneser III

Shalmaneser III needed 3 years, from 858 to 856, to defeat and conquer Til Barsib where Ahuni had organized his resistance to the invader.[1] As soon as Til Barsib was in his hands, Shalmaneser renamed it *Kar-Shalmaneser*, made it one of his royal cities and entrusted its management to the *turtānu,* the main dignitary of the empire after the king. Til Barsib/Kar-Shalmaneser remained a regional centre until the fall of the Assyrian Empire at the end of the seventh century.

Can we expect to find archaeological evidence of the conquest? In the inscription carved on the stele commonly called the *Kurkh Monolith*, probably written in 853, Shalmaneser says:

> I <approached> Til Barsib, the fortified city of Ahuni, son of Adini, conquered <the city>. Ahuni son of Adini, <became afraid> of the splendour of my raging weapons and fierce battle, [abandoned his ci]ty, crossed the Euphrates to save his life. He moved into other countries. By the command of Ashur, the great lord, my lord, I took Til Barsib, Alligu, [Nappigi] and Rugulitu to be my royal citi(es), settled Assyrians therein (and) founded therein palaces as my royal abode(s). I changed the name of Til Barsib to Kar-Shalmaneser, Nappigi to Lita-Ashur, Alligu to Asbat-la-kunu, Rugulitu as Qibit-[DN].[2]

Further down, Shalmaneser, before reporting how he defeated Ahuni in 855, recalls the siege and capture of Til Barsib in the previous years in the following words:

> In the beginning of my reign, in the eponym year of my own name, I departed from Nineveh (and) besieged Til-Barsib, his [= Ahuni's] fortified city. I let my warriors surround it, set a battle in its midst, cut down its orchard (and) rained fire (and) arrows upon it. He became frightened before the brilliance of my weapons (and) the splendour [of] my lordship and abandoned his city. He crossed the Euphrates to save his life.[3]

Two conclusions can be drawn from these accounts. The first is that there was apparently no major destruction in Til Barsib and the other conquered cities. Shalmaneser only mentioned à battle inside Til Barsib, probably to find his way into the settlement after Ahuni had left it. Nothing more can be drawn from a literary text found in Sultantepe in Turkey, which referred to the burning of Til Barsib at the time of the conquest:

> The arrogant slave of Bit Adini (and) his companions, [they (the gods) defeated],
> the city Til Barsib, the fortified town, they (the gods) burned,
> the kings of the land Hatti, they (the gods) destroyed their abodes.
> He (Shalmaneser) spoke ... to Ashur-belu-ka'in, the turtānu:
> "The forts/districts are entrusted to you, make your guard strong,
> keep your companies secure in order to take their tribute,
> the prince of the land Hatti I made bow down at my feet".[4]

Ashur-belu-ka'in was eponym for the year 856, year of the capture of Til Barsib.[5] The "obstinate slave of Bit Adini" mentioned together with Til Barsib cannot be but Ahuni and he is probably also the "prince of the land Hatti" who bowed down at the feet of Shalmaneser. The burning of Til Barsib was nothing more than a hyperbole in a text that had epic overtones. The *Kurkh Monolith* spoke only of "fire (and) arrows" (or "flamed arrows"). If there had been a fierce resistance, Shalmaneser would not have failed to mention it. In other circumstances, he emphasized the massacres, looting and destructions that occurred during the battle. At

Til Barsib, things seem to have happened as if Assyrian troops had entered the city deserted by Ahuni almost without opposition. The rest of the story concerns the re-organization of the conquered cities, not their dismantling or the massacre of their populations. One should thus not expect to find a stratigraphic disruption marked by a layer of destruction.

The second conclusion concerns possible constructions undertaken by Shalmaneser. The *Monolith* is not unambiguous. It speaks of "palaces", in the plural, which the context invites us to place in each of the conquered cities, but the expression "in the middle of it" is in the singular, as if only one city was involved. If this was the case, this city must have been Til Barsib, whose conquest was the main achievement of the campaign, an achievement that opened the way to the other cities. Be that as it may, the text states that at least one palace was erected at Tell Ahmar. Are there archaeological traces of this?

The only vestige that can be attributed with certainty to Shalmaneser is a stone inscription, which reproduces the introduction to the *Kurkh Monolith* and appears to be unfinished.[6] Like the *Monolith*, it should date from 853 or shortly afterwards. This text has not been found in its original context. It had been transported near the modern cemetery, where the Thureau-Dangin expedition dug it out. As for the palace(s), nothing has been uncovered during the French excavations nor during the renewed excavations. The palace excavated by the French expedition was probably built about a century after Shalmaneser's conquest of the city. The renewed excavations have shown that this palace was erected immediately above earlier Iron Age constructions, which have been levelled to make room for the new building. In other words, if there were any changes, they are more likely to have concerned the re-organization of existing structures rather than the construction of one or more prestigious buildings on the Acropolis. It can therefore be assumed that the buildings mentioned in the previous chapter remained in use during the time of Shalmaneser.

Actually, Shalmaneser does not seem to have spent much time in Til Barsib. After conquering the city, renaming it and counting it as one of his royal cities, he says that he received the tribute of kings collectively designated as "kings of the coast and kings of the banks of the Euphrates". He then turned his heels and headed for Urartu to the north-east of Assyria. He certainly returned to Til Barsib in the following years, as the town offered him the crossing point on the Euphrates – otherwise blocked by the power of Carchemish – which he needed to launch his numerous military campaigns to the west but his inscriptions never mentioned a vast building programme. The name of the city was only occasionally mentioned in the account of the campaigns that followed its conquest, although the king crossed the river many times.

The exact status of Tell Ahmar after the conquest is not known. Shalmaneser just said that he promoted it to the rank of "royal city". A royal city was a place where the king could stay when journeying throughout his empire, not a component of the administrative system. However, an interesting detail is given by the literary text from Sultantepe quoted above. It says that the *turtānu* was entrusted with the task of presiding over the subdued cities and collecting tribute from them. This link between Til Barsib/Kar-Shalmaneser and the *turtānu* official was to prove a long-lasting one as is shown by the *turtānu* Shamshi-ilu.

2. The *turtānu* Shamshi-ilu

The special link between Shamshi-ilu and Til Barsib/ Kar-Shalmaneser is shown by the two lions erected at the eastern gate of the city, each bearing a long inscription which, as we saw, made it possible to identify the site.[7] Shamshi-ilu had a long career. Already active in the early eighth century, he was still active in 752,[8] which gives him a career of about half a century. The tone of his inscription is royal. Shamshi-ilu celebrates his victory over Argishti, king of Urartu, in epic terms and in royal phraseology but without mentioning any king's name. He even goes so far as to call Kar-Shalmaneser "my lordly city" as a king would say "my royal city".

The phrase "my lordly city" is usually taken as evidence for Shamshi-ilu's decision to reside in Kar-Shalmaneser and make it the capital of his domain. However, considering that Shamshi-ilu adopts the style of the royal inscriptions, there is no reason to believe that he means anything different from what a king has in mind when he refers to one of his "royal cities". Shamshi-ilu might have had several "lordly cities" in the same way as kings had several "royal cities". This is especially likely if we consider the territory that he is supposed to have controlled. The inscription engraved on the lions of the eastern gate of Tell Ahmar presents him as being in charge of the land of Hatti to the west – where Tell Ahmar was – and of the Guti and the entire land of Namri to the east of Mesopotamia. He thus claims authority over the marches of the empire. His power was such that Stephanie Dalley regards him as "king of Hanigalbat", *i.e.* king of the western part of the empire, on a par with the king who resides in Ashur.[9] Anyhow, whatever the extent of his power, his domain was vast enough to allow Shamshi-ilu to have more than one "lordly city" at his disposal.

In point of fact, inscriptions discovered at Arslan Tash show that Shamshi-ilu was not directly involved in the management of Til Barsib/Kar-Shalmaneser.[10] The inscriptions were written on behalf of one Inurta-belu-usur who presented himself as governor of Kar-Shalmaneser and eunuch of Shamshi-ilu. The city had thus acquired the rank of provincial capital but power at the local level was in the hands of a governor who acted under the authority of the *turtānu*. Another example of a local governor under a *turtānu*'s authority would have been Mushezib-Shamash, governor of Duru, according to Karen Radner.[11] This makes it very unlikely that Shamshi-ilu had his principal residence at Til Barsib/Kar-Shalmaneser. He probably delegated to local governors the control of the cities placed under his authority. Harran, which will be the last place of resistance of the Assyrian kings after the fall of Nineveh in 612, was probably a better candidate for the *turtānu*'s residence.[12]

Inurta-belu-usur's inscriptions, especially the trilingual inscription, shed an interesting light on the status of the Kar-Shalmaneser province within the framework of the Assyrian administration. Significant is the tone adopted by Inurta-belu-usur. If in the Assyrian and Aramaic versions he defines his position as that of a "governor", in the Luwian version he uses the much more ambiguous term "Country-Lord". Although Country-Lords, in the second millennium, were local officials or governors, in the first millennium the title had evolved to the point that independent kings, especially at Carchemish and Malatya, could assume it.[13] Inurta-belu-usur also mentions his place of origin, refers to "his father's house" and, in the final curses, curses the prince (Akkadian *rubû*/Aramaic SRN) who, in the future, would want to erase his name. Such details are typical of royal inscriptions. Moreover, it is quite remarkable that, besides Assyrian and Aramaic, he also uses Luwian, and even more remarkable that, in the Luwian version of the inscription, unfortunately badly damaged, he refers to Tell Ahmar by its old name Masuwari, whereas in the Assyrian and Aramaic versions he uses the official name Kar-Shalmaneser. If the hypothesis, formulated in the previous chapter, that a local dynasty ruled Tell Ahmar/Masuwari within the wider framework of the tribal state of Adini, is correct, it is not impossible that this dynasty, or another that would have replaced it, remained in power after the defeat of Ahuni and went on with the local administration under the *turtānu*'s authority. The case would not be unique. It seems that the Assyrian empire in its early stages was satisfied with the submission of local rulers. This saved it to delegate a representative, who would have had little knowledge of local realities and would not have been very popular with the local populations. A famous example is that of Hadad-yis'i, king of Guzana (modern Tell Halaf) in the ninth century, whose statue was found at Tell Fekheriye in Northern Mesopotamia. The statue bore two inscriptions, one in Aramaic – in which Hadad-yis'i called himself "king" –, the other in Assyrian, in which the same Hadad-yis'i called himself "governor".[14] The case of Inurta-belu-usur at Kar-Shalmaneser/Masuwari may not have been very different.

The extent of the province of Kar-Shalmaneser is not known. The inscriptions of Inurta-belu-usur show that it included Arslan Tash/Hadatu. The other place names mentioned in these inscriptions are impossible to situate on a map. The only possible exception is Sirani, which could be Serrin to the south-east of Tell Ahmar.[15]

There results from all this that Til Barsib/Kar-Shalmaneser was already an Assyrian province in the first half of the eighth century, contrary to the common opinion that holds that the province was created by Sargon II,[16] and it looks as if Shamshi-ilu's "lordly city" had been under the rule of a local dynast.

3. The Lion Gate and the city-wall of Til Barsib/Kar-Shalmaneser

The most impressive archaeological remains of the early phase of the Assyrian domination were Shamshi-ilu's large basalt lions that were guarding the eastern city gate. The gate was excavated by the French in 1931[17] but the fragments of the two lions remained in place. They could be studied in 1988 before they were transferred to the Aleppo University a few years later.[18]

The gate as well as the section of the rampart on either its sides were considerably damaged, but enough remained to give an idea of their layout (*Fig. 145*). The gate was of the so-called "three entrances" type, consisting of two oblong chambers communicating through openings in the middle of the walls separating them. On the south-eastern side of each chamber was a smaller room. The southernmost of them was accessed directly from the inner town through a door in the south-east wall. This room probably led to an upper floor by means of wooden stairs, which have not been preserved. The other, set against the rampart, was accessible from the north-east chamber of the monumental gate. It probably housed the gatekeepers that were controlling the comings and goings. On the outside, the door was flanked by two towers. The base of the north-west one was partly preserved. The entire structure must have been crowned by battlements.

The section of the rampart adjoining the gate can be reconstructed with a certain degree of credibility, although an anomaly in the plan inserted in the publication of the French excavations makes the exercise somewhat hazardous. The plan was published in three parts, namely the gate, the section of rampart extending to the north-west of the gate and the section extending to the south-east. Moreover, the plan of the gate was reproduced on a larger scale than that of the wall sections. By adapting the scales, the plan of the south-east section can be connected to that of the gate without too much difficulty. The task is much more difficult for the north-west section. The connection between the wall and the door forms a right angle on the plan of the north-west segment, but it forms an obtuse angle on the plan of the gate. The reconstruction offered on *Figure 145* is based on the assumption that the plan of the gate is more accurate, and that, in all three cases, the north direction is adequately indicated on the plans. The end result is a gate that, quite surprisingly, appears askew in the rampart. The reason for such an arrangement is unknown.

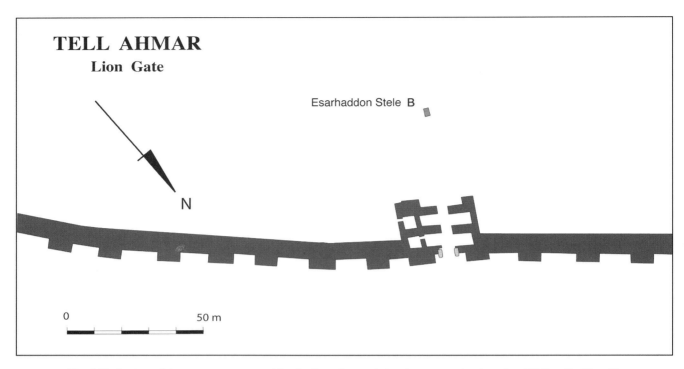

Fig. 145. Section of the rampart excavated by the French expedition (reconstruction based on Til-Barsib, *Plan E).*

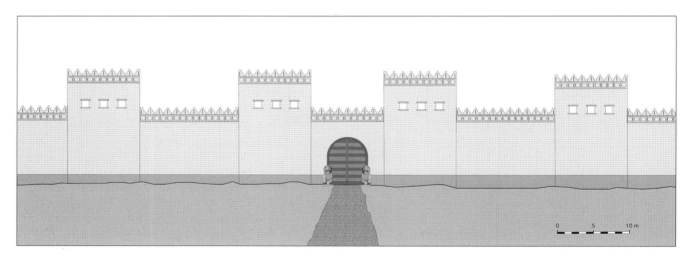

Fig. 146. Lion Gate: Tentative reconstruction of the gate and adjoining sections of the rampart (drawn with the assistance of F. De Backer). The reconstruction is based both on the plan published in Til-Barsib *(Plan E) and on depictions of city walls on Assyrian reliefs. The greyish band at the base of the wall represents the stone base of the mud-brick wall.*

The rampart seems to have been flat inside. Outside, however, salients about 8.50 m wide and 3.50 m deep followed one another at intervals of about 12.50 m. They were obviously the base of towers whose height is impossible to estimate (*Fig. 146*).

The two lions lay at the gate site, where David Hogarth had seen them and where the Thureau-Dangin expedition found them again (*Fig. 147*). They were still there in 1988.

However, the French archaeologists had turned them over to preserve the inscription. Originally, the lions, sculpted in the round, were partially engaged in the gate wall.

The best preserved is the one set against the north-west side of the gate (*Fig. 148*). It is broken into several pieces but could be almost entirely reconstructed (*Fig. 149*). Only the lower hindlegs have been lost. The south-east lion is more damaged (*Fig. 150*). The head and left hindleg are missing.

Fig. 147. Lion Gate: NW lion at the start of the French excavations (photo: Georges Dossin archives).

Fig. 148. Lion Gate: Forepart of the NW lion (now at the University of Aleppo).

Stylistically, these sculptures mix Assyrian features with more western traits. The proportions of the two lions, more stocky than their Assyrian counterparts, are closer to the Syro-Hittite canon. The details, however, point towards Assyria. The tongue, for example, is not visible, whereas the Syro-Hittite lions often have their tongues hanging out. The linear stylization of the musculature as well as the pincer-like pattern engraved on the front paw are also Assyrian features. These lions can therefore be regarded as local works produced by artists familiar with Assyrian models.

The inscription carved on the lions give broad chronological indications. Shamshi-ilu said that he erected the two lions after a military campaign against Argishti of Urartu, which must have taken place during one of the campaigns conducted against Urartu within the time span 781–776 according to the Eponym Chronicle.[19]

Did Shamshi-ilu re-use existing lions to carve an inscription to his glory? Although this is possible, the political situation does not make it very likely. As we saw, it does not seem that Shalmaneser III had the possibility of undertaking a vast construction programme in Til Barsib/Kar-Shalmaneser. On the death of Shalmaneser III, Assyria entered a long period of crisis from which it only gradually emerged during the eighth century. Shamshi-ilu, although not a king, contributed, with great energy combined with an exceptional longevity, to strengthening the power of the nascent empire. It would therefore not be surprising that he was responsible not only for the carving of the inscription but also for the erection of the lions. The names he gave them underscore their power and effectiveness as guardians as well as, *ipso facto*, they persuade us of their master's determination to defend Assyria. One was called "Raging storm, with unrivalled attack, who overwhelms the insubmissive, who brings success" and the other "Who charges

through battle, who flattens the enemy land, who expels criminals and brings in good people."[20]

For the same reasons – the active participation of the *turtānu* in the re-invigoration of Assyria – it can be suggested that not just the gate but the entire rampart was built on Shamshi-ilu's initiative.

The rampart was still recognizable at the time of the French excavations. Three depressions marked the site of three gates that were giving access to the town from west, north and east. The east gate, called here the "Lion Gate", is the only one to have been excavated. The rampart can still be seen in the photograph taken by satellite in 1968 and even, more recently, in the photographs taken after the completion of the Tishrin Dam (*Figs 4a* and *5*). According to the villagers, most of the remains of the rampart had been levelled shortly before excavation resumed in 1988 to make room for arable land. Almost nothing was visible on the ground at that time.

It is sometimes argued that the rampart extended into the lower valley of the Euphrates so as to form a circular settlement.[21] It is true that the site seems to be poorly protected on this side and it is natural to think that the valley, which gave direct access to a navigable river, had been included in the

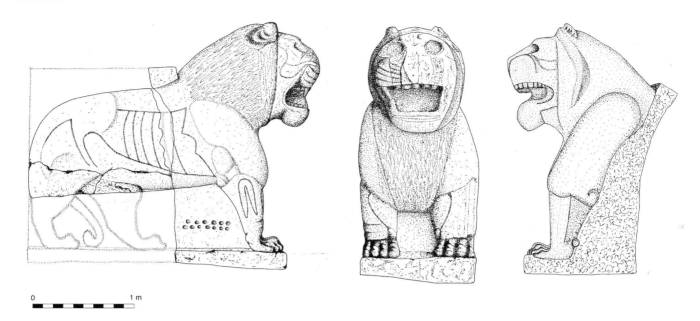

Fig. 149. Lion Gate: Reconstruction of the NW lion (right side and front, drawing: Greg Wightman; left side, drawing: Jenny Leimert). The dark dots behind the right paw are modern; they belong to a popular game.

Fig. 150. Lion Gate: SE lion (Aleppo University) (photo: Hamido Hammade); a) front view; b) side view.

urban settlement in order to take advantage of the benefits it offered. Besides this, circular cities are well attested in ancient Western Asia. However, geography does not favour such a reconstruction. Until recently, the lower valley was not suitable for the establishment of a permanent settlement. The riverbed, as seen above (pp. 2–3), often changed its course and the flooding of the valley, still observed at the time of the French excavations, was frequent. All this contributed to making the valley inhospitable. It is therefore difficult to believe that permanent constructions – walls or even residential quarters – have ever been erected in the lower valley of the Euphrates. More acceptable would be the hypothesis of a semicircular rampart. It must be remembered that the entire southern part of the site was considerably eroded at some time in the past as can be inferred from the plan of the preserved remains of the Assyrian palace.

A quarter or a fifth of the palace, and thus of the Acropolis, has been washed away by erosion. On the other hand, a fortification system, to which the so-called *pilier de soutènement* may have belonged, seems to have already protected this part of the Acropolis in the Bronze Age. It is therefore quite possible that another fortification system was built along the edge of the terrace in the Iron Age.

As a matter of fact, semicircular plans are not unknown. The site of Ziyaret Tepe, the ancient Tushhan, offers another example, all the more significant as Tushhan was, like Tell Ahmar, a provincial capital of the Assyrian empire.[22] Another provincial capital, Qasr Shemamok identified as Kilizu, further east in Iraqi Kurdistan, offered another example of a semicircular city.[23] To the north of Tell Ahmar, in the region of Samsat, the Iron Age site of Şaşkan Kuçuktepe seems to have been built on the same model.[24] We should resist the temptation to explain all these examples as resulting from erosion. The existence of semicircular cities is well established by the site of Ashqelon, one of the main cities of the Philistines, whose semicircular rampart, dated to the Middle Bronze Age, can be followed all around the city.[25] There are therefore reasons to believe that the rampart of Til Barsib/Kar-Shalmaneser was conceived from the start as a semicircular enclosure.

4. The Assyrianization of Masuwari/Til Barsib

Several of the reliefs discovered at Tell Ahmar were at the crossroads of Syro-Hittite and Assyrian traditions. They compare, in this respect, with the lions that decorated the

Fig. 151. Orthostat showing figures carrying tribute or offerings (Aleppo M 7499) (photo: Anwar Abd el-Ghafour).

Fig. 152. Relief showing a winged genie with a bird's head performing a rite of purification (Aleppo M 7498) (photo: Anwar Abd el-Ghafour).

Lion Gate but, unlike these, they were found out of context and bear no inscription. It is thus difficult to assign them a date. However, the Syro-Hittite features they include suggest that they are later than the large stelae of the Storm-God and the reliefs contemporary with the Suhi/Katuwa period at Carchemish. It seems more appropriate to place them in the early period of Assyrian domination, all the more so as the Inurta-belu-usur inscriptions show that the Assyrian conquest did not put an end to the Syro-Hittite tradition at the site.

On an orthostat, which is assumed to have come from the tell, two figures marching to the left are holding objects that are difficult to identify (*Fig. 151*). Both these figures are wearing shoes with upturned toes, typical of the Syro-Hittite period, but their hairstyle form a puffy mass in the nape of the neck closer to Assyrian conventions.

Another orthostat with a mythological or religious theme is also evocative of the Syro-Hittite tradition. It depicts a genie with the head and wings of a bird, holding a conical object in his right hand and a small bucket of the type commonly known as *situla* in his left hand (*Fig. 152*). This motif was already attested in the temple of the Storm-God in Aleppo[26] – among reliefs that K. Kohlmeyer dates to around 900[27] – and it became common in Assyria during the time of Ashurnasirpal II. It is often associated with the Assyrian stylized tree. The style of the relief, however, differs considerably from that of Aleppo and is similar, especially in the details of the head, to comparable figures shown on Assyrian reliefs. There is little doubt that we

are in the presence of a local work but under Assyrian influence.

Some works look more Assyrian. Two stelae have been found on the territory of Zerkotak, a village to the north-west of Tell Ahmar. According to the villagers, however, they were found on the borders between the two villages, at some distance to the north-west of the ancient city wall, approximately in the area where the large Storm-God Stele B was found.

On one of these stelae, two men stand in a chariot drawn by two horses (*Fig. 153*).[28] This may be a funerary monument. The details, especially the treatment of the hair and beard of the two figures and the clothing of the figure in the foreground, are Assyrian, but the general execution of the sculpture differs considerably from known Assyrian reliefs. For example, the size of the two figures, much larger than the chariot and the horses, is foreign to Assyrian art, but can be found, for instance, on the reliefs of Karatepe in Cilicia. The stylization of the hands is also closer to Syro-Hittite tradition than to Assyrian art. This is clearly a work of Assyrian inspiration but executed by a sculptor familiar with the Syro-Hittite tradition. The wheels of the chariot, which have six spokes as in the time of Ashurnasirpal II and not eight as in the time of Tiglath-pileser III, show that this relief probably predated the middle of the eighth century.

The second stele is decorated with the standard of the Moon-God, a pole topped by a crescent standing on a stepped pedestal (*Fig. 154*).[29] Two tassels are attached to a discoid or spherical ornament inserted between the crescent and the pole. Such standards were the symbol of the Moon-God of Harran, one of the major deities, together with the Storm-God of Aleppo, of Northern Syria. The stele is more difficult to date but could be contemporary with the one with which it was found.

The place of discovery of these two stelae suggests that, like the Ahmar/Qubbah Stele, they may have been roadside monuments, perhaps the remains of an extramural shrine with a stele commemorating the memory of a deceased person and another honouring the Moon-God.

These works, some of which perpetuate aspects of the Syro-Hittite tradition, were increasingly reflecting Assyrian conventions. They can therefore be dated to the period following the conquest of 856, but before the second half of the eighth century, when Assyrian domination became more effective.

* * *

Assyrian control seems to have extended gradually over Til Barsib, renamed Kar-Shalmaneser by its conqueror Shalmaneser III. The city had the great advantage of providing a permanent crossing point on the Euphrates while avoiding the powerful Carchemish, which could manage to retain its independence until 717.

Til Barsib/Kar-Shalmaneser is probably illustrative of the evolution of the practice of power of the emerging Assyrian empire. Immediately after the conquest, it was entrusted to the *turtānu*, probably the most powerful military official of the Assyrian empire, especially in charge of the defence of the marches. It was still under this official's authority at the time of the *turtānu* Shamshi-ilu in the first half of the

Fig. 153. Stele depicting two men in a chariot (Aleppo M 10172) (photo: Anwar Abd el-Ghafour).

Fig. 154. Stele with the standard of the Moon-God (Aleppo M 10171) (photo: Anwar Abd el-Ghafour).

eighth century. However, the city had become a provincial capital ruled, on behalf of Shamshi-ilu, by a governor called Inurta-belu-usur. This Inurta-belu-usur, although a eunuch, may have been a local ruler administering the province as his own possession but under Assyrian authority, according to a practice adopted by the Assyrians before they acquired enough resources to exert a direct control.

Material evidence to some extent corroborates this scenario. The first architectural manifestation of Assyrian presence was the erection of a rampart, probably by Shamshi-ilu. On the Acropolis, nothing seems to have changed from the preceding period. Figurative art still displayed characteristics belonging to the Syro-Hittite tradition. Inurta-belu-usur himself still used the Luwian language in one of his inscriptions and called Tell Ahmar by its Luwian name Masuwari. In other words, the conquest of 856 can no longer be considered the end, or the *terminus ante quem*, of the Luwian-Aramaean culture at Tell Ahmar.

Notes

1   All accounts of Til Barsib's conquest are analysed by S. YAMADA, The conquest of Til-Barsib by Shalmaneser III: History and historiography, *Acta Sumerologica*, 20 (1998), pp. 217–225 and ID., *The Construction of the Assyrian Empire: A Historical study of the inscriptions of Shalmaneser III (859–824 BC) relating to his campaigns to the west*, Culture & History of the Ancient Near East 3, Leiden-Boston-Cologne 2000, pp. 120–129.

2   RIMA 3, A.0.102.2, ii.31–35; translation S. YAMADA, *op. cit.* (n. 1), p. 374.

3   RIMA 3, A.0.102.2, ii 67–69; translation S. YAMADA, *op. cit.* (n. 1), pp. 376–377.

4   Translation A.K. GRAYSON in RIMA 3, A.0.102.17, 7–13.

5   A.L. MILLARD, *The Eponyms of the Assyrian Empire 910–612 B.C.*, State Archives of Assyria Studies II, Helsinki 1994, pp. 27, 82

6   RIMA 3, A.0.102.4, pp. 25–26.

7   RIMA 3, A.0.104.2010, pp. 231–233.

8   PNA 3/ii, s.v. Šamšī-ilu, p. 1226 (R. Mattila).

9   S. DALLEY, Shamshi-ilu, language and power in the western Assyrian empire, *Essays on Syria in the Iron Age*, Ancient Near Eastern Studies Supplement 7, Leuven-Paris-Sterling (VA) 2000, pp. 83–86.

10   I thank W. Röllig and H. Galter for having shown me copies and translations of these inscriptions. A bilingual inscription, Assyrian and Aramaic, known through two copies has been published by W. RÖLLIG, Die Inschriften des Ninurta-bēlu-uṣur, Statthalters von Kār-Salmānu-ašarēd, Teil I, *Of God(s), Trees, Kings, and Scholars: Neo-Assyrian and related studies in honour of Simo Parpola*, ed. M. LUUKKO, S. SVÄRD & R. MATTILA, Helsinki 2009, pp. 265–278. A trilingual inscription, Assyrian, Aramaic and Luwian, also exists. The Luwian version was published by J.D. Hawkins (CHLI, pp. 246–248). A hand copy of the Aramaean version can be found in A. ABU ASSAF, Inscriptions d'Anraphalazar,

roi de Hadatu (Arslan Tash), *Annales archéologiques arabes syriennes* 45–46 (2002–2003), p. 30 (Arabic section).

11   *RlA*, 11/1–2 (2006), p. 48 (K. Radner).

12   Many years ago E. FORRER, *Die Provinzeinteilung des assyrsichen Reiches*, Leipzig 1921, p. 22, had suggested that Harran was the capital of the *turtānu*'s province.

13   J.D. HAWKINS, 'Great Kings' and 'Country Lords' at Malatya and Karkamiš, *Studio Historiae Ardens: Ancient Near Eastern studies presented to Philo H.J. Houwink ten Cate*, Istanbul 1995, p. 75.

14   PNA 1/I, s.v. Adda-it'i, p. 47 (D. Schwemer).

15   Perhaps the same place as Sirina mentioned in a contract from Nineveh (RGTC 7/1, s.v. Ṣirina p. 233 [A.M. Bagg]).

16   For instance K. RADNER, *art. cit.* (n. 11), pp. 48 and 56.

17   *Til-Barsib*, pp. 125–132 (G. Dossin).

18   A. ROOBAERT, The city gate lions, *Tell Ahmar 1998 Season*, Abr-Nahrain Supplement Series 2, Leuven 1990, pp. 126–135.

19   A. MILLARD, *op. cit.* (n. 5), pp. 36–39, 58.

20   Translation after A.K. Grayson in RIMA 3, p. 233.

21   For instance H. KÜHNE, The urbanization of the Assyrian provinces, *Nuove fondazioni nel Vicino Oriente antico: Realtà e ideologia*, ed. S. Mazzoni, Pisa 1994, p. 60; J.-C. MARGUERON, Urbanisme syro-mésopotamien et géométrie, *Ktèma* 35 (2010), fig. 21, p. 21; ID., *Cités invisibles: La naissance de l'urbanisme au Proche-Orient ancien*, Paris 2013, pp. 329–331.

22   T. MATNEY et al., Excavations at Ziyaret Tepe, Diyarbakir Province, Turkey, 2009–2010 seasons, *Anatolica* 37 (2011), fig. 22, p. 114.

23   O. ROUAULT, Qasr Shemamok (ancient Kilizu), a provincial capital east of the Tigris: Recent excavations and new perspectives, *The Provincial Archaeology of the Assyrian Empire*, ed. J. MacGINNIS, D. WICKE & T. GREENFIELD, Cambridge 2016, pp. 159–160, who thinks that the site might have been circular.

24   T.J. WILKINSON, Late-Assyrian settlement geography in Upper Mesopotamia, *Neo-Assyrian Geography*, ed. M. LIVERANI, Rome 1995, p. 156 and fig. 12.

25   L.E. STAGER, The impact of the Sea Peoples in Canaan, *The Archaeology of Society in the Holy Land*, ed. T.E. LEVY, London 1995, fig. 4, p. 340 and pl. 3, p. 343; L.E. STAGER & J.D. SCHLOEN, Introduction: Ashkelon and Its Inhabitants, *Ashkelon 1: Introduction and Overview (1985–2006)*, ed. L.E. STAGER, J. D. SCHLOEN & D.M. MASTER, WINONA LAKE (IN) 2008, pp. 3–4, figs 1.3 and 1.4.

26   J. GONELLA, W. KHAYYATA & K. KOHLMEYER, *Die Zitadelle von Aleppo und der Tempel des Wettergottes: Neue Forschungen und Entdeckungen*, Münster 2005, fig. 14, p. 100.

27   K. KOHLMEYER, Der Tempel des Wettergottes von Aleppo: Baugeschichte und Bautyp, räumliche Bezüge, Inventar und bildliche Ausstattung, *Temple Building and Temple Cult: Architecture and cultic paraphernalia of temples in the Levant (2.–1. mill. B.C.E.)*, ed. J. Kamlah, Wiesbaden 2012, p. 68.

28   K. KOHLMEYER, Drei Stelen mit Sin-Symbol aus Nordsyrien, *Von Uruk nach Tuttul: eine Festschrift für Eva Strommenger*, ed. B. Hrouda, S. Kroll & P.Z. Spanos, Munich-Vienna 1992, p. 94–95, pl. 39/4.

29   K. KOHLMEYER, *art. cit.* (n. 28), pp. 94–95, pl. 39/3.

Part Three

Tell Ahmar in the Assyrian empire:
Birth of an imperial *koine*

The effort to strengthen Assyrian power, which began at the time of the *turtānu* Shamshi-ilu and king Adad-nirari III, continued throughout the eighth century and culminated in the Sargonid dynasty which was founded by Sargon II in 721 and lasted for more than a century until the collapse of the empire at the end of the seventh century. The date generally chosen for the end of the empire is that of the capture of Nineveh by the Medes in 612. However, this date, although it corresponds to the actual end of the empire, does not mark the end of Assyrian power. The Sargonid dynasty continued for a few more years in the region of Harran to which Til Barsib/Kar-Shalmaneser belonged.

Paradoxically, this period of political and administrative centralization also witnessed an increase in the influence western regions exerted on the Assyrian centre. The intensification of economic and cultural exchanges between dominating Assyria and dominated provinces favoured a back-and-forth movement whereby Assyrian models were exported to the provinces at the same time as customs from the provinces found their way towards the Assyrian core. Aramaic, for example, became one of the two administrative languages of the empire, on a par with Assyrian. A cultural *koine* started to spread to the whole of the Assyrian domain. This movement became particularly noticeable during the reign of Sennacherib (704–681) and lasted until the end of the empire.

5

Ashur imposes its mark: The Palace and the high dignitaries

The consolidation of imperial power deeply affected Tell Ahmar from the mid-eighth century onwards. Documents of the time refer to it either by its traditional name Til Barsib, sometimes spelt Tarbusiba, or by its Assyrian name Kar-Shalmaneser. Masuwari now seems forgotten.

The most visible manifestation of Assyrian power is found on the Acropolis, which was the focus of attention within the urban fabric. The Acropolis dominated the city and travellers marching along the Euphrates or across the plain could see it from afar. There stood a palace, which, as we shall see, had all the characteristics of a royal palace. But the Assyrian presence was also perceptible in the city. The official buildings that must have existed there have not

yet been found, but sculptures found scattered throughout the site attest to their existence and extend to the entire city the discourse of power that the new organization of the Acropolis manifested.

1. The Assyrian administration

The Palace, as can be expected in a city that Shalmaneser III raised to the rank of "royal city", symbolized the royal presence. However, the king was to reside in this palace only occasionally. He was represented locally by a provincial governor (*bēl pīḫāti*), some of whom gave their name to a year, according to the system of *limmu* or yearly eponyms.

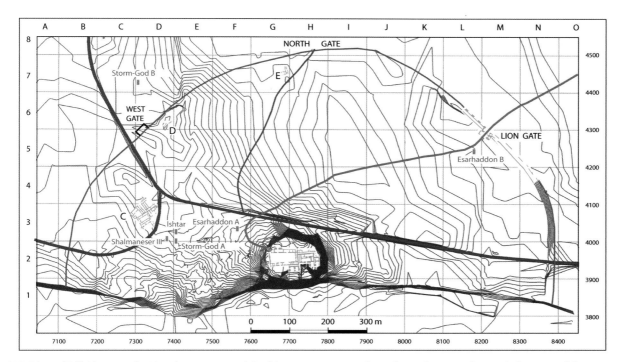

Fig. 155. Plan of Tell Ahmar in the Neo-Assyrian period. Building remains are indicated in red. Rectangles mark the point of discovery of the main stelae including the stelae of the Storm-God which were probably still visible. The dark red line that runs through the East Gate, or Lion Gate, and goes to the Acropolis marks the possible course of the road coming from Assyria. The dark green lines correspond to modern roads.

So, Hananu gave his name to year 701 and Nabu-nadin-ahi probably to year 647.[1]

The administration of Til Barsib/Kar-Shalmaneser was, however, more complex than just a governor administering the city and its province. Cuneiform tablets, both from the site and from Assyria itself, shed some light on the complexity of local government. Tablet T14 from Building C1a is particularly informative:

> Seal of Shulmu-ahhe the deputy of Tarbusiba, seal of Iqbi-Ashur the scribe.
> On the day when Hanni and Hashana come to Tarbusiba, (neither?) the deputy (governor) of Tarbusiba, (nor?) the ...., (nor?) the mayor, (nor?) the city overseer of Tarbusiba shall speak with them until the sealed order arrives from(?)/to(?) the palace and they verify(?) (it). Nobody whatsoever (?) shall speak with them.
> Before Sangu-Ishtar, before Nabua, before Salam-sharri-iqbi, before Dani.
> Month Shabatu, 7th day, limmu Sha-Nabu-shu (658)[2]

This document prohibits the local authorities from talking to Hanni – who is assumed to have resided in the building where the tablet was found – and a certain Hashana until written instructions have arrived from the Palace, *i.e.* from the central administration in Ashur, or, perhaps, to the palace, *i.e.* to the Palace of Til Barsib. This implies that Hanni and Hashana were sufficiently important figures for the central administration, *i.e.* the king, to take a personal interest in them. They had probably been granted a privilege that a document from the central administration would confirm. Tablet T14 gives information about the civil servants in place in the city. It lists successively the "deputy (governor)" (*šanû*) of Tarbusiba (Til Barsib), a civil servant whose name of function is lost in a break, the "mayor" or "town manager" (*hazannu*) and the "city overseer" (*ša muḫḫi āli*). Although the nature of the functions performed by these magistrates is not always very clear, it can be seen that several civil servants were assigned to the management of Tarbusiba/Til Barsib. On the other hand, it is surprising that the governor is not mentioned in Tablet T14, because the governor was the chief magistrate whose authority extended not only over the city but also over the province of which Til Barsib/Kar-Shalmaneser was the capital. Perhaps the governor devoted himself to the province, as well as to other tasks in the central administration, and his "deputy" replaced him in the management of local problems.

Another text mentions the "female administrator" (*šakintu*). Tablet T13 records the purchase of a slave by this officer.[3] The title *šakintu* was held by administrators working in the Palaces of the centre of the empire as well as in the provinces. They seem to have been in charge of the queen's interests. The *šakintu* of Tablet T13 could have been the representative of the Queen's house in Til Barsib/Kar-Shalmaneser.[4]

Texts found in Assyria itself show that more officials participated in the local administration. We know of a "village manager" (*rab ālāni*),[5] perhaps in charge of the countryside, and a "chief singer" (*rab zammāri*)[6] who shows that musicians or singers functioned as an autonomous body. There was also a "city emissary" (*ṣīr āli*) who appears in the list of witnesses in the documents that mention the "chief singer".

Lastly, the presence of an Assyrian military contingent at Til Barsib/Kar-Shalmaneser, which can be expected in a provincial capital controlling a major crossing point of the Euphrates, finds epigraphic support in the texts of Tell Shiukh Foqani, according to Mario Fales.[7] It must be noted that, if no barracks were found at the site, military equipment has come to light in Areas C and E.

2. The Acropolis

The Acropolis was completely reorganized in the eighth century. Its sides were consolidated and a Palace replaced the buildings that stood on its top in the previous period.

a. Consolidation of the Acropolis

The long trench (Area S) that was excavated on the eastern flank of the Acropolis during the renewed excavations made it possible to identify, among other things, a reddish mud-brick structure that covered the entire slope of the tell (*Fig. 156*). It formed a series of large steps climbing up the mound's surface. The brick layers were reinforced at intervals of about ten layers by a compact horizontal line of large stones mixed with gravel (*Fig. 157*). This structure was clearly intended to strengthen the sides of the tell. At the foot of the mound, the structure was protected by a small stone glacis. Flat, irregularly shaped slabs covered a 45° slope going down towards the east (*Fig. 158*). At the furthest end of the wall, the slope of the glacis was steeper, either to make it more difficult to climb or to line a ditch. The presence of a modern house and an orchard unfortunately did not allow the excavation to extend in this direction to reach the base of the glacis.

It is difficult to get an idea of the original appearance of the entire structure. However, immediately behind the glacis, the red bricks formed an almost vertical wall. The preserved part of the structure, however, showed slight indentations, which were probably levelled by a thick mud plaster, so that one can imagine a slightly slanting wall face.

To the west of the Acropolis, in Area M, reddish bricks were also recognized. Trench M1 (a 10 × 10 m square), the westernmost trench of Area M, was covered with mud bricks over most of its extent (*Fig. 159*). These bricks covered the level of the pebble mosaic of the Aramaean period (*Fig. 160*) and extended into the western slope of the tell, where they were clearly visible after a heavy rainfall.

There is little doubt that this reddish brick structure is the counterpart of the structure found on the eastern slope of the tell. We can thus hypothesize that the sides of the Acropolis were entirely reinforced with a thick covering of reddish

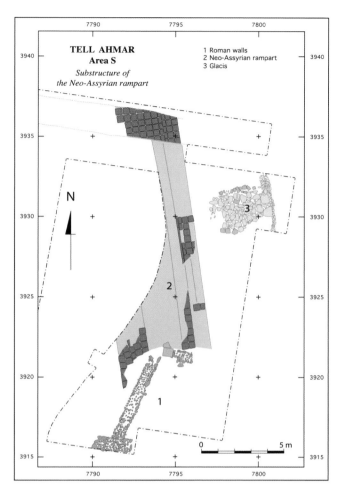

Fig. 156. Area S: Plan of the exposed section of the Neo-Assyrian brick structure protecting the Acropolis. The light brown marks places where the structure was recognized but individual bricks could not be traced. Actual bricks are in dark brown.

Fig. 157. Area S: Section through the Neo-Assyrian brick structure protecting the south-east slope of the Acropolis (looking W). The stone facing of the podium that supported the third millennium temple is visible to the left.

Fig. 158. Area S: Glacis at the foot of the SE side of the Acropolis (looking SW).

Fig. 159. Area M: Neo-Assyrian brick structure and Iron Age mosaic uncovered below the Assyrian palace (looking W).

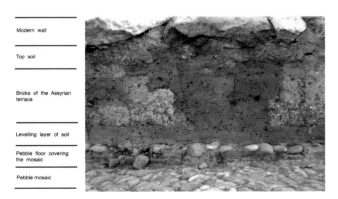

Fig. 160. Area M: Section showing the archaeological deposits immediately above the Iron Age pebble mosaic.

bricks. From this probably comes the name Tell Ahmar, the "Red Hill", given to the site. As the remains found on this massif were in direct contact with the Palace, it can be assumed that they both belonged to the same architectural programme.

What was its function? It probably served to counterbalance the considerable pressure that the Palace must have exerted. Was it also used to support a rampart, or even two, one protecting the foot of the hill and the other enclosing its top? The excavations do not make it possible to decide.

b. The Palace

The most important of the discoveries made by the Thureau-Dangin expedition is, without doubt, the Assyrian Palace (*Fig. 161*)[8] which, at the time of discovery, was one of the best preserved, if not the best preserved, of the provincial palaces of the empire especially if we admit that the "palace" of Arslan Tash, also very well preserved, should rather be understood as a temple as G. Turner has argued.[9]

Unfortunately, today almost nothing remains of this imposing construction. The French excavators removed it almost entirely in order to explore the underlying levels and recent levelling for military purposes during the recent civil war must have made the situation still worse. The renewed excavations could only expose a fragment of the pebble mosaic pavement of Courtyard XLIII, mentioned above (p. 88), and the north-eastern corner of Room XLV (*Fig. 162*). As the French had noticed, a band of bitumen

about 40 cm high ran at the base of the wall. It could also be observed that a few terracotta tiles were lying on the floor and, above all, that the ground had been levelled by filling a depression with large stones (*Fig. 124*), the surface of which was smoothed by a layer of bricks on which the mud plaster of the floor was applied. These observations showed that the palace was resting directly on the remains of the Iron Age II period, thus confirming the observation made by the French excavators that it was built without foundations. This is not surprising as the red brick massif ensured the stability of the whole structure.

Regarding the relation between the brick massif and the palace, the renewed excavations have revealed a

Fig. 162. Assyrian Palace: NE corner of Room XLV in 2002 (looking NW). The pit on the left was dug by the villagers to install a cowshed in the ruins of the Palace.

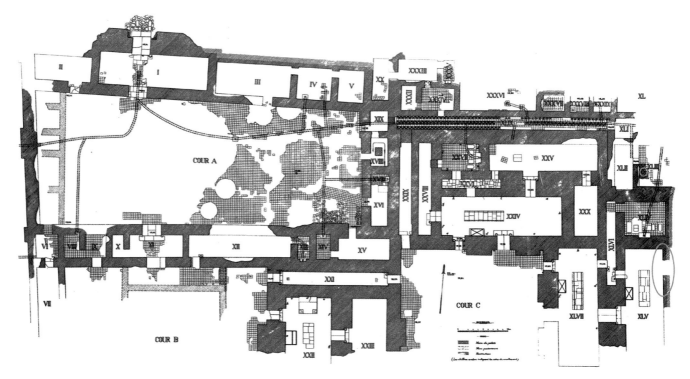

Fig. 161. Assyrian Palace: Plan drawn by the Thureau-Dangin expedition (Til-Barsib, Plan B). The parts of the Palace that were extant at the time of the renewed excavations are circled in red.

curious contrast between the north wall of Room XLV, made of greyish-brown bricks, and the east wall of the same room, which was made of reddish bricks identical to those of the red brick massif. It should also be noted that, contrary to what can be observed in the west, the brick massif does not extend, here, under the Palace. We can assume that it formed the outer wall of the Palace towards the east.

The Assyrian Palace covered the entire surface of the Acropolis, in sharp contrast to the previous period when the Acropolis seems to have included several separate buildings. The entire southern part of the Palace, about a quarter or a fifth of the whole, was destroyed, washed away by the erosion of the hill due to the floods of the Euphrates.

The building stood on an uneven surface, which was sloping down from south-east to north-west. The difference in height was significant. The passageway between Corridor XXI and Courtyard B was at 18.24 m in the reference system adopted by the French expedition; this was 1.83 m higher than the north-west corner of Courtyard A (16.41 m).

By far the most noteworthy of the Palace's features was its decoration of murals which, to this day, represent the largest group of paintings ever found in the ancient Near East.[10] It is all the more unfortunate that only a small number of fragments have been preserved, which were shared between the Aleppo Museum and the Louvre. Fortunately, the copies made by Lucien Cavro at the time of the discovery give an idea of the original compositions.[11]

In the most important rooms, a black bitumen band, 40 or 50 cm high, ran at the base of the walls. Immediately above it was a narrative register, about 1.30 to 1.50 m high, involving several figures. The whole was crowned by a frieze that could be 2.30 to 2.50 m high. The frieze itself consisted of a band of alternating geometric and protective figures, with strips at the top and bottom that were combining geometric and vegetal motifs. The proportions lower band–narrative register–frieze were approximately 1 × 3 × 5, which is somewhat surprising to the modern viewer, since the middle register, which was the most important in terms of ideological content, appeared to be somewhat squashed by the frieze (*Fig. 163*). It should be noted that the range of colours was limited. The artists used only black, red and blue on a white background.

The themes dealt with in the narrative middle register in the main rooms were all aimed at glorifying the person of the king. In the passageways connecting the rooms, the representations included deities and animals whose magical powers were supposed to ward off evil. In secondary rooms, the middle register could be absent altogether. The frieze, in all painted rooms, combined geometric patterns with animals or protective figures.

These paintings played the same role, but at a lower cost, as the carved orthostates of the palaces of Assyria itself. Their effect on the viewer, however, must not have been very different, as the orthostates were also painted.

Fig. 163. Assyrian Palace: Arbitrary reconstruction of a painted panel (after Cavro's copies, courtesy of Elisabeth Fontan).

The problem raised by the Tell Ahmar paintings is the same as the one presented by any kind of propaganda art that develops in a closed environment with carefully controlled access. At whom is it aimed? While it is clear that the scenes depicted are all intended to magnify royal power, one wonders who, in everyday reality, had the opportunity to linger in front of them to appreciate their artistic quality and extract its deep meaning. The people admitted to the Throne Room were carefully chosen and, in any case, they were all already persuaded of what the paintings wanted them to be convinced of. As for the residents, they had no need to be reminded of the power of the owner of the place. It rather looks as if such a decoration was to function as a sort of aide-memoire, a way for the ruling class to strengthen their convictions and create an environment that justified their actions. The governing body, by means of images apparently intended for its subjects, spoke above all to themselves.

The Palace of Til Barsib/Kar-Shalmaneser consisted of six sectors that can be grouped into three larger units.

A. The public unit

This can be seen as the part of the Palace where the public had access, either to settle personal or administrative problems (Courtyard A) or to submit problems or perform duties more directly related to the royal authority (Courtyard B).

SECTOR 1 – COURTYARD A (OUTER COURTYARD)

The palace entrance was located near the north-west corner of Courtyard A. It was flanked by two buttresses, possibly towers. On either side of the entrance, the floor was covered with a pebble mosaic arranged in a checkerboard pattern. This is the only place in the Palace – apart from the north-eastern sector, which is probably older – where this type of decoration appears. It shows that the technique continued to be used. The entrance hall (Room I) was decorated with paintings, fragments of which were found in the debris that filled the room. One fragment, preserved in the Aleppo Museum, depicted a naval combat scene (*Fig. 164*). Such a scene, so geographically marked, may come as a surprise in a place so far from the sea, but maritime scenes, admittedly earlier than the Assyrian period, are also known from Tell Halaf and Karatepe, whose link with the sea is no more obvious. The aim of the painting was undoubtedly to remind the visitor, as soon as he entered the palace, of the extent of the royal power.

Courtyard A was lined with a series of offices and guard-houses on the north, east and south sides. The fact that the staff engaged in administrative and supervisory activities spent long periods of time in these rooms is evidenced by the existence of toilets adjoining most of the offices. This is the case for Groups III+IV+V in the north, Groups XVI+XVII in the east and Groups XIV+XV in the south.

A staircase on the eastern side (Room XVIII) must have given access to an upper storey that covered all or part of the building.

Fig. 164. Assyrian Palace: Scene of a naval battle (Room I) (Aleppo M 512) (photo: Anwar Abd el-Ghafour).

SECTOR 2 – COURTYARD B (AUDIENCE COURTYARD)

As this courtyard was adjacent to the throne room, it can be considered to be the place where matters more directly relevant to the king – or to his local representative – were dealt with. People waiting for an audience must have been waiting here.

The passage from Courtyard A to Courtyard B was made through a rather similar device (Room XI), but smaller in size, than that of the main entrance (Room I). The courtyard was almost completely destroyed. Only the offices consisting of Groups VIII+IX, X+XI and XII+XIII were preserved. They too were equipped with toilets.

SECTOR 3 – THRONE ROOM COMPLEX

The Throne Room (XXII), on the east side of Courtyard B, was only preserved in its northern part (*Fig. 165*). As in other

Fig. 165. Assyrian Palace: NE corner of the Throne Room (Room XXII) at the time of the French excavations (photo: Georges Dossin archives).

Assyrian palaces, two doors would have given access to it, and its length would have been about three times its width, *i.e.* 9 × 27 m. The stone pedestal on which the throne stood was placed against the north wall of the room so that, as in other Assyrian throne rooms, the visitor entering the room would have had to make a quarter turn to the left to see the king.

Against the west wall, immediately south of the only preserved doorway, was a stone slab on which a jar filled with water could be placed, perhaps to allow the people coming in to purify themselves and surely to provide water for drinking. Such a device was also found in domestic architecture. A good example has been found at Tell Ahmar in Building C2 (below, p. 142). Until recently, houses in Syrian villages still had a large jar full of water placed next to the door of the main room, together with a bowl to draw water from it.

In the middle of the room, a pavement made of large flat stones must have supported a mobile hearth of the kind of the device found in the "Temple-Palace" of Tell Halaf.[12] It was mounted on wheels and could be pushed back and forth according to the desired heat intensity and the part of the room to be heated. Building C2 also revealed such a pavement.

Part of the painted decoration survived in the north-east corner.[13] Horses were shown that were probably participating in the procession that accompanied the king. According to Thureau-Dangin's description, it seems that lions were depicted behind the throne. The frieze consisted of alternating bulls and squares with curving sides.[14]

Another room (XXIII), parallel to the Throne Room, separated it from the inner Courtyard C. This is also a common feature in Assyrian palaces, in which a room of varying width and length was located between the throne room and the private sector of the palace.

B. The private unit

The rooms situated to the east of the Throne Room Complex obviously had a residential function. They were closed to the public.

SECTORS 4 AND 5 — APARTMENTS I AND II

Both apartments, which present strong similarities, will be considered together.

Apartment I, located to the north of Courtyard C, had its plan entirely recognized. However, enough has been discovered of the second apartment, to the east of the courtyard, to realize that they were both designed on the same model and had a common core. A first room, which served as a living/reception room (Room XXIV in Apartment I, XLVII in Apartment II), was followed by a second room (XXV in one case, XLV in the other), which was the most secluded part of the apartment. A corridor (XXVI and XLVI respectively) gave access to a bathroom (XXVII and XLIV respectively). To this ensemble, Apartment I added a fourth room, Room XXX, on the east side of Room XXIV and accessible from Room XXV. Apartment I also included a corridor, Corridor XXVIII, which provided direct access to Bathroom XXVII from Room XXIV. Such a corridor was absent from the second flat. At some stage, however, the door connecting Corridor XXVIII and Bathroom XXVII was blocked.

Apartments with one or more parallel rooms and a bathroom accessible through a corridor are common in both palatial and domestic architecture in the Neo-Assyrian period.[15] Moreover, hearths, mobile or not, as well as stone slabs near a doorway were also common features at the time. More examples will be discussed below when commenting on the residential buildings excavated at Tell Ahmar.

The presence of two apartments suggests that two different groups of people were expected to reside in the Palace. One naturally thinks of the men's apartment for one and the women's residence for the other. It should be noted, however, that the small number of rooms in either did not allow large numbers of people to live there. It is not very likely that all the royal court could be accommodated in these apartments. Kat-Shalmaneser/Til Barsib was just a stopover in the king's journeys to the west.

The painted decoration of the two apartments does not help to clarify the problem. In Apartment I, the main scene was set against the eastern end of Room XXIV.[16] It showed the king sitting on his throne, accompanied to the left by officers and soldiers. On the right, officers led prisoners to the king. Three fragments of the royal escort have been preserved: the bust of an officer (*Fig. 166*), the legs of a soldier (*Fig. 167*) and the bust of another soldier holding a shield (*Fig. 168*). The other walls of Room XXIV were decorated with more scenes involving the king, either sitting on a throne placed on a chariot and inspecting prisoners,[17] with a lion at his feet and inspecting other prisoners,[18] or else greeting dignitaries leading a procession of figures who had come to deliver weapons.[19] The glorification of the king went as far as the bathroom, where a hunting scene, reminiscent of those of Ashurbanipal at Nineveh, had been painted.[20]

Fig. 166. Assyrian Palace: Military officer of the royal escort (Apartment I, Room XXIV) (Aleppo M 7508) (photo: Anwar Abd el-Ghafour).

Fig. 167. Assyrian Palace: Legs of a foot soldier of the royal escort (Apartement I, Room XXIV) (Aleppo M 7505) (photo: Anwar Abd el-Ghafour).

Additionally, it must be noted that a fragment of the frieze of Room XXV, showing a winged genie (*Fig. 169*),[21] could be lifted. Two others, from the frieze of Corridor XXVI (*Fig. 170* and *171*), which showed wild goats originally associated with a motif in the shape of a square with rounded sides, could also be rescued.[22]

In Apartment II, the main scene was very similar to that of Room XXIV of Apartment I and it was also placed at one end, the north end in this case, of the main room (Room XLVII). However, the king here was not receiving prisoners but tributaries. Four fragments have been preserved: the bust of the two eunuchs standing behind the royal throne (*Fig. 172*),[23] the head of one of the officers

Fig. 168. Assyrian Palace: Soldier of the royal escort (Apartement I, Room XXIV) (Aleppo M 7507) (photo: Anwar Abd el-Ghafour).

Fig. 169. Assyrian Palace: Winged genie from a frieze (Apartment I, Room XXVII (Louvre A 23009) (photo: © RMN-Grand Palais [Musée du Louvre]/Franck Raux).

of the royal escort (*Fig. 173*), the heads of two of the dignitaries leading the procession of tributaries (*Fig. 174*) and the head of one of the tributaries (*Fig. 175*).[24] Panels adorning the other walls of Room XLVII included the king standing in front of prisoners[25] and the king in his chariot greeting male figures that may represent foreign ambassadors.[26]

The intention was obviously to illustrate the king's omnipotence, which extended to all the peoples of the earth as well as to the animal world. An intention that was even manifested in a bathroom! However, it cannot give any clue as to the function of the apartments.

Fig. 172. Assyrian Palace: Two eunuchs standing behind the king's throne (Apartment II, Room XLVII) (Louvre AO 23011) (photo: © RMN-Grand Palais [Musée du Louvre]/Franck Raux).

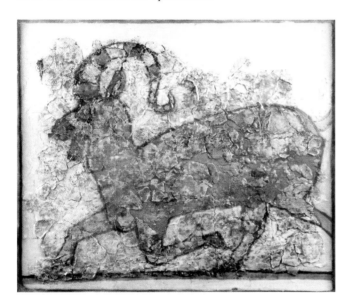

Fig. 170. Assyrian Palace: Wild goat from a frieze (Apartement I, Corridor XXVI) (Aleppo M 7511) (photo: Anwar Abd el-Ghafour).

Fig. 171. Assyrian Palace: Another wild goat from the same frieze (Apartement I, Corridor XXVI) (photo: © RMN-Grand Palais [Musée du Louvre]/Franck Raux).

Fig. 173. Assyrian Palace: Military officer of the king's escort (Apartement II, Room XLVII) (Aleppo M 7510) (photo: Anwar Abd el-Ghafour). As F. Thureau-Dangin observed (Til-Barsib, p. 64), this officer has puffy features and his beard seems to have been added to the original painting, which was probably portraying a eunuch.

Fig. 174. Assyrian Palace: High dignitaries (Apartement II, Room XLVII) (Aleppo M 7509) (photo: Anwar Abd el-Ghafour).

Fig. 175. Assyrian Palace: Head of a tributary (Apartment II, Room XLVII) (Louvre AO 23014) (photo: © RMN-Grand Palais [Musée du Louvre]/Mathieu Rabeau.)

C. A secondary unit

SECTOR 6 – WALLED OFF SECTOR

To the north of Apartment I was a series of rooms separated from it by Corridor XLIX. Very ruined, these rooms seem

to have been organized into two apartments formed, on the one hand, by Rooms XX and XXXII to XXXV and, on the other, by Rooms XXXVII to XL. Each was grouped on either side of a possible courtyard (XXXVI). A third apartment, comprising rooms XLI to XLIII, could have existed further to the south-east.

This ensemble was clearly isolated from the rest of the Palace. In its original state, it was accessed from Courtyard A via Room XIX and Corridor XLIX, and from Courtyard C via Corridor XXIX. However, these accesses were blocked at some stage so that the area became inaccessible. It is impossible to restore an access from other directions. To the east the system of consolidation of the Acropolis, revealed by the renewed excavations, was too close to the palace to give way to even one access corridor. The possibility of access from the north, if it cannot be excluded, is hardly likely either. It would imply that the entire sector functioned independently from the palace.

One possible reason for the abandonment of this sector could be the dilapidated state of the construction. Dunand considered this part of the Palace to be older than the rest, as if an existing building had been integrated into the new structure.[27] In fact, as he notes, the level of the rooms in the north-east corner was 40–80 cm lower than that of the neighbouring rooms to the south-west. The walls were narrower. It is probably, as seen above (pp. 87–88), a building that pre-dated the Palace and was integrated into it for some time before being abandoned.

c. Function of the Palace

From an ideological point of view, the Neo-Assyrian palace of Til Barsib/Kar-Shalmaneser marked in a solemn and spectacular way the Assyrian hold not only on the site, but on the whole region.

The existence of the Palace helps to replace Tell Ahmar in the settlement hierarchy of the empire. There were four levels. At the top were the great cities of Assyria and, first of all, Ashur. Next were the "royal cities". These were cities where the king was supposed to reside during his travels throughout the empire. They had a palace to accommodate the royal person. Thirdly, there were "fortified cities". These were settlements from which subdued areas could be controlled, but they were not specifically associated with the person of the king. Finally, there were the ordinary towns and villages. Til Barsib/Kar-Shalmaneser, since Shalmaneser III, belonged to the second level, that of the royal cities. In addition, at least since the first half of the eighth century, it was also the capital of a province. The palace was thus the material manifestation of the imperial power in one of its essential components, which happened also to be the gateway to the western provinces of the empire.

For the same symbolic reasons, it is very likely that, in the absence of the king, the palace was the place where the governor had his office and administration, possibly also his residence.

d. Dates of construction and abandonment of the Palace

The date of construction of the Palace is uncertain. As we saw above, it is unlikely that Shalmaneser III built it at the time of the conquest but any date from the beginning of the eighth century onwards is possible, be it at the time of the *turtānu* Shamshi-ilu or of kings Adad-nirari III, Tiglath-pileser III or even Sargon II. However, one thing emerges with certainty from the study of the building: it had a relatively long history, which Julian Reade tried to reconstruct.[28] This is demonstrated, among other things, by the closing of the access to the north-eastern sector and by the existence of different styles in the execution of the paintings. There are even traces of superimposed painted decoration, such as the horsemen discovered in Room XXII under a more recent decoration,[29] or two small grotesque heads that appeared under the paintings of the frieze in Room XXIV (*Fig. 176a*)[30] and in the passage-way between Rooms XXIV and XXV (*Fig. 176b*),[31] although these small heads could be nothing more than the drawings of an artist wanting to relax as Thureau-Dangin suggested.[32]

The end of the palace must have coincided with the end of Assyrian domination in the late seventh century. There are no signs of violent destruction.[33] Actually, new and thinner walls were built on the western side of Courtyard A and the northern side of Courtyard B as if the Palace, or parts of the palace, had remained in use.[34] There results from this that the palace was probably abandoned by the Assyrians but still occupied by unknown settlers. A similar observation was made in Building C1a in the Middle Town (below, p. 138). The only marks of violence concern the paintings. The faces of many of the figures have been mutilated, either by erasing them entirely or by scratching the nose, mouth, eyes or ears of the figures.[35]

a

b

Fig. 176. Assyrian Palace: Drawings covered by the painting of a frieze: a) Apartment I, Room XXIV (Louvre AO 32443) (photo: © Musée du Louvre, Dist. RMN-Grand Palais/Thierry Ollivier); b) Apartement I, passageway between Rooms XXIV and XXV (Aleppo M 7506) (photo: Anwar Abd el-Ghafour).

Tentative reconstruction of the Assyrian palace (Guy Bunnens)

The building (*Fig. a*) may have been modified several times over time as Julian Reade has suggested.[1] However, the reconstruction offered here will only consider the last stage of its occupation before it was abandoned. In the process, four criteria need to be met:

1) The southern and eastern boundaries cannot be restored too far from the preserved remains, to the south because the tell could not have extended over a long distance towards the river and to the east because the palace seems to be bounded by the mass of red mud-bricks discovered on the slope of the mound.

2) Having said this, there needs to be rooms to form the southern boundary of the building. A construction of such a standard can hardly be expected to have been closed by a simple wall over such a length.

3) There must be enough space to accommodate domestic services, especially considering that the excavated rooms of the Private Unit are entirely residential in nature.

4) Lastly, the possible existence of an upper storey, made likely by the staircase in Room 18 on the east side of Courtyard A, requires that appropriate accesses to this floor are restored wherever there might have been a need for it.

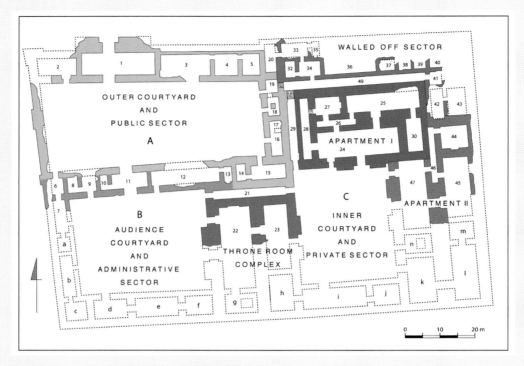

Fig. a. Reconstructed plan of the Assyrian palace.

With these prerequisites in mind, the following reconstruction may be suggested for the sectors as they were when the palace was abandoned:

The public unit

Sector 1 – Courtyard A (outer courtyard)

It is almost entirely preserved and shows that the sector did not extend further north.

Sector 2 – Courtyard B (audience courtyard)

On the contrary, this sector around Courtyard B is almost entirely destroyed. The reconstruction is inspired by the internal organization of Sector 1. The rooms on the west side of Courtyard B have about the same width as those on the east side of Courtyard A. Wider rooms are impossible to restore because their width is indicated by the remains of Rooms 6 and 7 to the north-west. The rooms to the south are assumed to have had about the same width as the rooms on the northern side of Courtyard A. All rooms are arbitrarily distributed into units of two or three rooms. Rooms 6 and 7 may have belonged to a secondary access to the sector, whilst Room 11 acted as its ceremonial entrance.

Sector 3 –Throne Room Complex

The length of throne rooms is often about four times their width. A similar ratio has been adopted here. Opposite the throne, royal palaces usually include a staircase, hence the reconstruction of Room *g*. Often an antechamber separates the throne room from the staircase. It has not been included here, both for lack of space and because the palace is of more modest proportions than the great Assyrian palaces. In most cases, the room that links the throne room with the private sector, here Room 23, is of different size. The length adopted here is three times the width.

The private unit

Sectors 4 and 5 – Apartments I and II

Apartment II can be partly reconstructed on the model of the better preserved Apartment I. Only one doorway is preserved in the living/reception room (Room 47) of Apartment II. A second can be hypothesized and a room length of about three times the width of the room can be restored to match the layout of Room 24 of Apartment I. The length of the parallel Room 45, however, is more difficult to figure out. It should be shorter than Room 47, like its counterpart, Room 25, in Apartment I, but this is hardly possible considering the position of the doorway connecting Room 45 with Room 47. It has thus been decided to make it only slightly shorter. This, in turn, prevents from suggesting the addition of a room on the south side of Room 47, which, with Room 45, would replicate the group Rooms 25 and 30 of Apartment I. It is therefore likely that Apartment II was smaller than Apartment I.

The southern part of the private unit has been arbitrarily reconstructed with two series of three rooms, Rooms *h–i–j* and Rooms *k–l–m*, where servants and domestic services might have been located. No bathroom has been included although there is enough space for one or two of them. These rooms are set in line with the reconstructed southern rooms of the Public Unit so as to form the southern boundary of the palace. In addition, a staircase (marked *n* on the plan) has been suggested, because, if the hypothesis of an upper storey were confirmed, the Private Unit must have had access to it. Its exact location, however, is anyone's guess.

Secondary unit

Sector 6 – walled off sector

In contrast with the public sector, the walled off sector seems to have included rooms extending northwards, in such a way that the north wall of the palace did not make a straight line. It is impossible, however, to offer any reconstruction of these rooms.

There remains the problem of a possible upper storey. Room 18, east of Courtyard A, and Room *g*, whose existence is almost certain to the south of the Throne Room 22, point to its existence. There might be another indication of its existence. In both Apartment I and Apartment II, the wall that separates the living/reception room from the more private room is so thick that, in both cases, a corridor could be arranged within it. The function of such thick walls is puzzling. A possibility would be to provide support for the upper floor or for a special feature of the upper floor. To allow convenient communication in the private unit between the ground and upper floors without going through the Throne Room Complex or Courtyard A, a third staircase must be restored. It is suggested that it was to the south of Room 47, in Room *n*. There are other possibilities, but this one has the advantage of resolving the problem of the absence of a third room in Apartment II, south of Room 47, which the configuration of the excavated remains makes difficult to restore.

Note

1   J. Reade, Assyrian palaces reconsidered: Practical arrangements at Til-Barsib, and the Garden-Gate and Canal at Khorsabad, *State Aechives of Assyria Bulletin* 25 (2019), pp. 73–85.

3. The empire and the city

The pre-eminence of the Acropolis was emphasized by a theatrical process that imposed the king's presence on the visitor who went from the Lion Gate to the Acropolis along a road, which, as will be seen below, appears to have connected one to the other. The ideological role of this road was shown by two stelae that King Esarhaddon (680–669) erected on this way.

a. The stelae of Esarhaddon

One of the stelae – Stele B, about 2.5 m high (*Fig. 177*) – was located immediately to the west of the Lion Gate, inside the city, and must have been the first thing travellers saw when entering the town. It depicted the king standing and holding by a leash Ushanahuru, son of Tarqu, king of Nubia and Egypt, and a prince who may have been Abdi-Milkutti,

king of Sidon, or Baalu, king of Tyre. On the sides were the sons of Esarhaddon, Ashurbanipal on the left side and Shamash-shum-ukin on the right.

The other stele – Stele A, more than 2 m high (*Fig. 178*) – stood at the foot of the Acropolis, to the west, where the road from the Lion Gate made a turn before climbing up to the Acropolis. The carved motifs were the same but an inscription was added, in which Esarhaddon explained how he organized the succession of an Arab leader named Hazael.[36]

Stelae A and B were found near the bases on which they stood. The basalt base of stele A was 2.14 m long, 1 m wide and 1.10 m high, and that of stele B 2.40 m long and 1.25 m wide (its height is not mentioned).[37] These two stelae were very similar to a third, also inscribed, which Esarhaddon had erected in Zincirli, further west, on the borders of Syria and Asia Minor. However, the style of the latter was much more elaborate and the king, instead of looking to the left as in Tell Ahmar, looked to the right.[38] The smooth surface of the Tell Ahmar stelae, especially compared with the one from Zincirli, may be due to the

Fig. 177. Esarhaddon's Stele B (Aleppo M 7497) (photos: Anwar Abd el-Ghafour).

Fig. 178. Esarhaddon's Stela A (Aleppo M 7502) (photos: Anwar Abd el-Ghafour).

fact that they were left unfinished,[39] perhaps because of the death of Esarhaddon on his way to Egypt in 669. Although his successor Ashurbanipal did not complete the job, the stelae remained in place.

Travellers arriving at Til Barsib/Kar-Shalmaneser through the Lion Gate were welcomed – and dominated in the literal sense of the word – by the king of Assyria at two key points along the way: on entering the city and on their way up to the palace. The ideological use of the space is obvious. The more so as the Lion Gate being the eastern access to Til Barsib/Kar-Shalmaneser, it was the place through which people coming from, or going to, Assyria had to pass.

b. Assyrian dignitaries

Assyrian officials also left a trace of their presence in the city. Ashur-dur-paniya, who was governor of Kar-Shalmaneser, dedicated a stele to Ishtar of Arbela (*Fig. 179*). The names of the dedicator and the dedicatee are known through an inscription carved on the stele:

> To Ishtar who resides in Arbela, his Lady,
> Ashur-dur-paniya, governor of Kar-Shalmaneser,
> dedicated (this stele) for his life.[40]

The exact date of the monument is unsure. According to Karen Radner, it could date from the time of Sargon II (721–705).[41] However, the stone it is carved in might point to a later date. It is not carved in the basalt or limestone normally used for the sculptures of Tell Ahmar, but in a reddish breccia. This kind of stone is probably the same as the stone called *turminanbandû* discovered in the region of Til Barsib during the reign of Sennacherib (see above p. 6). The qualities of this stone were so remarkable that the king brought it to Assyria to be used in local works. If the identification of the stone is correct, the stele could not be earlier than the reign of Sennacherib (704–681) and possibly later.

The goddess is shown standing on the back of a lion that she is holding on a leash with her left hand. A flower is shown above the same hand, while she makes a gesture of blessing with her right hand. A radiating disc surmounts her crown. To outline her military appearance, she carries a sword at her side and, on her back, not two crossed quivers as is commonly believed, but rather two bows inserted in a case.[42] Between the bow on the left and the sword, a fringed object could indicate the presence of a nimbus or, more simply, it could be part of the goddess' military equipment.

Ashur-dur-paniya's stele is at a crossroads of traditions. The name of the dedicator is Assyrian. The dedicatee, Ishtar of Arbela, is one of the most revered of the Assyrian deities. However, the style of the sculpture departs from Assyrian standards inasmuch as it adopts more rounded contours and slightly stockier forms than those of the works of Assyria proper. Additionally, the representation of a deity standing on the back of an animal is part of a tradition that, even though it goes back to the third millennium in Mesopotamia, was especially popular in the Hittite and Syrian tradition. At Tell Ahmar, it is attested by the large stelae of the Storm-God (see Chapter 3). In Assyria, the reign of Sennacherib (704–681) seems to have marked a renewed interest in the motif as is shown by the processions of deities standing on animals illustrated on the famous reliefs of Maltai/Halamata, Bavian/Khinis and other places, usually attributed to the king. Ashur-dur-paniya's stele thus testifies to the adaptation of elements of the Assyrian imperial ideology to a provincial capital. Besides the style and the stone, the local nature of the work is emphasized by the fact that Ashur-dur-paniya dedicated the stele "for his life" and not, as one would expect, for the life of the king who is not even mentioned. It is a local work commissioned by a local Assyrian dignitary.

Another stele, discovered in a house of the village during the renewed excavations, is made from the same stone.[43] It also bears an inscription, unfortunately almost completely illegible, and also portrays a deity. In this case, it is the Moon-God that is depicted. The dedicant is unknown, given the poor state of preservation of the inscription, but there is little doubt that he must have been another high dignitary. Only the upper part of the stele has been preserved (*Fig. 180*). The god is easily identified by the crescent above his crown. Two bows in their case, similar to those on the stele of Ishtar, emerge from behind his back. One is still clearly visible, the other has left faint traces. The style of the sculpture, like that of the stele of Ishtar, is of Assyrian inspiration, but the god depicted may have been local. The particular aspect of the god illustrated here might have been that of the Moon-God of Harran who was especially venerated in northern Syria in the first half of the first millennium. If it were so, we would have another possible example of the interpenetration of cultural elements from the core of the empire with others from the West.

A small and rather enigmatic stele was discovered in two parts on separate occasions (*Fig. 181*). The lower part was found out of context on the Acropolis by the Thureau-Dangin expedition and is now in the Louvre (AO 26555). The top, of unknown provenance, arrived several decades later at the Aleppo Museum (M 4526).[44] The original object, carved in limestone, was approximately 39 cm wide, 60 cm high and 7 cm thick. Very strangely, it was carved on both sides. It must therefore have been a free-standing object.

On one side, the Moon-God, carved in low relief, stands above a monumental gate flanked by two crenellated towers which, in all probability, represent the façade of his temple.

The god, who raises his right hand in a blessing gesture, can be identified by the many crescents that surround him, one above his crown, another at the end of his sword, a third as part of his sceptre and, most visible of all, the two large crescents supported by tasselled staffs, which stand on either side of the building. On the other side, a four-winged genie is portrayed carrying a *situla*, or ritual bucket, in his left hand and raising his right hand in the same gesture as the god. He is wearing a horned cap – a sign of divinity – topped with a floral motif. The style of the work is of Assyrian inspiration. It probably offers another witness of the popularity of the god of Harran.

The function of the stele is difficult to determine. Its execution with two decorated sides sets it apart from other

Fig. 179. Stele dedicated to Ishtar of Arbela by Ashur-dur-paniya, governor of Kar-Shalmaneser, (Louvre AO 11503/16083) (photo: © RMN-Grand Palais [Musée du Louvre]/Franck Raux).

Fig. 180. Fragment of a stele portraying the Moon-God.

a   b

Fig. 181. Small stele carved on both sides (upper part: Aleppo M 4526; lower part: cast of the fragment in the Louvre, AO 26555) (photo: Anwar Abd el-Ghafour).

Fig. 182. Fragments of the statue of an Assyrian dignitary at the time of its discovery near the entrance shaft of an Assyrian burial vault (C54 O.1007, Aleppo). One of the slabs covering the access shaft to the burial vault in Area C appears in the background.

sculptures, statues and reliefs. Its execution (which requires a skilled craftsman), its subject (which combines Assyrian motifs), its technique (which denotes provincialism), all point to a work commissioned by a local Assyrian resident. Could it be an offering deposited in a temple by a member of the Assyrian ruling class?

A last dignitary has left a material testimony of his existence. During the renewed excavations, a basalt statue, broken into three pieces, came to light immediately to the south of a burial vault in Area C (on which see below, pp. 145 and 147) (*Fig. 182*).[45] The statue portrays a life-size standing figure with clasped hands (*Figs 183* and *184*). Only the feet are missing. The height of the statue in its present state is 1.45 m. Everything – hairstyle, clothing, jewellery – is typically Assyrian. Although parallels from the centre of the empire are rare, a statue found in Nimrud provides an excellent point of comparison.[46]

The figure has no beard, indicating that he was a eunuch. Assyrian texts make a clear distinction between the *ša ziqni*, *i.e.* men with beards, and the *ša rēši*, *i.e.* eunuchs. Remembering that Inurta-belu-usur, governor of Kar-Shalmaneser at the time of Shamshi-ilu, was also a eunuch, one might wonder whether the statue is not

Fig. 183. Life-size basalt statue of an Assyrian dignitary (C54 O.1007, Aleppo).

Fig. 184. Drawing of the statue of an Assyrian dignitary (C54 O.1007) (drawing: Sarah Myers).

that of a governor of the city and province of Til Barsib/Kar-Shalmaneser.

Although the statue is almost complete, it is not intact. The facial features have been erased. A hole has been hammered in the top of the skull and another in the right chest. This cannot be due to chance. As a matter of fact, monuments of this kind were intended to perpetuate the existence of the deceased beyond death. If its features were

erased, the person was made unable to express itself or to be recognized. Furthermore, the blows, aimed at vital organs, performed a kind of ritual murder of the eunuch. Even his memory was deleted. Such harshness would tend to confirm that the statue depicted a person who played an important role in the exercise of imperial domination.

The original location of the statue is not known. The place of its discovery, near a monumental tomb, might give an indication. The statue could have been a memorial to the person buried in the tomb. A limestone slab with a central perforation found together with the statue may have served as a pedestal. If this were the case, however, one wonders why the feet were not found. It is therefore possible that the statue did not belong to the funerary installation but was brought from elsewhere, possibly from a temple in which it would have been placed as a sign of devotion. Anyhow, whatever its exact origin, the presence, in a funerary context, of a statue that had been "ritually killed" deserves to be noticed.

c. Fragments of the decoration of official buildings

It is difficult to imagine that all the officials contributing to the administration of Til Barsib/Kar-Shalmaneser resided in the Palace. The existence of other official buildings is therefore extremely likely. Fragments of their decoration have been found out of context. They necessarily come from still unexcavated buildings because the Palace, which covers the entire surface of the Acropolis, did not receive any sculpted decoration, at least in its preserved parts.

A basalt column base, with a maximum diameter of 72 cm, was found in the village during the renewed excavations (*Fig. 185*). Globular column bases are found in Assyria proper as well as in the provinces. An almost identical base was found at Carchemish.[47] They were often placed in monumental entrances of buildings.

Another basalt piece must come from a bull that guarded a monumental gate (*Fig. 186*). The sculpture is of little interest in itself, given its state of preservation, but it bears an inscription worthy of attention. The inscription can be attributed to Sargon II (721–705)[48] and demonstrates that Sargon erected or at least renovated buildings in Til Barsib/ Kar-Shalmaneser.

More fragments belonged to orthostats adorning the walls of buildings. A limestone relief could portray the king himself (*Fig. 187*). It shows a bearded figure holding two arrows in his right hand and, presumably, a bow in his left. These attributes are generally those of the king. However, a difficulty arises from the fact that the figure does not wear a crown nor the two ribbons that usually fall into the king's or crown prince's back. Identification is therefore not certain. F. Thureau-Dangin wondered whether this was not a portrait of Shamshi-ilu who, as we have seen, behaved like a king in the province under his control.[49] Nothing, however, confirms the hypothesis.

Another orthostat, made of basalt, comes from a composition in which prisoners or tributaries were brought before the king (*Fig. 188*). An Assyrian official raises his left hand to give a signal to the procession behind him. Only the first figure in the procession, in an attitude of supplication, is shown. A third orthostat, also made of basalt, shows the siege of a town whose inhabitants are depicted begging for mercy from the top of their ramparts (*Fig. 189*).

Fig. 187. Fragment of limestone orthostat portraying a high dignitary, possibly an Assyrian king (Aleppo M 7500) (photo: Anwar Abd el-Ghafour).

0   50 cm

Fig. 185. Basalt column base discovered in the modern village.

Fig. 188. Fragment of basalt orthostat with an Assyrian officer introducing a procession of tributaries or prisoners (Aleppo M 7501) (photo: Anwar Abd el-Ghafour).

Fig. 186. Fragment of portal bull with an inscription of Sargon II (Aleppo M 9944).

Fig. 189. Fragment of basalt orthostat depicting a besieged city (Aleppo M 9956) (photo: Anwar Abd el-Ghafour).

These three orthostates illustrate well-known themes in the decoration of Assyrian palaces. They seem to complement each other. The king, if it is really he, looks to the right and the prisoners or tributaries are moving to the left. The figures standing on the city walls also look to the left. It all looks like the surrender of a city with the delivery of tribute. However, apart from the stones they are made of (basalt and limestone), the style of the individual reliefs is too disparate to assume that they all come from the same composition. The figure that could represent the king is sharper than that of the tributaries and the besieged city is a little stiffer in its execution.

* * *

The Assyrian control over Til Barsib/Kar-Shalmaneser was thus materialized by monuments using the themes and style that the masters of the empire developed at the very heart of their power. Be it the Palace that dominated the city on top of the Acropolis, or the stelae that Esarhaddon placed along what appears to be the main road to the Acropolis, or the sculpted works – statue, stelae and reliefs – scattered over the site, all these works proclaimed the sovereignty of Ashur. If the local style could surface here and there, a definitely Syro-Hittite component seems to have vanished altogether.

Notes

1   A. Millard, *The Eponyms of the Assyrian Empire, 910–612 BC*, State Archives of Assyria Studies II, Helsinki 1994, pp. 94 and 105. The date of Nabu-nadin-ahi adopted here follows a suggestion of J. Reade, Assyrian eponyms: Kings and pretenders 648–605 BC, *Orientalia* NS 67 (1998), pp. 256–257.

2   S. Dalley, Neo-Assyrian tablets from Til Barsib, *Abr-Nahrain* 34 (1996–1997), pp. 84–85 (available online at <http://oracc.org/atae/P522605/>).

3   S. Dalley, *art. cit.* (n. 2), pp. 82–84 (available online at <http://oracc.org/atae/P522604/>).

4   S. Teppo, The role and the duties of the Neo-Assyrian *šakintu* in the light of archival evidence, *State Archives of Assyria Bulletin* 16 (2007), pp. 257–272 (pp. 258–259 for Til Barsib's *šakintu*).

5   S. Parpola, *The Correspondence of Sargon II, Part I, Letters from Assyria and the West*, State Archives of Assyria I, Helsinki 1987, Text 183, Rev. 15–16 (available online at <http://oracc.org/saao/P334830>).

6   T. Kwasman & S. Parpola, *Legal Transactions of the Royal Court of Nineveh, Part I*, State Archives of Assyria VI, Helsinki 1991, Texts 312, 1–2, and 313, 1–2 (available online at <http://oracc.org/saao/P335652/>).

7   F.M. Fales in F.M. Fales, K. Radner, C. Pappi, & E. Attardo, The Assyrian and Aramaic texts from Tell Shiukh Fawqani, *Tell Shiukh Fawqani 1994–1998*, II, ed. L. Bachelot & F.M. Fales, Padua 2005, n. 103, p. 609 and pp. 620–621.

8   *Til-Barsib*, pp. 8–42 (M. Dunand).

9   G. Turner, The Palace and Bâtiment aux Ivoires at Arslan Tash: A reappraisal, *Iraq* 30 (1968), pp. 62–65.

10   *Til-Barsib*, pp. 42–74 (F. Thureau-Dangin).

11   Colour reproductions of the copies have been published by A. Thomas, *Les peintures murales du palais de Tell Ahmar: Les couleurs de l'empire assyrien*, Paris-Dijon 2019.

12   F. Langenegger, K. Müler, R. Naumann, *Tell Halaf* II, *Die Bauwerke*, Berlin 1950, pp. 45–50, pl. 12.

13   *Til-Barsib*, pl. liii top left; Thomas, *op. cit.* (n. 11), figs 16 and 17, p. 36; fig. 19, p. 38.

14   *Til-Barsib*, pl. xlv (centre); Thomas, *op. cit.* (n. 11), fig. 22, p. 40. Cavro's drawing does not show the bulls.

15   They form a variant from the units called "unité F" of Neo-Assyrian palaces by J.-C. Margueron, Du *bitanu*, de l'étage et des salles hypostyles, *Syria* 82 (2005), pp. 108–109.

16   *Til-Barsib*, pl. xlix (Panels a–c); Thomas, *op. cit.* (n. 11), fig. 46, p. 65; figs 54–56, p. 76.

17   *Til-Barsib*, pl. li (Panel i); Thomas, *op. cit.* (n. 11), fig. 47, p. 65; fig. 59, pp. 78–79; fig. 60, p. 79.

18   *Til-Barsib*, pl. l (Panels g–h); Thomas, *op. cit.* (n. 11), fig. 58, p. 77.

19   *Til-Barsib*, pl. l (Panel d); Thomas, *op. cit.* (n. 11), fig. 57, p. 77.

20   *Til-Barsib*, pl. liii (Panels a–c, e); Thomas, *op. cit.* (n. 11), figs 26–27, p. 42–43 (and fig. 41, p. 54); fig. 73, p. 104.

21   *Til-Barsib*, pl. xliii/1; Thomas, *op. cit.* (n. 11), fig. 31, p. 45.

22   *Til-Barsib*, pl. xliii/4; Thomas, *op. cit.* (n. 11), fig. 30, p. 44 and fig. 35, p. 48.

23   *Til-Barsib*, pls xliv/3–4 (eunuch's head); Thomas, *op. cit.* (n. 11), fig. 36, p. 49.

24   Thomas, *op. cit.* (n. 11), figs 37–38, p. 50.

25   *Til-Barsib*, pl. lii (Panel d); Thomas, *op. cit.* (n. 11), figs 78–79, p. 111.

26   *Til-Barsib*, pl. lii (Panel f) (Thureau-Dangin thinks that the male figures represented prisoners [p. 66]); Thomas, *op. cit.* (n. 11), fig. 20, pp. 38–39.

27   *Til-Barsib*, pp. 25–26.

28   J. Reade, Assyrian palaces reconsidered: Practical arrangements at Til-Barsib, and the Garden-Gate and Canal at Khorsabad, *State Archives of Assyria Bulletin* 25 (2019), pp. 73–85.

29   *Til-Barsib*, fig. 16, p. 70; Thomas, *op. cit.* (n. 11), fig. 21, p. 39.

30   *Til-Barsib*, pl. xliii/2; Thomas, *op. cit.* (n. 11), fig. 39, p. 52

31   *Til-Barsib*, pl. xliii/3.

32   *Til-Barsib*, p. 57.

33   *Til-Barsib*, p. 79 (M. Dunand).

34   *Til-Barsib*, pp. 13 and 15 (M. Dunand).

35   G. Bunnens, Facial mutilations on the Til Barsib wall paintings, *Fundstellen: Gesammelte Schriften zur Archäologie und Geschichte Altvorderasiens ad honorem Hartmut Kühne*, ed. D. Bonatz, R.M. Czichon & F.J. Kreppner, Wiesbaden 2008, pp. 145–153.

36   RINAP 4, Text 97, pp. 179–181 (available online at <http://oracc.org/rinap/Q003326/>).

37   *Til-Barsib*, pp. 151 and 155 (F. Thureau-Dangin).

38   Text, photograph and bibliography in RINAP 4, no 98, pp. 181–186. B.N. Porter, Assyrian propaganda for the West: Esarhaddon's stelae for Til Barsip and Sam'al, *Essays on Syria*

in the Iron Age, ed. G. BUNNENS, Leuven 2000, pp. 143–176; EAD., The importance of place: Esarhaddon's stelae at Til Barsip and Sam'al, *Historiography in the Cuneiform World*, ed. T. ABUSCH, Bethesda 2001, pp. 373–390.

39 *Til-Barsib*, p. 156 (F. Thureau-Dangin).

40 *Til-Barsib*, p. 157; RINAP 2, Text 2010, pp. 495–496 (available online at <http://oracc.iaas.upenn.edu/rinap/rinap2/Q006652/html>).

41 K. RADNER, Aššur-dūr-pānīya, Statthalter von Til-Barsip unter Sargon II. von Assyrien, *Baghdader Mitteilungen* 37 (2006), pp. 185–195.

42 G. BUNNENS, A stela of the moon god from Tell Ahmar/Til Barsib: Contribution to the iconography of the moon god in the Neo-Assyrian period, *Travels Through the Orient and the Mediterranean World: Essays presented to Eric Gubel*, ed. V. BOSCHLOOS, B. OVERLAET, I.M. SWINNEN & V. VAN DER STEDE, Orientalia Lovaniensia Analecta 302, Leuven-Paris-Bristol (CT), pp. 99–110.

43 G. BUNNENS, *art. cit.* (n. 42).

44 Both fragments were joined by K. KOHLMEYER, Drei Stelen mit Sin-Symbol aus Nordsyrien, *Von Uruk nach Tuttul: eine Festschrift für Eva Strommenger*, ed. B. HROUDA, S. KROLL & P.Z. SPANOS, Munich-Vienna 1992, pp. 99–100 and pls 40–41, and, apparently independently, by U. SEIDEL, Kleine Stele aus Til Barsib, *NABU* 1993/3, no 85, p. 72.

45 A. ROOBAERT, A Neo-Assyrian statue from Til Barsib, *Iraq* 58 (1996), pp. 79–87.

46 C.J. GADD, *The Stones of Assyria: The surviving remains of Assyrian sculpture, their recovery and their original positions*, London 1936, p. 228 and pl. 8/2.

47 C.L. WOOLLEY, *The Town Defences*, Carchemish: Report on the Excavations at Djerabis/Djerablus on Behalf of the British Museum II, London 1921, fig. 61, p. 155.

48 RINAP 2, Text 107, p. 417 (available online at <http://oracc.iaas.upenn.edu/rinap/rinap2/Q006588/html>).

49 *Til-Barsib*, p. 158.

6

Urbanism and residential buildings

1. Urbanism

The approximately 60 hectare in extent, semicircular city has every chance of being a Neo-Assyrian creation, as we have seen above (p. 107). A pair of test soundings (G and H) carried out in the Middle and Lower Towns showed that it was not entirely built over. There must have been open spaces, perhaps gardens or orchards, or just land awaiting construction. The research carried out in Areas C and D in the Middle Town and Areas E and F in the Lower Town gives the impression that the constructions were not erected according to a pre-established development plan. No specialization seems to have guided the choice of the location and the types of buildings. Both the excavated remains and the geophysical survey conducted by John Russell in the western part of the Middle Town (see pp. 148–152) show that there was no regularity in the urban fabric. Large residences, adapted from Assyrian models, were erected in both the Middle and Lower Towns. They have been observed in Areas C and D for the first, and in Area E for the latter. More modest constructions were encountered in the eastern part of the Lower Town, in Area F. Metal workshops existed in Areas CJ and L in the Middle Town. The temple of the Storm-God, the existence of which has been suggested in Chapter 3, may still have existed, perhaps, as we have seen, in the western part of the city, close to or under the modern cemetery.

There might have been an important access road connecting the Lion Gate to the Acropolis (*Fig. 155*). The topographical survey shows a shallow depression that starts from the gate, passes in front of one of the stelae of Esarhaddon (Stele B), crosses the Lower Town obliquely, goes up towards the Middle Town, turns near the second stele of Esarhaddon (Stele A) and climbs the western slope of the Acropolis to reach the point where the entrance of the Palace was. Although a road crossing the Lion Gate was still in use at the time of the French excavations, there is no reason to think that the depression visible on the map could not have started to form in antiquity as a result of the repeated passage of men, beasts and chariots. This would show that the main access to the city was from the east, that is, quite unsurprisingly, on the road coming from Assyria.

2. "Hanni's house"

The most extensively excavated of the large residences was the complex C1a–C1b–C2 in Area C (*Fig. 190*). The remains of other constructions, collectively designated as Building C5, have also been exposed, but they could not be explored in sufficient detail to allow a plausible interpretation of their remains. As for Building C4, to the south-west of C1a, only one corner was recognized. The discussion will therefore concentrate on the C1a-C1b-C2 complex.

The stratigraphy of Area C included a shallow Roman level, called Stratum C/1, covering the much thicker Assyrian occupation, Stratum C/2. Most of Stratum C/2 rested on virgin soil but evidence for an earlier level, Stratum C/3, was found in some places under Building C1a. A sounding at the foot of the south-east wall of Room 1 hit the bedrock immediately below the base of the wall. There were therefore no foundations on this side. On the contrary, the exploration of the layers underlying Room 15 and the northern corner of Courtyard 13 revealed walls which must have belonged to an earlier occupation level, Stratum C/3, on which they had been erected (*Figs 192* and *199*).

The material found in the three interrelated units C1a–C1b–C2 can be dated to the seventh century. Tablets found on the C/2c1 floor in and around the doorway connecting Room 11 with Room 12 of Building C1a allow a more precise date (*Figs 195* and *201*). Some of these texts are dated in according to the Assyrian system of yearly eponyms in which each year was designated by the name of an official that had been selected for this purpose. As some of these eponyms belong to the so-called post-canonical period, *i.e.* to the period following the year 649 (see below, p. 171), which is the last year documented by the eponym lists that have come down to us, we must admit that the oldest phase of occupation of Building C1a ended after 649, in the second half of the seventh century and, as it was followed by one or possibly two phases of occupation, Building C1a must have remained in use until the end of the Assyrian empire and perhaps even for some time after this major event. This chronological conclusion can be extended to the entire C1a–C1b–C2 complex.

Another conclusion that is made possible by the tablets concerns the personality of the owner of the complex. He seems to have been a certain Hanni mentioned in several tablets, among which T14 already referred to above (p. 115).

The three units do not appear to have been built at the same time, although at one point they very clearly co-existed and functioned as an organic whole. The oldest but unfortunately most poorly preserved building is Building C1b. Building C1a was built against it. Its walls were set against the exterior wall of C1b, which retained its plaster at the junction of the two buildings. Later, at a time difficult to specify but slightly after C1a was built, C2 was erected against the northwest side of C1a.

To the north-east of Building C1b was a large, vaulted tomb whose relationship to surrounding buildings is problematic (see below).

a. Building C1b

The presence of a modern road, which extended along the excavation area to the north-east and, of a large sandy pit dug along the road prevented from fully exploring Building C1b. Three rooms were identified, of which only Room 2 was relatively well preserved. Evidence is lacking to recognize their function. In Room 2, a terracotta basin was set against the south-west wall, that terracotta tiles protected against splattering. The dimensions of the room suggest that it was a workshop rather than a bathroom.

b. Building C1a

This building has not been completely exposed either, for the same reasons that prevented the complete exploration of C1b. However, the excavated rooms seem to constitute the main part of the construction. Only a few more rooms could have extended to the south-east under the modern road.

Like many Neo-Assyrian residences, Building C1a, in its original conception, was organized around two large courtyards: an outer courtyard (13) (*Fig. 192*), accessible to visitors, and an inner courtyard (3) around which one or more apartments were grouped. A close parallel to Building C1a of Tell Ahmar is to be found in Residence J on the acropolis of Khorsabad (*Fig. 191*),[1] the ancient Dûr-Sharrukin founded by Sargon II of Assyria. However, Residence J is larger. It consists of two apartments located to the north-west and south-west of the inner courtyard (called "central court" *Fig. 191*), whereas Building C1a seems to have had only one apartment. It should be noted, however, that the width of the outer courtyard is about 23 m in both

cases. Nonetheless, the plans of the two buildings present interesting similarities.

Entry to C1a must have been originally through Room 15 as it was through Room 1 in Residence J. From there one could cross the outer courtyard (13) towards two groups of parallel rooms: 9–11–12 and 8–10–14 in Building C1a, corresponding to 14–15–16–17 and 18–19–20 in Residence J. In Khorsabad, there was a staircase (14) at the end of the first series of rooms. At Tell Ahmar, Room 14 – a small room filled with bricks that might have supported steps – might also have been a staircase. It does not seem, however, to have been accessible from Room 10 but rather from the opposite side where a secondary access to the building seems to have existed.

In standard Assyrian residences, the normal way to get from the outer to the inner courtyard was through the two largest of the parallel rooms between the outer and inner courtyards, *i.e.* Rooms 16 and 19 in Residence J, and, one would have expected, Rooms 11 and 10 in Building C1a. However, no doorway seems to have existed between Rooms 11 and 10. The passage was through Rooms 9 and 8. Nonetheless, a passage through rooms 11 and 10 remains a possibility because only the northern half of Room 11 could be excavated down to the level of the first floor. Only the top of the walls was recognized in the southern half and it is not impossible that, during the last phase of occupation, or reoccupation, of the building one or more doorways were walled up.

Assyrian apartments usually included at least four rooms, as Apartments I and II of the Palace on the Acropolis. They consisted of a reception/living room, a more private room behind it, an additional room on the side and a bathroom. This arrangement is found in both apartments of Residence J. However, in the original conception of Building C1a the rooms were slightly differently organized. The reception/living room (1), the private room (4), and the bathroom (5) were set in line. The secondary room (6) was placed at right-angles to the bathroom and a smaller fifth room, Room 7, was added to the south-east of Room 6.

Building C1a went through three phases of use, designated from the latest to the earliest as Phase C/2a, C/2b and C/2c. The building does not seem to have ever been used in the way the comparison with other Assyrian buildings would suggest. From the beginning of phase C/2c, structural changes were observed. For example, the door connecting Room 15 to Courtyard 13 was blocked. A carefully built wall coated with mud plaster rested directly on the threshold slab without any accumulation having had time to form (*Fig. 196*). This is an indication that the changes occurred early in the life of the building. Room 15, which should have been the entrance hall, was converted into a workshop – probably a weaving workshop – as we shall see below. Similarly, the door that allowed the passage from Room 10 to Courtyard 3 was walled up and a staircase was built in

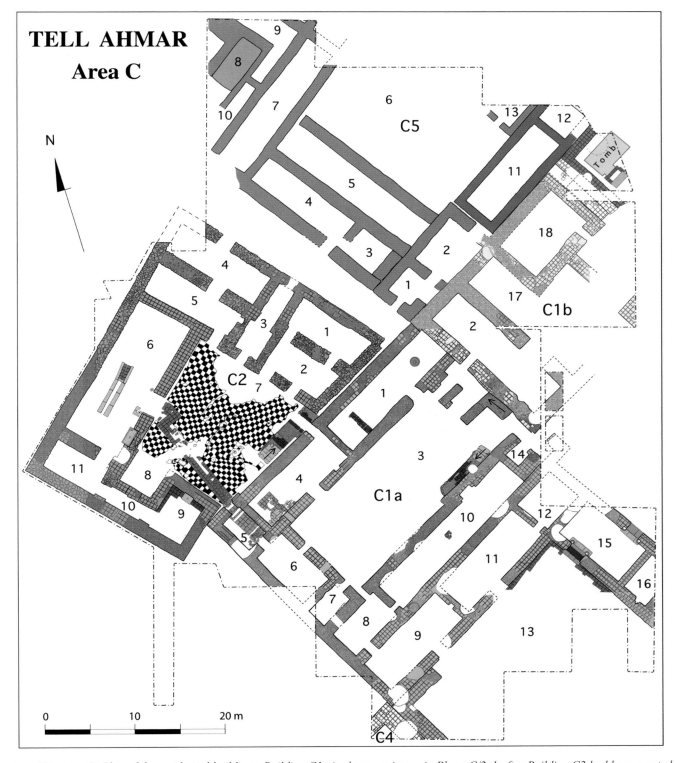

Fig. 190. Area C: Plan of the residential buildings. Building C1a is shown as it was in Phase C/2c1 after Building C2 had been erected against its north-west wall.

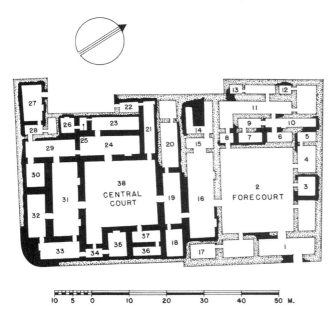

Fig. 191. Khorsabad/Dur-Sharrukin: Plan of Residence J (adapted from G. LOUD & C.B. ALTMANN, Khorsabad, Part II, Chicago 1938, pl. 71, courtesy of the Oriental Institute of the University of Chicago).

Fig. 192. Area C: Building C1a: NE corner of Courtyard 13 (looking SE). The base of the walls was protected against infiltration by an alignment of terracotta tiles. A test trench, visible in the upper right corner of the photo, exposed the building's substructures.

the courtyard, which definitively condemned the use of the door. Similar conclusions can be drawn from the pits dug in the earliest floor of Room 1 – some of them containing large bowls – an unusual feature in an Assyrian reception/living room (*Fig. 204*). It must therefore be admitted that, shortly after its construction, Building C1a was converted into a workplace. The residential function was transferred to Building C2, which was constructed shortly after the start of Phase C/2c, hence the subdivision of this phase into Phase C/2c2 (before the construction of Building C2) and Phase C/2c1 (after the construction of Building C2).

Fig. 193. Area C: Building C1a: NE corner of Courtyard 13 and adjoining rooms (looking S). Room 15 is in the background to the left, Courtyard 13 to the right, Room 12 in the foreground to the left, and Room 11 in the foreground to the right. The installations set against the south wall of Room 11 and the partitioning wall in Room 12 were added in Phase C/2c1.

The building was probably not violently destroyed but only abandoned. The only traces of destruction observed are those that caused the end of the earliest phase, Phase C/2c. No evidence of violent destruction appears in phases C/2b or C/2a. Moreover, it seems that the last inhabitants had time to remove most of the contents and of the wooden parts of the building. There is good evidence that Phases C/2c and C/2b were unquestionable phases of occupation and use of the building. As for phase C/2a, it is not known whether it represents the last phase of occupation or a reoccupation after abandonment and partial destruction of the building, in a process that recalls the end of the Assyrian Palace on the Acropolis (Chapter 5).

A few rooms deserve special attention.

Room 15. It is in this room, which had originally been devised to be the main access to Building C1a, that the most surprising discoveries were made (*Figs 194* and *195*). First, its two doorways displayed similarities with doorways of Assyrian monumental buildings. In the doorway leading to Courtyard 13, the threshold consisted of a large basalt slab in front of which lied three smaller basalt slabs (*Fig. 197*). The southernmost of them, when removed and turned over, revealed the Luwian inscription now known as TELL AHMAR 5 mentioned in Chapter 3. The doorway in the north-eastern wall was less elaborate, with a threshold consisting of only two basalt slabs (*Fig. 198*). In front of each of the doorways, on the inner side, three limestone slabs were set in line. At either end the slabs were pierced with a large semicircular opening lined with concentric circles, which was intended to receive the door hinges and allow them to pivot on a brick placed about 30 cm below the slab.

The position of these door sockets shows that, in the original layout, both doors were designed to be closed from inside the room, contrary to the common practice which organizes the closing of the doors in such a way that it blocks the progression of anyone coming from the outside to the inside. In other words, the door-sockets should have been placed inside the room for the door in the north-east wall – as they actually were – but outside the room for the door in the south-west wall, which led into Courtyard 13. It is as if the staff that closed the doors remained locked in the room, preventing anyone from both coming in and going out. The only possible way out might have been in the north-east corner, now destroyed, towards Room 12, but there is no evidence to support the hypothesis.

The earliest phase was destroyed by a heavy fire. Its floor was littered with debris (*Figs 194* and *195*). They even covered the door sockets, showing that they were no longer in use.

Charred logs lay on the ground and clay loom-weights had been piled up in various places. In addition, fragments of bowls and large jars were found among the debris. Two large jars were sunk in the ground. The best explanation for the presence of this material is that of a weaving workshop (more on this below).

Furthermore, among the debris from Room 15 was a clay tablet bearing signs of Aramaic writing (T23). Although difficult to read, the text could be that of a contract.

Also surprising was the discovery of several carved ivories, which will be examined more in detail in Chapter 7. We must wonder, however, why they were there. Obviously, they were not in the place where they were usually kept. One of them, the ivory carved with a procession of servants (*Fig. 252*), was used to wedge one of the jars sunk into the ground (*Fig. 200*). Another, the small Egyptianizing head (*Fig. 254*), had fallen into one of the door-sockets of the east door. The other ivories were either on the floor of the room or in the debris accumulated on the ground. On the other hand, a great variety of styles existed between them. The collection was therefore not the product of a workshop working at Tell Ahmar and kept in Room 15 for further use. Nor was it a collection of ivories of various origins stored in Room 15. They were more likely discarded objects intended for a different use than that for which they were originally made.

Courtyard 13. Only the northern corner of the courtyard, between Rooms 11 and 15, could be exposed (*Fig. 192* and *Fig. 193*). The base of the walls was lined with terracotta tiles placed slightly at an angle to the walls. Most of the courtyard seems to have been covered by a mud floor.

Rooms 11 and 12. Room 11 must also have been used as a weaving workshop, after the reorganization of the building,

judging by the many loom-weights found in it. Room 12, adjoining it to the north-east, has only been partially excavated due to the large sandy pit dug on the side of the modern road which had destroyed almost the half of it. The excavation of this room was nonetheless particularly rewarding because of the tablets that were found on its floor, as well as on the floor of the doorway that connected it to Room 11 (*Fig. 201*).

Courtyard 3. In phase C/2c2 the floor of the courtyard consisted of a pavement of irregular limestone slabs. In phase C/2c1 the pavement was covered with a thick layer of earth, the surface of which was consolidated by a layer of river pebbles (*Fig. 202*).

The most notable feature of Courtyard 3 is the presence of two staircases. One, very badly preserved, was built on the north-east side of the courtyard and rested on the limestone floor of Phase C/2c2. It started against the outside wall of Room 2 of Building C1b and may have made a turn south-westwards over a small brick wall and a buttress set against the outside wall of Room 1. A calculation of the height reached by these stairs would be too speculative. Different is the case of the other, better preserved, stairs that were built against the north-west wall of Room 10 (*Fig. 203*). These stairs belong to Phase C/2c1 as is evidenced by the fact that they rest not on the stone pavement but on the pebble floor. The first four limestone steps are preserved and measure 30 cm high and 30 cm deep. The total length of the stairway is about 6.80 m and, assuming a landing about 1 m wide at the top, it must have consisted of about 19 or 20 steps over 5.80 m leading to a height of about 6 m. Did it give access to an upper storey? The problem is complicated by the possible existence of an internal staircase not far away in Room 14. There are two possibilities: (1) either the internal staircase led to an upper floor and the outside stairs led to a roof terrace and one could reconstruct a ground and an upper floor about 3 m high each; (2) both stairs were leading either to a second floor of unknown height or to a roof terrace, which, in either case, would imply a ground floor about 6 m high. The first possibility relies on figures that are more realistic.

After the reorganization of the residence, the courtyard was crammed with ovens and low walls. These were probably facilities intended to feed the personnel employed in the workshops.

Room 1. In its original design, Room 1 was intended to serve as a living/reception room. In the north-eastern third of the room, a terracotta circle about 1.10 m in diameter was provided with a hemispherical depression in its centre. It was probably intended to support a fireplace. When the room was, like the others, converted into a workshop, large bowls were sunk into the ground and a partitioning wall was built towards the south-western end of the room (*Fig. 204*).

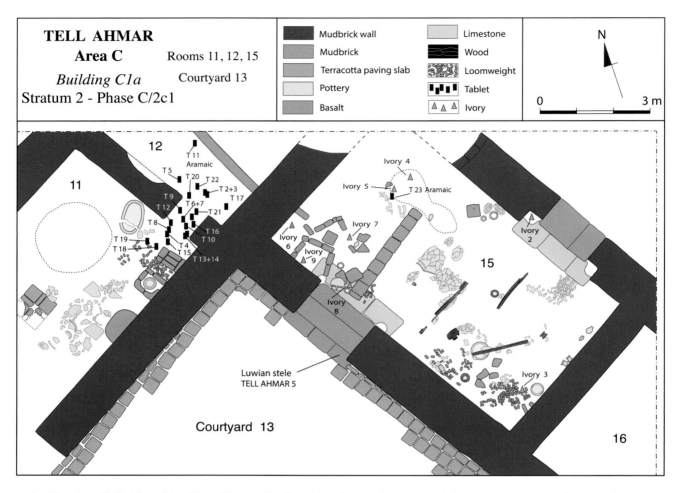

TELL AHMAR
Area C   Rooms 11, 12, 15
Building C1a   Courtyard 13
Stratum 2 - Phase C/2c1

Mudbrick wall | Limestone
Mudbrick | Wood
Terracotta paving slab | Loomweight
Pottery | Tablet
Basalt | Ivory

N

0 _____ 3 m

Fig. 194. Area C: Building C1a: Plan of Rooms 11, 12 and 15 after the destruction of Phase C/2c1 (after Sarah Myer's drawing).

Fig. 195. Area C: Building C1a, Room 15: Debris from the destruction of Phase C/2c1 (looking SE).

Fig. 196. Area C: Building C1a: The walled doorway which originally connected Room 15 with Courtyard 13 (Phase C/2c1) (seen from inside Room 15).

Fig. 197. Area C: Building C1a: Doorway connecting Room 15 with Courtyard 13 in its original state (Phase C/2c2) (seen from inside Room 15).

Fig. 200. Area C: Building C1a: Big jar sunk into the ground of Room 15 in Phase C/2c1. The object under the jar, to the left, is the large ivory with the procession scene (see below, p. 165) used to wedge the vessel.

Fig. 198. Area C: Building C1a: Doorway in NE wall of Room 15 (seen from inside Room 15).

Fig. 201. Area C: Building C1a: Floor of the doorway between Rooms 11 and 12 (north at top left corner). Cuneiform tablets were scattered in and around the doorway connecting Rooms 11 and 12 in Phase C/2c1. One is visible next to the bristles of the red handle brush on the left and another next to the handle of the smaller red brush.

Fig. 199. Area C: Building C1a: Test trenches in Room 15 (looking SE).

Fig. 202. Area C: Building C1a: Courtyard 3 near the entrance doorway of Room 1 (north to top). The pavement of irregular limestone of Phase C/2c2 is visible to the right. In Phase C/2c1 the pavement was covered with a thick layer of soil whose surface was consolidated by Euphrates pebbles (visible on left).

Fig. 203. Area C: Building C1a: Stone steps of the stairs laid on the south-eastern side of Courtyard 3 in Phase C/2c1 (looking S).

A small ivory head, possibly a seal box (see below, p. 159) was found in the debris accumulated in Room 1 (*Fig. 240*).

Rooms 4 and 5. Both rooms are particularly illustrative of the changes undergone by Building C1a during its three phases of use. Initially, in Phase C/2c2, Room 5 was designed as a bathroom, with a floor of terracotta tiles coated with bitumen and a stone slab with an opening to let wastewater flow away (*Fig. 205*). In Phase C/2c1, after the construction of Building C2, a doorway was opened in the north-west wall and steps were built on the tiled floor to facilitate the access to the new Building C2, which was situated a little higher (*Fig. 206*). Phases C/2b (*Fig. 207*) and c/2a (*Fig. 208*) were each marked by the building of a new floor, which progressively reduced the number of steps.

In Phase C/2c1, at the same time as a doorway was opened to get into Building C2, the bathroom was transferred to the south-west part of the adjacent Room 4 and a thin wall was built to separate this new bathroom from the rest of the room (*Fig. 209*).

c. Building C2

Building C2 was designed from the start as a complement to Building C1a. This is shown by the fact that Courtyard 7 was closed to the south-east by the outer wall of Building C1a. Two doors, one in Room 4, the other in Room 5 of C1a, allowed communication between the two buildings.

It is not known why the orientation of C2, which led to its trapezoidal shape, was slightly different from that of C1a. The plan is typical of Assyrian houses.

Residential complex (Rooms 6, 9, 10, 11). Four rooms were arranged in an L-shaped unit characteristic of Neo-Assyrian architecture.

Room 6 was the living/reception room with, in its middle, a device conceived to accommodate a mobile hearth (*Fig. 210*), similar to those already encountered in the Assyrian Palace. It included a small quadrangular platform

Fig. 204. Area C: Building C1a: Room 1 in Phase C/2c1 (looking NE).

made of terracotta tiles framed with limestone slabs and complemented, to the south-east, by two kinds of rails also made of limestone slabs, on which a mobile hearth could be driven. On either side of the doorway were door-sockets covered by perforated slabs similar to those found in Room 15 of Building C1a. To the left of the entrance, for anyone coming from the courtyard, a niche in the wall contained a rectangular limestone slab (*Fig. 211*). A jar containing water was almost certainly placed there.

A doorway linked Room 6 to Room 11, in the west corner of the building, from where a small corridor, Room 10, led to a bathroom, Room 9, situated in the south corner of the building. Terracotta tiles still ran alongside Room 9's north-west and north-east walls and a large limestone slab with a central perforation was set against the north-east wall (*Fig. 212*). It is likely that, in its original state, the room was entirely covered with terracotta tiles, like Room 5 of Building C1a, but that most of them had been removed. Such L-shaped units are attested at several sites of the Assyrian

Fig. 205. Area C: Building C1a: Room 5 in its original configuration (Phase C/2c2) (looking SE).

Fig. 206. Area C: Building C1a: Room 5 in Phase C/2c1 (looking NW).

Fig. 207. Area C: Building C1a: Room 5 in Phase C/2b (looking NW).

Fig. 208. Area C: Building C1a: Room 5 in Phase C/2a (looking NW).

Fig. 209. Area C: Building C1a: Room 4 in Phase C/2c1 (looking S).

empire.[2] They are generally associated with an open space opening into a courtyard (marked 8 on *Fig. 190*). In Assyria, it is found, for instance, in the already mentioned Residence J (*Fig. 191*, Rooms 31–33–34–35). It does not seem to have been used in the great palaces of Nimrud, Khorsabad or Nineveh. It could therefore be a formula originating in the western provinces, which had not really taken root in the heart of the empire.

Entrance unit (Rooms 4 and 5). These are the rooms through which visitors had to pass to enter the house. They were therefore not intended to have a residential function and may have had the same function as the two rooms that were placed between the outer and inner courtyards in other buildings of the same period.

A staircase? (Room 3). Room 3 is particularly enigmatic. It consists of two parts. One, which opened into the court-yard, was wider than the other to the north-east. The latter

seemed to open onto the exterior through an opening which, however, was too narrow to be a real doorway. The reason for its existence might be looked for in a pipe that passed under the room and went down to the courtyard. The damp rising from the pipe probably considerably damaged the outer wall, thus giving the impression of the existence of a doorway. Similar damage was observed above other pipes in Corridor 10 of Building C2 and in Room 4 of Building

Fig. 210. Area C: Building C2: Installation for a mobile hearth in Room 6 (looking SW).

Fig. 211. Area C: Building C2: Doorway and niche in the south-eastern wall of Room 6 (looking SE).

C1a. On the other hand, the narrowness of the north-eastern part of the room precludes the possibility that any significant activity could have taken place in it. A likely function for Room 3 would be that of a staircase whose steps may have been made of wood because no earth or brick filling intended to support the steps were found. If this is correct, the steps were probably in the narrower part of the room, which is about 5.50 m long. Assuming that the steps were about 20 or 25 cm high and 30 cm deep, and deducting from the entire length a landing of about 1 m that would have been necessary for turning either to the left or right, this staircase could have consisted of about 15 steps that could have led to a height of about 3–3.75 m.

The domestic quarters (Rooms 1 and 2). These two rooms contained jars, basins and ovens. It is the kind of material that can be expected in a service area.

Courtyard 7. Trapezoidal in shape and measuring about 15 m on its longest side, the courtyard of Building C2 was covered with a mosaic of pebbles set in a checkerboard pattern (*Fig. 213*). The pebbles, placed on their edge, formed squares, alternately white and black, about 20 cm wide. There is only one exception. Some pebbles to the east of the paved way that crossed the courtyard, about halfway along the route, were arranged in concentric circles (*Fig. 214*).

Fig. 212. Area C: Building C2: Pavement and perforated slab in Room 9 (looking N).

It will be remembered that earlier pebble mosaics were found on the Acropolis (above, pp. 88–89) and more were associated with Buildings E1 and E2 (below, pp. 152, 154). This form of decorative pavement, probably of Hittite origin, seems to have been quite widespread in the western provinces of the Assyrian empire.

Circulation must have been intense in the courtyard, to the point that the mosaic is completely destroyed in a few places. This is particularly clear on the north-eastern side in front of Rooms 2 and 3, to the south-west in front of Room 8 and in front of the stairs to the south-east. The most frequently used passage, however, was most likely between Room 6 and Building C1a, because a path paved with terracotta tiles linked the two places.

External stairs. Stairs were set on the south-east side of the courtyard against the wall of Room 4 of Building C1a. A passage had been left free under the stairs to access the door that opened in the north wall of Room 4 of Building C1a. The total length of the staircase was about 8 m and the preserved stone steps were about 40 cm deep with

risers about 20 cm high. As the stairs led straight to Room 2, it is not necessary to restore a landing at the end of the staircase. The stairs could therefore have consisted of about 20 steps leading to a height of about 4 m, that is, to a height that is somewhat higher than that of the possible staircase of Room 3. However, taking into account the uncertainties of these calculations, it can be assumed that the height of the ground floor of Building C2 was in the range of 3–4 m. Where did these stairs lead to? A roof terrace is a possibility. However, as in the case of Building C1a, an upper storey covering at least a part of the house is an option worth considering.

The foundations. Building C2 differs from buildings C1a and C1b in its construction technique. Its mud-brick walls stand on a base of irregular stones, which in turn rest on foundations that were originally made of mud-bricks (*Fig. 215*). The irregularity of the facing shows that these are foundations and do not belong to an underlying level. There was no need to protect the wall against run-off water and the aesthetic aspect was of no importance. This type of foundation is relatively rare, but it is found, in particular, in the *bâtiment aux ivoires* at Arslan Tash.[3]

3. A burial vault

A break in the small irrigation canal running along the road bordering Area C let water rush into a hole in the field below and revealed the existence of an underground vaulted chamber. It was a monumental tomb built of terracotta tiles (*Fig. 216*). The hole through which the water had flown was a breach made in antiquity by grave robbers. The chamber measured approximately 2.70 × 4.50 m and partly extended under the road. A brick case occupied the north-eastern half of the chamber and a terracotta sarcophagus of the so-called "bathtub" type was placed on top of it (*Fig. 217*). The sarcophagus was obviously intended to be deposited in the case and either never reached its destination or was removed by the looters.

The ceiling consisted of a flat vault made of the same material as the walls (*Fig. 218*). The tiles were arranged in a fan-shaped pattern, with only their edges visible. It was therefore not a corbelled vault but a real vault. The weight of the tiles ensured the stability of the whole by pressing on each other, which explains the good state of preservation of the construction. This is all the more remarkable since the vault partly extended under a road frequented by lorries and tractors.

A small niche in each of the four walls, about 60 cm above the floor, was certainly intended to accommodate a lamp. In fact, the only find made in this tomb was a pedestal terracotta lamp (*Fig. 220*).

Fig. 213. Area C: Building C2: Pebble mosaic of Courtyard 7 (looking N).

To the south-east, an entrance shaft about 2.40 m deep was covered by two large limestone slabs, of which one was still in place (*Fig. 182*). Seven steps reaching a height of about 1.30 m had been set at the bottom of the shaft (*Fig. 219*). It was therefore necessary to jump more than 1 m to get into the tomb.

Fig. 214. Area C: Building C2: Pebbles assembled in concentric circles in Courtyard 7.

Fig. 215. Area C: Building C2: Foundations under the south-eastern corner of Room 2 (looking SW).

The relationship between this tomb and Buildings C1b and C5 is unclear. The three structures apparently coexisted but it is impossible to tell whether the tomb was part of one of them or whether it was an independent structure. Similarly, as we already observed (p. 131), the link between the statue found to the south of the tomb and the tomb itself remains unclear. Tombs of this kind were well known in Assyria, especially in Ashur.[4]

4. Another residence

In Area D, at a short distance to the north of the Area C complex and near the rampart, another residence was uncovered. The few ruined walls that were excavated belonged to a building that included an Assyrian-type living/reception room with a large, perforated slab placed in a niche (*Fig. 221*).

However, the Area D architectural remains stand out among the Neo-Assyrian vestiges so far excavated at Tell Ahmar as the only ones whose last occupation phase vanished in a violent destruction. It is possible that the place, close to the western city gate, which was the gate opening into the road to Carchemish, fell victim to the fighting that erupted between the Egyptians and Babylonians in the region of Carchemish in 605.

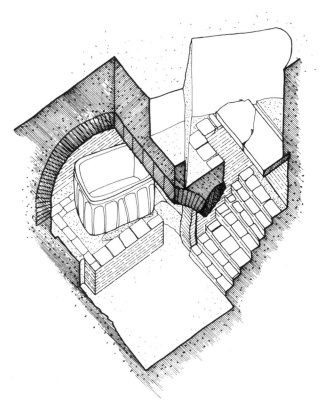

Fig. 216. Area C: Burial vault: Axonometric view (drawing: Barry G. Rowney).

Fig. 217. Area C: Burial vault: "Bathtub sarcophagus" against the NE wall.

Fig. 219. Area C: Burial vault: Entrance shaft and stairs giving access to the burial.

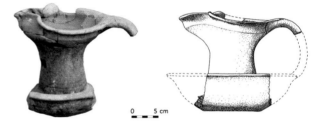

Fig. 220. Area C: Burial vault: Pedestal lamp (C54 PL6042) (drawing: Andrew S. Jamieson).

0   5 cm

Fig. 218. Area C: Burial vault: SW wall.

Fig. 221. Area D: Remains of an Assyrian residence (looking SE).

Geophysical survey of the Middle Town (John M. Russell)

A large-scale geomagnetic survey of the urban area of Tell Ahmar, including both the surviving intramural city and parts of the extramural suburbs, was carried out in 2000 and supplemented in 2001 by electrical resistance survey in selected areas. The goal of the survey was to recover enough of the city plan to determine the overall distribution of building types and open spaces within the city walls and in the city's immediate environs, providing the larger urban context for the Neo-Assyrian remains that had been excavated at the site to date. As time and resources permitted, we hoped to be able to ground-truth the results of the geophysical survey by carrying out pinpoint excavations in selected areas.

Methodology

By the time the survey was conducted, geomagnetic sensing had reached a level of precision that had produced remarkable results at a number of Middle Eastern archaeological sites, often revealing buried architecture almost as clearly as if it had been excavated. Geomagnetic sensing is the most efficient ground-based geophysical survey method, with the capability of covering large areas quickly, up to 1 ha/machine/day. Under ideal conditions, its results can be very clear, as it is sensitive to a variety of culturally-generated archaeological features. Magnetic highs are generated by burning, including hearths and baked clay, areas with concentrated organic decay, and igneous and metamorphic stones in cultural patterns. Under certain conditions, limestone and mud-brick may also show as magnetic lows. Limitations of this method include the potential for significant interference from surface features such as modern iron and agricultural furrows, the fact that highly magnetic cultural features can mask less pronounced features in their immediate vicinity, and the method provides no indication of the depth of cultural features, which may be anywhere between 0.5 and 2.5 m below the surface.

Fortunately, Tell Ahmar proved to be well-suited to geomagnetic sensing techniques. Its soil is fairly magnetic, which provides ideal conditions for high quality survey results. The surface of the town has been graded and terraced as farmland, with the result that the Assyrian foundations are invisible to the eye but well within the range of the magnetometer. Many of the walls have stone foundations, often incorporating highly magnetic imported basalt, which makes them easily visible to magnetic sensing. Architectural features such as baked brick pavements, basalt fittings, large storage jars, and ovens are readily visible, and sometimes mud-brick walls and streets of compacted earth can be seen as well when they are close to the surface.

The geophysical survey in 2000 was carried out over a period of four weeks from late May to June, followed by three weeks in June 2001. The survey was conducted by two professional geophysical surveyors, David Maki and Geoffrey Jones of Archaeo-Physics LLC, working under the general direction of this author. As the city area is intensively cultivated and it is impossible to conduct survey in fields covered with large plants, the seasons were timed to coincide with conditions that permit field walking; surveying cotton fields during the early stage of cotton growth and wheat fields immediately following the harvest. The principal limiting factors were the late harvest of some wheat fields, a considerable number of modern houses, especially on the main tell and Middle Town, and impassable obstacles, such as irrigation works, orchard tree lines, ditches and ridges. Modern iron features on the surface, including electrical utility poles and metallic objects and debris near houses, are extremely magnetic and tended to mask any subsurface features in their vicinity.

The survey collection units were adapted to field size and ground cover. The survey teams walked traverses set 1 m apart, collecting data at a rate of eight samples per linear meter, for a total of 80,000 data samples per hectare. Field plans of the day's work were generated each day. Significant magnetic features were then checked out on the ground to see if they could be explained by surface features or if surface finds could provide a clue to what is beneath. Thirty-one plots were surveyed, ranging in area from 170 m² to 3.9 ha, for a total area of some 27 ha, comprising most of the unflooded area of the Lower Town inside the city wall and much of the adjacent suburban area (*Fig. a*).

During the 2001 season, the geomagnetic survey was complemented in selected areas with electrical resistance survey. The value of this method is that it can often highlight different materials than does the magnetometer, including being more sensitive to mud-brick. Limitations are that it is relatively slow, it is impractical under some ground conditions, including hard dry and soaking wet ground, and it gives no indication of the depth or composition of features. For these reasons, this method was only used in areas where the geomagnetic survey suggested there might be more to be revealed. For example, the electrical resistance method showed an apparent mud-brick mass at the south-western end of the city wall where the geomagnetic survey shows nothing but where we might expect a continuation of the wall or a city gate. While this feature is tentatively reconstructed as a city gate in our plan, the true nature of this apparent mass must remain speculative until test excavations can be conducted in the area.

A sample density of one sample per m² was generally sufficient for detecting architectural features but data could be collected at differing probe spacings and data sample densities to optimize depth of penetration and resolution.

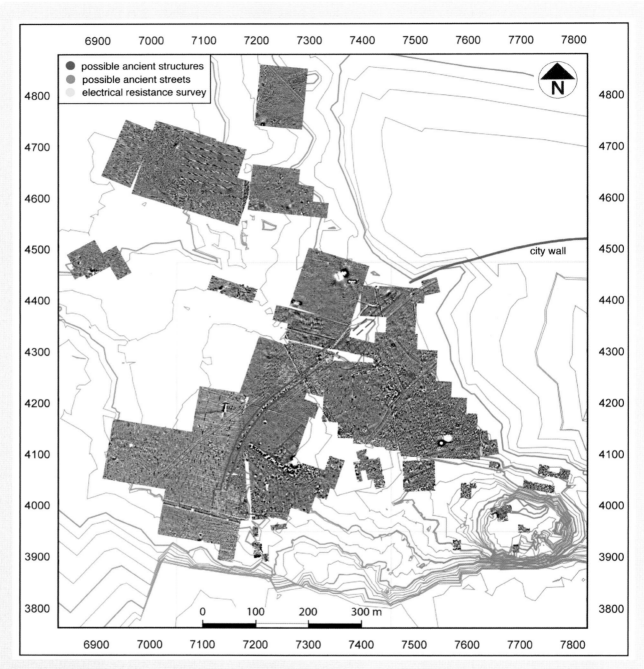

Fig. a. Plan of the geophysical survey (surveyed by Archaeo-Physics LLC). The yellow patterns indicate the zones surveyed by electrical resistivity. The red lines indicate possible streets and the blue lines possible constructions. The line of the western section of the rampart, indicated by a double blue line, is easily recognizable.

Electrical resistance survey was conducted in whole or in part on seven of the geomagnetic plots, totalling 2.6 ha, often complementing the geomagnetic results by suggesting the presence of mud brick not visible in the geomagnetic survey.

Results

A large number of features were readily identifiable in the geomagnetic printouts. The most exciting discovery was the western line of the city wall, completely invisible from the surface (*Fig. b*). A test trench (CJ1) revealed that the wall was 8 m thick and preserved to a height of nearly 3 m at its outer face, with a massive stone foundation (*Fig. c*). The ancient ground level inside the wall was 2 m higher than that outside, suggesting either that the area inside the wall was a low tell, or that the area outside was a ditch, a point that could be clarified through future excavations. This discovery finally permits the full extent of Tell Ahmar's intramural area to be defined.

A variety of structures was revealed inside the wall. Most surprising was a massive stone wall at the west side of the city, perpendicular to the city wall, running for a length of 100 m and ending in a corner (CJ4 and CJ5) (*Fig. b*). It has the appearance of a fortification, but in an unexpected location. Projecting northward from this is a long rectangular structure some 20 × 60 m in extent, subdivided into three 20 × 20 m units. In 2002 an 18 × 4 m trench (CJ4) was excavated at the southern end of this structure, confirming the walls visible in the geomagnetic plan, which belonged to a building devoted, at least in this area, to metalworking (see pp. 175–179). Small test soundings, CJ5 and CJ6 to the west and north of CJ4, were also excavated where the geomagnetic plan showed the continuation of what appeared to be walls of this structure. In both soundings, mud-brick walls were found just below the surface, confirming that the plan of this structure as visible in the geomagnetic survey is at least generally correct.

The geomagnetic plan of the field immediately to the east, across the modern road, appears to show the intersection of two streets. At the north-east street corner is a building with a large courtyard, apparently similar to examples excavated elsewhere at the site, and at the north-west corner are the massive stone foundations of another building (*Fig. b*). Most of the remaining area within the city wall shows linear and rectangular magnetic features, permitting the hypothetical layout of the city to be reconstructed to a much greater degree than was previously possible.

The area outside the city wall seems to have been much less densely settled, with two apparent houses on slight rises to the west of the modern road and a very clear rectangular structure just to the east of the road (*Fig. d*). They have the general appearance of farmhouses, similar to those that dot the landscape

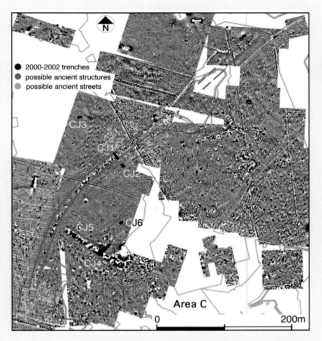

Fig. b. Sector of Areas C and CJ (surveyed by Archaeo-Physics LLC). Note the possible presence of vestiges near the western section of the Assyrian rampart. The rampart itself is clearly visible, as is the West Gate. The rampart ends in a brick massif to the SW, which could be either a tower or another gate.

Fig. c. Area CJ : Trench CJ1 across the rampart (photo: John M. Russell).

today, but their dates need to be ascertained with test soundings. If ancient, then their distribution near the road may suggest that the modern road follows the track of the ancient one, in which case we might seek a gate in the vicinity where the modern road crosses the city wall. Indeed, the geomagnetic plan shows what appears to be a large rectangular structure straddling the city wall just north-east of where the wall crosses the modern road, and this may well be a city gate.

The geophysical survey of Tell Ahmar demonstrated that a comprehensive geomagnetic and electrical resistance survey can assist in distinguishing built areas from open ones, and can locate probable streets and structures, both inside and outside the city wall. This in turn gives some indication of the character of different neighbourhoods. The 2000–2001 geophysical survey of Tell Ahmar therefore provided the first comprehensive picture of spatial organization and typological variability of the architecture inside and around a Neo-Assyrian city.

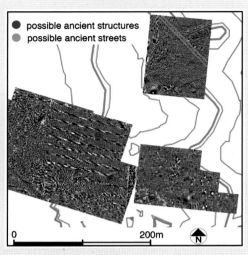

Fig. d. Area situated NW of the rampart (surveyed by Archaeo-Physics LLC). The survey identified a few isolated structures to the NW of the city, perhaps isolated farms as there still were before the recent outbreak of violence.

5. Building E2: A *bit hilani*?

Prestige residences also existed rather far away from the Acropolis. Two of them were partially excavated in the Lower Town, not far from the possible location of the northern gate (*Fig. 222*). The layout of one of these houses, Building E2, excavated by J.M. Russell, is quite different from that of the Area C buildings. Its dimensions are also more modest. It is trapezoidal in shape, about 15 m long, but it may have extended further south and west. It is possible, that it included an Assyrian-style living/reception room (Room 5), the remains of which extended to the north.

The excavated remains are reminiscent of the so-called *bit hilani*, an architectural form typical of the Syro-Hittite regions.[5] A *bit hilani* consisted of an open entrance porch with one or more columns, on the side of which was often a staircase, and, behind it, broad rooms arranged in parallel lines. The essential elements of this plan can be found in Building E2. Room 3 was a broad room opening widely on Courtyard 4 (*Fig. 223*). A basalt column base indicated that it was a porticoed porch as is found in *bit hilani* buildings. Behind this porch was a broad room parallel to the line formed by the porch and Room 2, again in accordance with the traditional *bit hilani*.

However, this building cannot be considered a real *bit hilani*. There is no staircase on the side of the entrance porch. The small Room 2, which could have housed stairs, was either a shed or a kitchen. More generally, it is almost sure that Building E2 had no upper storey. Not only the absence of staircase but also the fragility of the walls rule

out such a possibility. Lastly, if the building included an Assyrian-type living/reception room (Room 5), comparable to Room 1 in Building C1a, it departed from the usual plan of the *bit hilani*s. The builders of Building E2 appear to have been inspired by a venerable tradition but did not entirely conform to it, somewhat like their nineteenth century colleagues, who revived the popularity of the Gothic style, but without faithfully reproducing models that belonged to the past.

Another possible western feature is the pebble mosaic that covered the floor of Courtyard 4. It consisted of large black and white squares made of fine, flat pebbles set on their edge, quite different from those of the Building C2 mosaic. The entrance cannot be identified with certainty. It could have been in the south side of the courtyard.

6. Building E1: An Assyrian shrine?

Only a small part of Building E1 could be explored before the waters of the Tishrin Dam started to rise. However, enough has been found to show that Building E1 found its place in the Assyrian tradition. Room 2, fully excavated, was a living/reception room of the type found in large Assyrian residences, including those of Tell Ahmar itself. The room was accessed through a large entrance with a threshold formed by two limestone slabs and two door-sockets protected by limestone slabs. Its originality lies in the presence of not one but two niches, one in the wall opposite the doorway (*Fig. 224*), the other in the eastern wall (*Fig. 225*).

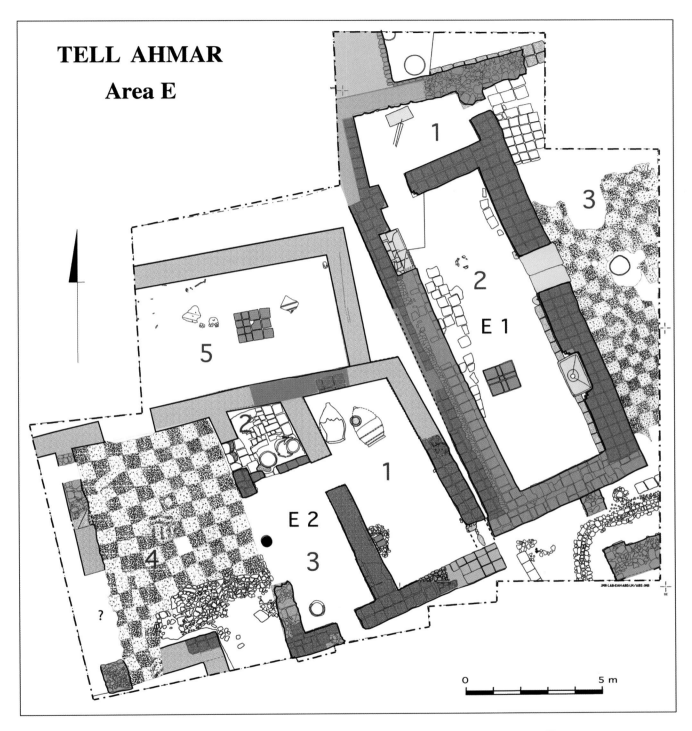

Fig. 222. Area E: Plan of the excavated buildings (original drawing: John M. Russell).

The bottom of each was covered with a limestone slab. Lastly, in the southern half of the room, a small platform paved with terracotta tiles was intended to accommodate a mobile fireplace. All these elements were characteristic of the architecture of the Assyrian period.

The room opened onto Courtyard 3, which was partially exposed, and offered another example of pebble mosaic (*Fig. 226*). The pebbles were laid in a black and white checkerboard pattern of a somewhat more expedient execution than that of the mosaics in Buildings C2 and E2.

A notable feature of Room 2 was its painted decoration. Fragments of it were found among the debris fallen on the floor. Most consisted of a series of concentric circles connected to each other by parallel horizontal lines (*Fig. 227*).[6] They must have come from a frieze.

Other fragments bore a figurative decoration. One shows the lower leg, from the calf to the foot, of a human figure facing right (*Fig. 228*). The stylization of the musculature is characteristic of Assyrian art, in particular the calf rendered by an oval. There is also a horizontal line slightly lower than the calf, which must have represented the fringe of a garment. The foot rests on an oblique line with triangular points, which suggest the mane of a lion. It is therefore easy to imagine that the scene, when complete, represented a deity standing on the back of a lion.

Another fragment of painting may belong to the same composition. It depicts a flower on the right and probably a nimbus, which takes the form of a sort of gear wheel, on the left (*Fig. 229*). The motif of a deity wrapped in a nimbus and holding a flower is common in Assyrian art, especially on cylinder seals. Considered together, the two figurative fragments could therefore come from a painting depicting a deity standing on the back of a lion, wrapped in a nimbus and holding a flower in one hand (*Fig. 230*). As the lion was the animal attribute of the goddess Ishtar, we may hypothesize that the deity was Ishtar. The stele of the governor Ashur-dur-paniya dedicated to Ishtar of Arbela gives a good example of a similar composition (above pp. 128–129).

Such a decoration seems more appropriate in a sanctuary than in a private house.[7] The holy nature of the Building might be confirmed by a discovery made in the small Room 1, north of Room 2. Lying on the floor of the room was an iron trident, about 1 m long (*Fig. 231*). The handle of the trident rested on a stone slab. Iron or bronze tridents of this kind were known long before the Assyrian

Fig. 223. Area E: Building E2 (looking NW).

Fig. 224. Area E: Building E1: Niche partly filled with mud-bricks in the west wall of Room 2.

Fig. 225. Area E: Building E1: Fireplace and niche in the east wall of Room 2 (looking NE).

Fig. 226. Area E: Building E1: Pebble mosaic in Courtyard 3 (looking SW).

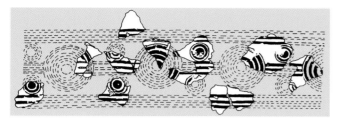

Fig. 227. Area E: Building E1: Reconstruction of the painted frieze of Room 2 (drawing: Lia Abbate).

Fig. 228. Area E: Building E1: Fragment of painted figurative decoration from Room 2 showing a foot resting on an animal's neck (drawing: Elizabeth Hendrix).

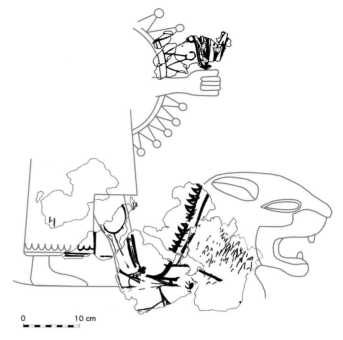

Fig. 230. Area E: Tentative reconstruction of the figure to which the fragments of Figs 228 and 229 belonged.

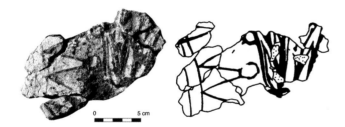

Fig. 229. Area E: Building E1: Fragment of painted figurative decoration from Room 2 showing part of a nimbus and a flower (drawing: Lia Abbate).

period, and many of them may have been of practical use. However, the tines of this trident seem too long for any obvious utilitarian purpose and its shape is very similar to the thunderbolt held by the Storm-God on the Syro-Hittite stelae found at Tell Ahmar. It is therefore not impossible that this trident had a symbolic value and personified the Storm-God. Often a trident fixed on a pedestal appears among the divine symbols engraved on Assyrian reliefs. The trident of Building E1 could have been fixed, for instance by a wooden device, on the stone slab with which it was found. There might therefore have been a second divine representation in this house.

Lastly, it is interesting to note that the niche in the west wall of Room 2 had been partially filled with mud-bricks (*Fig. 224*). These were not bricks that had fallen from the

Fig. 231. Area E: Building E1: Iron trident discovered in Room 1.

Fig. 232. Area E: Remains exposed under the floor of Room 2 of Building E1 (looking NW).

wall after the house had been abandoned but had been laid there intentionally. Whether one interprets this – as does John Russell, who excavated this part of the house – as a device intended for libations or, more probably, as a table – altar or offering table – the fact remains that a niche whose function was utilitarian was converted into a structure that could have had a religious function.

The logical conclusion of these observations is that a domestic building conceived in the Assyrian tradition had been converted into a holy place.

Building E1 was built over walls that certainly belonged to an earlier construction (*Fig. 232*). Not only they were of a slightly different orientation, but a smaller rectangular room appeared under the floor of Room 2, and fragments of pebble mosaic floors appeared under the east wall of Room 2.

Neither Building E1 nor Building E2 showed any sign of violent destruction.

* * *

Tell Ahmar, under Assyrian domination, does not seem to have been the subject of a systematic development plan. Inside the semicircular city wall, probably built during the Shamshi-ilu period, large residences were built freely. Their layout, with their different orientations, shows that they did not fit into a pre-established development scheme. A large, almost rectilinear road apparently connected the eastern gate, which seems to have been the main gate of the city, to the Palace built on the Acropolis.

The construction methods of the large residences of the seventh century bear witness to the interaction of cultures during the last century of Assyrian domination. The Assyrian influence is dominant, as is normal for the residences of a wealthy class that must necessarily have been close to the Assyrian ruling class, but the local tradition is not completely extinct. It can be recognized in the plan of Building E2, close to that of the *bit hilani*, probably also in the pebble mosaics, whose discoveries have been multiplying for several years in the provinces of the empire. As for the residential unit living room+additional room+corridor+bathroom recognized in Building C2, it could be a western formula occasionally adopted in the heart of the empire. The standardization of cultures was in progress within the borders of the Assyrian power.

The architectural evidence from the Middle and Lower Towns concur with the observations made in the Palace to suggest that the site was not violently destroyed but progressively abandoned after the fall of the Assyrian heartland to the Medes and Babylonians after 612. Only sporadic occupation might have continued, as Area C and E tend to show. Area D would offer another example of such continuity, but with the particular circumstance that its proximity to the West Gate may have made it more vulnerable to violence, for instance during the Egyptian-Babylonian war around Carchemish in 605.

Notes

1   G. LOUD & Ch.B. ALTMAN, *Khorsabad* II, *The Citadel and the Town*, Oriental Institute Publications 40, Chicago (IL) 1938, pp. 10–12, 65.

2   G. BUNNENS, Aramaeans, Hittites and Assyrians in the Upper Euphrates valley, *Archaeology of the Upper Syrian Euphrates: The Tishrin Dam area*, ed. G. del OLMO LETE & J.-L. MONTERO FENOLLÓS, Sabadell (Barcelona), 1999, p. 619.

3   F. THUREAU-DANGIN, A. BARROIS, G. DOSSIN & M. DUNAND, *Arslan-Tash*, Bibliothèque archéologique et historique 16, Paris 1931, pp. 49–50.

4   A. HALLER, *Die Gräber und Grüfte von Assur*, Ausgrabungen der Deutschen Orient-Gesellschaft in Assur A, Baudenkmäler aus assyrischer Zeit VII, Berlin 1954.

5   G. BUNNENS & J.M. RUSSELL, A bit-hilani at Til-Barsib? Clarifications and further evidence, *Ugarit-Forschungen* 43 (2011), pp. 31–35.

6   L. ABBATE, Wall-paintings from a Neo-Assyrian building at Til Barsib, *Abr-Nahrain* 32 (1994), pp. 7–16.

7   G. BUNNENS, *A New Luwian Stele and the Cult of the Storm-God at Til Barsib – Masuwari*, Tell Ahmar II, Leuven-Paris-Dudley (MA) 2006, pp. 67–69.

7

Images in everyday life

The figurative representations we saw in Chapter 5 were aimed at conveying ideas to an audience, even though the audience was not always easy to identify. Murals from the palace, royal stelae, carved orthostats and sculptures commissioned by high dignitaries were all parts of a system of communication, whatever their material support. The images we shall be concerned with in this chapter reverse the relationship. They decorate objects whose function as objects is more important than their decoration. They were all objects of everyday life. Seals were used to authenticate documents, carved ivories decorated pieces of furniture and clay figurines were objects of private use or domestic worship. This does not mean that their decoration was purely ornamental but the meaning of the decoration was not the primary reason that motivated the production of these objects.

1. Seals

Seals were an important vector of images in ancient Western Asia. They were found in fairly large numbers throughout

0   2 cm

Fig. 233. Uncarved stone cylinder with a bronze setting (C O.374; Aleppo M 12402).

the region. The reason for this may be that, in addition to its authentication function, the seal also served as a kind of personal talisman and a status symbol for its owner. Seals, both cylinders and stamps, were usually cut into hard stone, although some of them could be made of clay. Seals of the latter type are usually considered to be made of "frit" (also called "sintered quartz"), *i.e.* terracotta covered with a glaze similar to glass. However, most of the terracotta seals found at Tell Ahmar lacked the characteristic glossy surface of "frit". Without excluding the possibility that the glaze had disappeared, it is probably better to consider that these seals were simply made of terracotta. Only two stamp seals seem to correspond to what "frit" must have looked like (*Fig. 247* and *Fig. a*, p. 162).

Cylinder seals were often fitted with a metal rod going through a perforation made along their vertical axis and holding two discs at both ends of the cylinder. This setting could be complemented by a loop through which a string could pass to enable the seal's owner to carry it with him. Two of the Tell Ahmar seals have preserved such a setting (*Figs 233* and *244*).

Stamp seals usually had an oval base, on which the decoration was carved, and a straight side (*Fig. 246, 248* and *250*). Their top was slightly rounded. Such seals are commonly referred to as "scaraboids", on the assumption that they would be a simplified form of the Egyptian scarabs. Genuine scarabs may occasionally be found.

a. The seals and their use[1]

The Neo-Assyrian period witnessed a major change in sealing techniques. It is the period during which the stamp seal gradually replaced the cylinder seal, in a trend parallel to the movement that saw the Aramaic language developing to the detriment of Akkadian in the imperial administration. Several stamps and cylinder seals were found in Areas C and E. The number of cylinders (nine) was almost equal to the number of stamps (eight). This is surprising, as the tablets found in Building C1a, when they

Fig. 234. Blank stamp seal impressions on Tablet T13 (Aleppo M 12406).

Fig. 236. Jar sealing (?) C O.1102: Cylinder seal impression.

Fig. 237. Jar sealing (?) C O.1102: Stamp seal impression. The decoration consists of three omega-shaped motifs and a pomegranate arranged in a cross-pattern.

Fig. 235. Jar sealing (?) seen from the side and below (C O.1102; Aleppo M 11585).

bore a seal impression, bore the mark of a stamp seal. Only two impressions made with a cylinder were found in the Assyrian levels, one on a door sealing (*Fig. 245*), the other on a possible jar sealing (*Fig. 235*).

It happened that cylinder and stamp seals were combined into the same object. An example can be reconstructed from impressions made on the possible jar sealing from Building C1a. The lower part of the impression of a cylinder seal

can be seen near the edge of the object (*Fig. 236*). This seal must have had a fairly thick frame, judging by the trace it left underneath the figurative scene. In addition, a stamp seal was applied several times to the soft clay (*Fig. 237*). The impression of this stamp partly covers that of the cylinder at least three times. It is most likely, as Madeleine Trokay suggested,[2] that this circular stamp was in fact the decoration applied to the base of the metal frame of the cylinder whose impression is also found on the object. Other examples of cylinder seals carved in such a way that they could also be used as stamp seals are known.[3] Such seals would bear testimony to the transition from the cylinder to the stamp seal.

The symbolic value of seals is illustrated by both a cylinder and a stamp seal. The cylinder was carved from a whitish stone. It was perforated and had a bronze setting with a suspension ring exactly as cylinder seals had. However, contrary to cylinder seals, its surface was flat and smooth with no trace of decoration (*Fig. 233*). More puzzling were the impressions of a stamp seal that was applied twice on Tablet T13 (*Fig. 234*). The two impressions were blank, a circumstance that cannot be explained by the fact that the pressure was not strong enough for the seal to leave a mark because the frame of the seal was clearly visible. It seems that the application of the seal, without an identification mark, was sufficient to bind its owner. In the case of both the cylinder and the stamp, the symbolic value of the object seems to have been the main concern.

Fig. 238. Impression of the fringe of a garment on Tablet T14 (Aleppo M 11589).

Fig. 239. Impression of the fringe of a garment on the envelope of Tablet T20 (Aleppo M 12408).

In this regard, they were not very different from another sealing technique that is represented by two examples at Tell Ahmar. The first was found on Tablet T14, on which two impressions had been made. One, on the left, was the impression of a regular stamp seal (*Fig. 251*) but the other, on the right, consisted of slightly undulating horizontal lines with kinds of hairy tufts at their left end (*Fig. 238*). The other example was found on the envelope of Tablet T20. One recognizes a sort of string wrapped around itself (*Fig. 239*). Although the texts of both tablets refers to these impressions by the word "seal", neither may have been made by an actual seal. They are best explained as the mark left by the fringe of a garment according to a practice called *sissiktu*, well attested in the Middle Bronze Age but much less so in later periods. A person involved in an agreement or contract could "sign" a document by applying a few threads of the fringe of his garment on the tablet instead of a seal. The operative strength of the sealing does not result from the object's individual identification marks but from the object itself.

Besides tablets, other objects could carry a seal impression. We already saw, p. 65, that doors, in the Middle Bronze Age, could be sealed by impressing a seal on a lump of clay that was applied to the stick around which the string that was holding the door was wrapped. A find from Area E shows that the system was still in use in the Iron Age (*Fig. 245*). On the other hand, the clay object from Area C that was impressed with the "stamp-cylinder" may have been used to seal a jar (*Fig. 235*). Traces of a string and of a piece of fabric were discernible on its flat base. The fabric probably covered the mouth of the jar and the string held it around the jar's neck. A third category of sealed object consisted of tags. We already saw Middle Bronze Age examples of tags (pp. 53, 61). These were in the shape of clay strips. Another kind of tag, closer to the so-called *bullae*, was found in Area C. An approximately conical clay object bore the impression of a stamp seal on its base (*Fig. 249*). The tip of the cone was broken off, but it is very likely that, when complete, it was pierced to allow a string to pass through it in a such a way that the bulla could be attached to a bag or a box.

Fig. 240. Ivory seal box (?) (C O.466; Aleppo M 12390) (drawing: Lia Abbate).

Lastly, an enigmatic object found in Room 1 of Building C1a may reflect still another sealing method. It is a small ivory, 2.3 cm high, figuring a female head carved in high relief (*Fig. 240*). The back of the ivory is flat with a cavity in its middle, which forms a kind of mortise giving the impression that the object is intended to be attached to a piece of furniture. More puzzling, however, is a perforation that runs through the object from top to bottom. To what purpose would such a perforation be drilled in an object whose function is to decorate a piece of furniture? François Popelin made a convincing suggestion to the author. According to him, this small ivory could be the ancestor of the seal boxes of the Roman period. The two ends of a string attached to an object could have been passed through the perforation and knotted in the cavity, which would then be filled with wax or some other malleable material on which a seal could be impressed. In this way, the knot would be protected and the safety of the object guaranteed. The ivory would therefore have been another kind of tag designed to seal objects such as a papyrus scroll, a bag or a box.

b. *The iconography of the seals*

The styles of the stamp and cylinder seals were quite different. The cylinder seals were carved with motives executed in the Assyrian style, the stamp seals offered a greater variety of styles.

The best-preserved cylinder seal, made of a very fine-grained black stone, shows two figures standing on either side of a tall jar (*Fig. 241*). The figure on the left is holding a square fan and the one on the right a bow in one hand and probably a cup in the other. This motif was very common. The figure holding a bow is usually seen as a representation of the king. A tall jar placed between the figures, a rhomboid motif, a "ball-staff" and a plant below a crescent complete the scene.

Hunting scenes are another popular theme, which is represented by one example (*Fig. 242*). A clay cylinder depicts an archer shooting an arrow at an ostrich. A small, stylized tree stands between the two figures.

Religious symbols and cultic scenes also appear on the Tell Ahmar seals. A well preserved cylinder seal, also made of a fine-grained black stone, is carved with a figure facing left and standing in adoration before the standard of the Moon-God, which consists of a crescent supported by a tasselled pole set up on a pedestal (*Fig. 243*). To the left of the crescent six small balls are surrounding a seventh ball to form the symbol of the *Sibittu* or Pleiades. Beneath the *Sibittu* is the frequent but enigmatic symbol of the "ball-staff". A winged disc above an animal completes the scene. Another cylinder seal, made of black stone, has retained the upper part of its setting (*Fig. 244*). Two standing male figures are looking to the left towards a deity that can no longer be identified due to a break. It is clear, however, that the deity was wrapped in a nimbus. Behind the divine figure, or behind the two worshippers depending on how the seal is unrolled, stands the standard of the Moon-God, here without a pedestal. The seal impressed on the door sealing mentioned above, which comes from Area E, also bore a cultic scene (*Fig. 245*). The centre of the scene is occupied by an offering table below a winged disc. On the right stands the Storm-God brandishing a thunderbolt in either hands and on the left a worshipper. Another worshipper stands behind the deity. Perhaps would it be far-fetched to relate this motif to the possible symbolism of the trident discovered in Room 1 of Building E1 (Chapter 6).

Stamp seals are too small for a complex scene to be carved on them. A scaraboid carved in a crystalline white

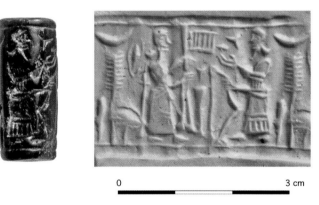

Fig. 241. Cylinder seal with a ceremonial scene (C O.591; Aleppo M 12393).

Fig. 243. Cylinder seal with a cultic scene (C O.345; Aleppo M 12391).

Fig. 242. Clay cylinder seal with a hunting scene (C O.659; Aleppo).

Fig. 244. Cylinder seal with a cultic scene (C O.348; Aleppo M 12401).

stone is decorated with a motif reminiscent of the standard of the Moon-God (*Fig. 246*). However, the crescent is almost closed as if it were a disc and the tassels that usually emanate from the top of the pole are replaced by small balls. Two more balls are placed on the pole itself, so that it cannot be ruled out that the six balls and the crescent/disc represent the Pleiades instead of the Moon-God. Another object, possibly but not necessarily a seal, has the shape of a bell (*Fig. 247*). It is made of "frit" as is shown by its greenish white glaze. Its base is decorated with a winged disc, very poorly executed.

Other stamp seals are decorated with human figures. A scaraboid, made of a very fine-grained black stone, shows a male figure walking to the right and holding a quadrangular object (*Fig. 248*). The figure seems to be dressed in the Assyrian way, wrapped up in a kind of shawl. On either side of the figure, four signs are carved in the Luwian script. This might be an indication that the Luwian tradition had not yet entirely died out. The tag already presented above

has the impression of a stamp seal with two standing figures facing each other (*Fig. 249*). They may be shaking hands in a gesture reminiscent of the central scene on the base of the throne dais of Shalmaneser III from Nimrud, unless it is a scene similar to a well known motif found on reliefs decorating Assyrian palaces, as well as the murals of the

0   3 cm

Fig. 247. Bell-shaped pendant with the representation of a winged disc (C O.1118; Aleppo M 11584).

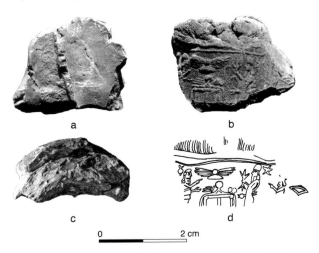

Fig. 245. Door sealing with the impression of a cylinder seal bearing a cultic scene (E15 O.13; Aleppo M 12403) (drawing: Elizabeth Hendrix).

0   2 cm

Fig. 248. Scaraboid with Luwian hieroglyphs (C O.347; Aleppo M 11587).

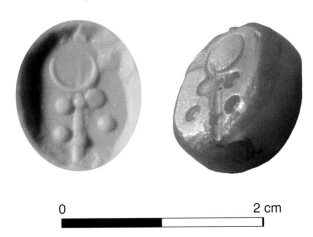

0   2 cm

Fig. 246. Scaraboid with a religious symbol (C O.65.17; Aleppo M 12415).

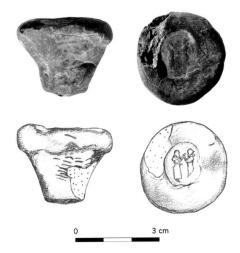

0   3 cm

Fig. 249. Bulla with a stamp seal impression (C O.92.5; Aleppo M 12404) (drawing: Lia Abbate).

Fig. 250. Scaraboid with a crouching caprid (C O.319; Aleppo M 12387).

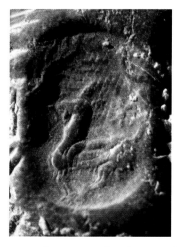

Fig. 251. Impression of a stamp seal with a caprid on Tablet T14.

Tell Ahmar palace, where the king is facing a high dignitary, possibly the crown prince.

Seals could also carry animal figures. A scaraboid is decorated with a recumbent caprid, one of the front legs of which is bent to suggest that the animal is about to stand up (*Fig. 250*). A triangular motif fills the void above the animal. The style of this seal, made of grey stone, places it in the Syrian tradition. Another caprid – a wild goat – decorates one of the seals impressed on Tablet T14 (*Fig. 251*).

The filling motifs, in this case, are a branch above the animal and a rosette behind its head. The style is also in the Syrian tradition.

One scarab and two seals known through their impression on a tablet bear Egyptian motifs. They are discussed by Vanessa Boschloos.

Egyptian and Egyptianizing seals (Vanessa Boschloos)

Egyptian and Egyptianizing glyptic evidence at Tell Ahmar is not plentiful but uniquely reflects the importance of the city situated at the crossroads of major roads between the Levant, Anatolia and Syro-Mesopotamia. Most notable are impressions of scarabs or scaraboids on two cuneiform tablets and a white faience scarab. Eight more scarabs were discovered in the tombs of the Persian Period, but none shows an Egyptian subject.[1] They are only slightly older or even contemporary with their archaeological contexts. With the exception of a scarab dating from the Egyptian Late Period (Twenty-fifth–Twenty-sixth Dynasties, c. 747–525) "found at Ahmar" by D.G. Hogarth during his survey for the British Museum in 1908,[2] the scarabs excavated at the site are not of Egyptian origin. Actually, besides Tell Ahmar, imported Egyptian scarabs are rare in this part of Syria during the Iron Age. Looking at the whole of Syria, scarabs dated to the Twenty-fifth–Twenty-sixth Dynasties have been found in eighth–sixth century contexts at Shiukh Foqani, Taʿyinat, al-Mina, Ras al-Bassit, Sukas, Neirab, Khan Sheikhun and, further south, Salahiya (near Damascus).[3]

The white faience scarab (*Fig. a*), discovered in Room 1 of Building C2, bears hieroglyphs that are difficult to identify with certainty. However, parallels found elsewhere in Syria,[4] but also in Egypt[5] and in the Western Mediterranean,[6] indicate that they form a proper name of the type *P3-dj-*[...], "The one given by [...]", the last part of which generally consists of the name of an Egyptian deity, such as Isis, Osiris, Bastet, Neith or Amun.[7] In this case, we propose to read the name *Padibastet* (Greek *Petubastis*), an Egyptian name prevalent in the Late Period.[8] At the top are the sign *p* and the arm *dj*, practically

Fig. a. Scarab in white faience (C O.369; Aleppo) (drawing: Vanessa Boschloos).

merged, while the long narrow sign represents the vase *b3s* next to two small signs *t*. Similar scarabs appear in the Egyptian production of the Twenty-sixth Dynasty (including Naukratis), but even more so in the contemporary Phoenician production (seventh–sixth century).[9] The poor state of preservation of the scarab, having lost its glaze, does not allow us to assign its morphological characteristics unequivocally to an Egyptian origin. It could date from the same period as the remains among which it was found.

Building C1 yielded objects of high quality, including a collection of cuneiform tablets probably belonging to a certain "Hanni" who is mentioned several times in these texts.[10] Only six tablets bear seal impressions, two of which have an Egyptian or Egyptianizing subject matter.[11] Tablet T8 (*Fig. b*) bears three impressions made by the same seal, an Egyptian scarab. The identification as a scarab and its origin are indicated by its composition in registers for which Egyptian parallels can be cited. Above a basket *nb*, two figures dressed in long robes stand on either side of a central motif, probably a third figure. A double line separates them from the upper part of the design where a falcon stands opposite two unidentifiable motifs. Similar scarabs show scenes with the Egyptian lion-headed goddess, Sekhmet, in the company of other deities or worshippers. These two-register compositions were particularly popular during the Twenty-fifth Dynasty (c. 747–656) and the following dynasty.[12] The seal appears to be contemporary with the document that was sealed with it. The tablet mentions the sale of a slave to Hanni and the seal belongs to its owner.[13] Such is also the case for the second tablet, T9 (*Fig. c*), which is only partially preserved and bears the impression (upside down) of an Egyptianizing seal, probably a scarab or a scaraboid.[14] Its base was decorated with hieroglyphs and Egyptian motifs, which are, from left to right, the ostrich feather as the sign of the goddess Ma'at, a circle probably representing the sign *ḥ* surmounted by a *t* sign, and finally an uraeus. The whole seems to form the phrase *ḥ.t m3ʿt*, "righteous things", as attested by similar scarabs attributed to a faience workshop that was probably located on the island of Rhodes. These scarabs are also known as the "Perachora/Lindos type", a mass-produced item found throughout the Mediterranean, mainly at Greek sites, and generally in contexts dated between the second half of the eighth and the first half of the seventh century.[15]

Fig. b. Tablet T8 stamped three times with the same seal (drawing: Vanessa Boschloos).

Fig. c. Tablet T9 stamped with a seal inscribed with Egyptian hieroglyphs (drawing: Vanessa Boschloos).

It thus seems that the two types of Egyptian or Egyptianizing seal impressions attested in the Hanni archives were made by scarabs of which the production periods correspond to the first phase (Phase C/2c1) of Buildings C1/C2, which ends in the second half of the seventh century. They bear witness to relations with coastal sites in northern Syria and Phoenicia, which played a major role in the dissemination of Aegyptiaca, and even with the Greek world, as suggested by the impressions on Tablet T9. The owners of the Egyptian and Egyptianizing seals of Til Barsib must have maintained relations with the Levantine coast, where larger numbers of such objects circulated. The white faience scarab supports this interpretation and the scarab collected from the surface by Hogarth may have reached its final destination around the same period. Only one other Syrian site yielded Egyptian scarabs of the Twenty-fifth Dynasty in contexts contemporary with their period of production: al-Mina, in the estuary of the Orontes River. Til Barsib was located on the road leading from north-west Syria to Syro-Mesopotamia and it cannot be excluded that a major coastal centre and trading post like al-Mina, also part of the Assyrian Empire, functioned as an intermediate distribution point for the Aegyptiaca that circulated in Neo-Assyrian Syria. Tell Ahmar/Til Barsib's favourable strategic position on the Euphrates, situated at the crossroads of the routes between Mesopotamia (Assyria) and Jezireh, Anatolia, inland Syria and the Mediterranean (notably the Phoenician city-states and the Aegean world), not only made it the gateway to the Levantine coast, but also a hub for people, goods and objects of various origins that crossed the Euphrates at this point. These Aegyptiaca can certainly not be considered as indicators of direct contact with Egypt, but they do bear witness to the existence of ever-expanding Phoenician and Greek trade networks, while reflecting the commercial activities as well as the international and inter-regional relations of their owners.

Notes

1   *Til-Barsib,* pp. 76–79.

2   R. Giveon, *Egyptian Scarabs from Western Asia from the Collections of the British Museum,* Orbis Biblicus et Orientalis, Series Archaeologica 3, Fribourg 1985, pp. 172–173, no 4.

3   V. Boschloos, *De geo-chronologische distributie van Egyptische scarabeezegels in de Noordelijke Levant (Syrië en Libanon) van het late 3e millennium tot de late IJzertijd,* unpublished PhD dissertation, Vrije Universiteit Brussel 2011–2012: pp. 568–570; ead., Egyptian and Egyptianising scarab-shaped seals in Syria and Lebanon, *Bibliotheca Orientalis* 69/3–4 (2012), p. 180, n. 16.

4   M. Dunand, A. Bounni & N. Saliby, Fouilles de Tell Kazel, *Annales Archéologiques (arabes) Syriennes* 14 (1964), p. 12, pl xx, no 5 (Tell Kazel); R. Giveon, *op. cit.* (n. 2), pp. 144–145, no 19 (Amrit).

5   For instance, W.M.F. Petrie, *Naukratis. Part I. 1884–5,* Memoir of the Egypt Exploration Fund 3, London 1886, pl. xxxvii, nos 116–118; id. *Hyksos and Israelite Cities,* British School of Archaeology in Egypt 12, London 1906, pl. xix, no 238 (Tell el-Yahudiya).

6   For instance, A. Feghali Gorton, *Egyptian and Egyptianizing Scarabs: A typology of steatite, faience and paste scarabs from Punic and other Mediterranean sites,* Oxford 1996, pp. 101–102, nos 17–20, 22–23; G. Hölbl, Ägyptisches Kulturgut im phönikischen und punischen Sardinien, Études préliminaires aux religions orientales dans l'empire romain 102, Leiden 1985, Taf. 101, 107, 133, no 3; J. Vercoutter, *Les objets égyptiens et égyptisants du mobilier funéraire carthaginois,* Bibliothèque Archéologique et Historique 40, Paris 1945, no 36–39 (Carthage).

7   H. Ranke, *Die Ägyptischen Personennamen,* Band I, *Verzeichnis der Namen,* Glückstadt 1935, pp. 121–126.

8   H. Ranke, *op. cit.* (n. 7), p. 123, no 5.

9   G. Hölbl, *op. cit.* (n. 6), pp. 181–182, 228–229, 256–257.

10 S. Dalley, Neo-Assyrian tablets from Til Barsib, *Abr-Nahrain* 34 (1996–1997), p. 66.

11 G. Bunnens, Sealing practices at Neo-Assyrian Til Barsib. Cylinders-stamps - *Sissiktu* - seal box, *The Ancient Near East: A Life! Festschrift Karel Van Lerberghe,* ed. T. Boiy, J. Bretschneider, A. Goddeeris, H. Hameeuw, G. Jans & J. Tavernier, Leuven 2012, pp. 75–89.

12 *E.g.* G. Hölbl, *op. cit.* (n. 6), Taf. 97, no 2; O. Keel, *Corpus der Stempelsiegel-Amulette aus Palästina/Israel. Von den Anfängen bis zur Perserzeit. Katalog,* Band 1, Orbis Biblicus et Orientalis, Series Archaeologica 13, Fribourg 1997, pp. 598–599, no 194; J. Vercoutter, *op. cit.* (n. 5), nos 251, 259, 408, 452.

13 S. Dalley, *art. cit.* (n. 10), pp. 76–77.

14 G. Bunnens, *art. cit.* (n. 11), p. 77, figs 5–6; S. Dalley, *art cit.* (n. 10), p. 78.

15 E. Apostola and P. Kousoulis, Aegyptiaca in archaic Greece: Preliminary remarks on scarabs and scaraboids from the Sanctuary of Ialysus (Rhodes), *Göttinger Miszellen* 258 (2019), pp. 9–20; A. Feghali Gorton, *op. cit.* (n. 6), pp. 53–72 (Group A).

2. Carved ivories

A collection of about 20 worked ivories has been found in Area C, most of them in the destruction debris of Phase C/2c1 in Room 15 of Building C1a.[4] Objects of this kind were generally used to decorate pieces of furniture, sometimes to make small boxes or caskets.

The largest of these ivories is a plaque 32.3 cm long, which depicts a procession of servants carrying provisions and led by musicians (*Fig. 252*). A guilloche runs along the upper and lower edges of the ivory. A rounded incision in the upper edge shows that the plaque must have been part of a more elaborate decoration. The nature of the object it decorated remains unknown.

The first figure of the procession, on the right, is almost completely lost. The second shows a female musician playing a double flute. She is followed by male figures, the first of whom may have been carrying bunches of grapes, the second pomegranates, the third small birds and the last, badly damaged, fish. The figures are separated from each other by lotus flowers. The procession must have been bringing food to a banquet that was represented on another ivory. The style is characteristic of northern Syria, particularly in the rendering of rather squat forms. The hairstyle and the loincloth of the food bearers are reminiscent of Egypt. The dress of the flautist, on the other hand, orientates more towards the Syro-Hittite world.

Another ivory, 15.9 cm high and carved on either side also comes from a north Syrian workshop (*Fig. 253*). The ivory was attached by tenons to a frame, possibly the armrest of an armchair. On one side, the decoration consists of a plant made up of a superimposition of palmettes. On the other, a similar plant supports a lotus flower on which stands a griffin. The north Syrian style is recognizable by the rounded forms and, more specifically, by the figure of the griffin. For instance, the stylization of the feathers of its wings, which form kinds of scales on its chest, is typical of north Syrian sculpture. The black colour and the shiny tone of the ivory seem to be due to the fire that ended the first phase of occupation of Building C1a. However, traces of polychromy remain in some places. The stem and peduncle of the flower buds emanating from the lower palmette are coloured in white and the stalk of the lotus flower on which the griffin stands is yellowish in colour.

A third ivory recalls the Phoenician or south Syrian style (*Fig. 254*). It shows a head whose wig and eye are stylized in a manner strongly reminiscent of the Egyptian style. Its style sets thus this ivory apart from the other two.

In addition to these three objects, several ivories show a wide variety of palmettes. Stylized bands of palmettes with large drooping leaves are a well known type at Nimrud (*Fig. 255d* and *255e*).[5] Another object consists of a double row of stylized flowers (*Fig. 255c*). More curious is an ivory whose left edge is lost. It shows a stylized palm tree on a mountain, the rocky aspect of which is rendered by a scale motif (*Fig. 255b*). Finally, a plaque decorated with palmettes is executed in the cloisonné technique (*Fig. 255a*). The details of the plants are indicated by hollows that must have been filled with coloured material. At the time of discovery, some yellowish glazed material was still present in one of the branches of the top middle palmette and a tiny fragment of gold leaf was still attached to its right outer branch.

Fig. 252. Ivory plaque depicting a procession of servants carrying provisions (C O.1708; Aleppo M 10982).

Fig. 253. Ivory carved on either side and showing stylized trees and a griffin (C O.817 + 1445; Aleppo M 10981).

Fig. 254. Egyptianizing head (C O.1417; Aleppo M 10980).

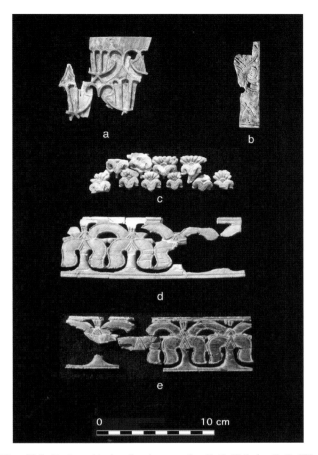

Fig. 255. Various kinds of palmettes (a: C O.686; b: C O.680; c: C O.1008; d: C O.1009; e: C O.690; Aleppo).

3. Terracotta figurines and plaques

Terracotta figurines, human or animal, are one of the most frequent finds made on archaeological sites in Western Asia, often in a poor state of preservation. Tell Ahmar is no exception. However, the function of these figurines remains enigmatic. Toys? Idols? One and the other, depending on the circumstances? The same questions that arose for the Bronze Age figurines (above pp. 34–35) also apply here. A definite answer has not yet been given.

Among the human figurines, several represent female figures. Some of them have large, radiant headdresses (*Figs 256* and *257*). A comparison with the few complete examples found elsewhere in northern Syria, especially in the Carchemish region, shows that the head is the only part of the body that is rendered with any detail. The arms, generally bent on the chest, are roughly indicated and the lower part of the body is cylindrical, slightly flaring towards the base to ensure the stability of the object, hence the name "pillar figurines" often given to this type of figurine. No sexual characteristics are indicated. Fairly rare is a figurine showing a woman holding a child in her arms (*Fig. 257*). A complete figurine, except for the arms, could be reconstructed from

Fig. 256. Fragment of a terracotta female figurine (C O.80; Aleppo M 12382).

Fig. 257. Fragment of a terracotta female figurine with a child (C O.64.14; Aleppo M 12423).

Fig. 259. Moulded plaque showing a nude female C O.427; Aleppo).

Fig. 258. Terracotta pillar figurine (C O.486+590; Aleppo M 12394).

Fig. 260. Moulded plaque showing a nude female (D O.6; Aleppo).

two fragments – the body and the head – found respectively in Rooms 1 and 2 of Building C2 (*Fig. 258*). The figure has a quite different, less elaborate, hairstyle.

The clumsy execution of most of these figurines suggest that they are not the work of professionals. This, together with the absence of marked sexual characteristics, would give weight to the hypothesis that they were toys made in a domestic context.

The same cannot be said of another category of human figures: the moulded plaques. Some are naked (*Fig. 259* and *260*), others dressed (*Fig. 261*), but in all cases the emphasis is clearly on the femininity of the figures. It has therefore been assumed that these plaques were related in some way to the idea of fertility, hence the name of "Astarte plaques" arbitrarily assigned to these representations.

The mould manufacture implies mass production and its execution, often very elaborate, requires a know-how accessible only to a professional. Such a production certainly falls outside the domestic context. Moulded plaques must have been part of the pious imagery that the inhabitants of large residences – and no doubt also those of more modest dwellings – liked to keep at home. Incidentally, it is interesting to note that the figure illustrated on *Figure 261* holds a mirror in its left hand as many female figures do in Syro-Hittite art.

Animal figurines are often difficult to interpret, the more so as, in many cases, the head and legs are broken off. When details are preserved, they indicate that the figurine is that of a horse. A good example has a very complex harness represented by strips of clay applied on the animal's body (*Fig. 262*). Often these figurines are ridden by a horseman

Fig. 261. Moulded plaque showing a dressed female (C O.620; Aleppo).

Fig. 263. Fragment of a terracotta horse rider figurine (C O.515; Aleppo).

Fig. 262. Fragment of a terracotta horse figurine (C O.1510; Aleppo M 10983).

Fig. 264. Terracotta horse figurine (C O.65.10.2; Aleppo).

whose body merges with that of the animal. Only the rider's head and arms, holding the horse's collar, are clearly marked. No complete figurine of a horse with its rider has been found at Tell Ahmar, but several horses still present traces of the rider and several riders have obviously been torn away from a horse (*Fig. 263*).

Animal figurines probably bring us back to the field of domestic production. The ease of production and the clumsiness of execution of these figurines are better understood if they were made in a domestic environment, perhaps to be used as toys. It is tempting to think, but is not demonstrated, that some of the female figurines were not cultic objects but dolls for little girls and horseman figurines were toys for boys. In this regard, it should be noted that a fairly large horse figure (13.3 cm long) had both front and hind legs

bonded together and perforated as to allow wheel axles to pass through (*Fig. 264*). It is very likely that this object was used as a wheeled toy that a child could pull.

* * *

The images that decorated various devices in the Middle and Lower Towns at Tell Ahmar provide a good illustration of the cultural *koine* that united the heart of the empire to the regions it dominated. The ivories were all in various Western styles, but found parallels in other cities of the empire, especially in one of its capitals, Kalhu (Nimrud), where they were certainly imported from the West. The seals combined Assyrian, Egyptian and Syrian features as much as they reflected contacts with Phoenicia and the

Mediterranean. Only terracotta figurines, probably largely produced in domestic contexts, seemed to belong to a local tradition.

Notes

1   G. BUNNENS, Sealing practices at Neo-Assyrian Til Barsib: Cylinders – stamps – *sissiktu* – seal box, *The Ancient Near East, a Life! Festschrift Karel Van Lerberghe*, ed. T. BOIY, J. BRETSCHNEIDER, A. GODDEERIS, H. HAMEEUW, G. JANS & J. TAVERNER, Leuven-Paris-Walpole (MA), 2012, pp. 75–89.

2   M. TROKAY, Interconnections in glyptic during the Neo-Assyrian period, *Abr-Nahrain* 33 (1995), pp. 98, 105, and fig. 1, p. 99.

3   D. COLLON, *First Impressions: Cylinder seals in the ancient Near East*, London 1987, pp. 79, 80, 112 (see especially No 359, p. 79).

4   G. BUNNENS, Carved ivories from Til Barsib, *American Journal of Archaeology* 101 (1997), pp. 435–450.

5   G. HERRMANN, *Ivories from Nimrud (1949–1963)*, IV, 1, *Ivories from Room SW 37, Forth Shalmaneser. Commentary and Catalogue*, London 1986, p. 174.

People and crafts

The few written documents found in Building C1a and various objects found in the level from the Assyrian period give an idea of both the day-to-day life of the inhabitants of Til Barsib/Kar-Shalmaneser and of their craft activities.

1. Hanni's archive

Around 20 cuneiform tablets, including fragments, as well as two Aramaic tablets were found in Building C1a. With two exceptions (Tablet T1 discovered to the north-east of Room 14 and Tablet T23 from Room 15), they were all found on the oldest floor (Phase C/2c1) in and around the doorway between Rooms 11 and 12 (*Fig. 201*).[1] The fire that brought this occupation phase to an end helped to preserve them. They were not, however, in their original context, as they were lying in disorder on the floor, probably dropped there at the time of destruction.

These tablets form a relatively homogeneous group. Those that are dated follow the Assyrian system of yearly eponyms, *i.e.* a system in which imperial dignitaries give their name to a year.[2] The oldest tablet dates from the end of the reign of Sennacherib (T15: Mannu-kî-Adad, eponym in 683), the others can be attributed to the reign of Ashurbanipal (668–631). Two eponyms belonged to his reign: Sha-Nabu-shu (T14, eponym in 658) and Bel-Harran-shadua (T3 and T4, eponym in 650). Tablet T20 bore the date "after Bel-Harran-shadua", *i.e.* after 650, which means that it was written when the name of the year's eponym was not yet known. It should be noted that 649 is also the last year of the "canonical" period, *i.e.* the period for which the order of the eponyms is known through lists, or "canons", giving their names in chronological order. From 648 onwards, the order of succession of the eponyms is therefore hypothetical.[3] Two eponyms belonged to this period: Shamash-dainanni (perhaps eponym in 644) cited in Tablet T13 and Ashur-garua-niri (perhaps eponym in 640) whose name appears in the formula "after Ashur-garua-niri" in Tablet T6 (his name may have also occurred in T2).

One name, Hanni, appears several times in the documents (T2, T4, T6, T8, T9, T14).[4] Given the role played by this Hanni, one might think that the tablets belonged to his archives. Hanni would thus have been the owner of the C1a–C1b–C2 complex in the second half of the reign of Ashurbanipal.

The activities of this Hanni seem to be those of a businessman. We see him lending money (T2, T4, T6), and buying slaves (T8, T9). The tablets also include two very fragmentary ration lists (T1, T18), which could indicate that Hanni was also in charge of the distribution of foodstuffs. It is not known whether he exercised an official function, but Tablet T14, already referred to in Chapter 5, suggests that he was close to the central government. Finally, the craft activities that took place in his house – as will be seen later – seem to indicate that he derived part of his income from textile activities and the repair of military equipment.

2. Languages in use in Til Barsib/Kar-Shalmaneser

The tablets from the house of Hanni conform, for the most part, to Assyrian models – this should come as no surprise in a provincial capital of the empire – but there are also two Aramaic tablets among them. One (T11) is a sale contract with a witness list, whose form hardly differs from its Assyrian counterparts (*Fig. 265*). The other (T23), of which only one side is preserved, is much more original (*Fig. 266*). It is made of a clay that is coarser than usual and adopts an exceptional, almost oval shape. Its text, however, is difficult to understand. Whatever their aspect and contents, the merit of these two tablets is to add one more example, in addition to sites such as Tell Shiukh Foqani, Tell Halaf, Dur-Katlimmu and Maʾallanate, of the administrative use of Aramaic at the end of the Assyrian Empire.

No monumental inscription written in Aramaic, especially funerary inscriptions, has been found, although a couple of small inscriptions written in a Semitic language have come to light. Two fragments of limestone plaques bear alphabetical signs. These could be marks of ownership or small votive inscriptions. One was found during the French excavations of the Lion Gate,[5] the other was found in Area D (*Fig. 267*). In both cases, the first letter is L, meaning "(belonging) to" or "(dedicated) to". Only the first letter of the next word, B, is preserved in the inscription from the gate. The inscription from Area D has kept two more letters in the first line, which reads LBNŠ[and could be understood as "(belonging) to Bn-Š[…]". This proper name could mean "Son-of-Sh[…]". If this were the case, it would not be an Aramaic name – "son" is *bar* in Aramaic – but a name belonging to another West-Semitic language. Only one ostrakon bears an alphabetical inscription (*Fig. 268*). It too begins with the letter L, probably followed by a proper name (NGRD). It is surprising that in an environment where Aramaic is supposed to have been widely spoken and where Aramaic personal names were numerous,[6] so few of these small alphabetical inscriptions were found.

It is possible that Luwian, which was the language of the monumental inscriptions before the Assyrian conquest, had not been completely forgotten. A Scaraboid from the House of Hanni, which was presented in the previous chapter, bears four Luwian signs of which only the sign *sa* is of certain reading.

Fig. 267. Fragment of a limestone plaque with an alphabetic inscription (D O.1; Aleppo M 10463).

Fig. 265. Aramaic Tablet T11 (Aleppo M 11588).

Fig. 266. Aramaic Tablet T23 (Aleppo M 11591).

Fig. 268. Ostrakon with an alphabetic inscription (C64 PL146.1).

3. A cosmopolitan world

The texts highlight the cosmopolitan aspects of life in Til Barsib/Kar-Shalmaneser. Exchanges with the centre of the empire were quite naturally part of daily life. Tablet T22 mentions witnesses from Kalhu (Nimrud) and Dur-Sharrukin (Khorsabad).

The personal names might give evidence for relations with the western regions. Three witnesses to the contract T13 were sons of people whose names actually were ethnonyms. One was the son of a certain Hamataya, another of a certain Tabalaya and the third of a certain Samiraya. Hamataya means "inhabitant of Hamat", the great city of the Orontes valley, and Tabalaya "inhabitant of Tabal", a region of Asia Minor. Samiraya should be "the inhabitant of Samira", an unknown place unless it is a misspelling for Samirnaya, "inhabitant of Samaria". Although it is true that ethnic names were often used as personal names, the fact that all three ethnonyms are used to determine the name of the witnesses could indicate that they should not be taken literally, even though they are preceded by the determinative for personal names but should have kept their original meaning of ethnonyms. "Son of Tabalaya", for instance, could thus mean "son of the Tabalaean (people)" and the tablet could have been witnessed by people from Tabal, Hamat and Samir (Samaria?). The contract would have reflected Til Barsib/Kar-Shalmaneser 's cosmopolitan milieu.

The site was an almost inevitable stage for people travelling from the western provinces to the centre of the empire. One recalls, for example, the letter found in Nimrud, which signals the passage by Til Barsib of emissaries from Commagene, Marqasi, Sam'al, Ashdod and Moab (above, p. 5).

Archaeological finds confirm the cosmopolitanism of life in Til Barsib/Kar-Shalmaneser. We already saw, in the previous chapter, that Egyptian influence was noticeable in the city, probably through Phoenician intermediaries. In addition, fragments of Phoenician jars were found in the levels of the Assyrian period (*Fig. 269* and *Fig. b4*, p. 187). Pottery was imported from Cyprus, probably as luxury goods, as attested by a large fragment of a "White Painted" oenochoe (*Fig. 270*). On the other hand, a jug with a human head on its neck reflects a practice that has been documented as far away as Italy (*Fig. 271*). Although the human face is heavily damaged, the anthropomorphic decoration of the jug's neck is confirmed by the small dots at its base,

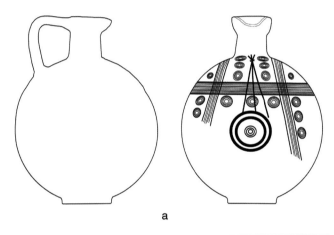

a

b

Fig. 269. Phoenician "torpedo jar" (C PL74.19.1) (drawing: Andrew S. Jamieson).

Fig. 270. "White Painted" Cypriot oenochoe (C PL2937): a) reconstruction; b) the actual fragment.

Fig. 271. Jug with a human face on the neck (C PL263).

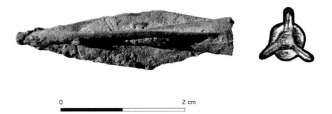

Fig. 272. Trilobate bronze arrowhead (C O.64.25).

Fig. 273. Iron spearhead (C O.513).

Fig. 274. Iron dagger (F O.21).

Fig. 275. Bronse armour scales (E O.54.5).

which figure a necklace. This jug gives further evidence of cultural links between Til Barsib/Kar-Shalmaneser and the Mediterranean world. Two cosmetic palettes, which will be discussed below, are of a type that was widespread in Phoenicia and Palestine (*Fig. 284*). Lastly, a jug whose spout and handle were on perpendicular axes recalls a pottery form that was used as far as Phrygia in the heart of Asia Minor (*Fig. 299a*).

4. Crafts

The domestic buildings of Tell Ahmar offer evidence for craft production.

a. Metallurgy

Military equipment, such as arrowheads (*Fig. 272*) and spearheads (*Fig. 273*), was stored in the residences of Areas C and E. A dagger was found in another context (*Fig. 274*). The number of these weapons is too small to suggest that they came from arsenals, but it is likely that repair work was carried out at least in Area C and E buildings.

Tablet T12 gives a list of various materials, including dye, nerves, leather, tree bark, copper, iron, which were entrusted to various people. S. Dalley suggests that some of these products are materials needed to make composite

0   5 cm

Fig. 276. Iron armour scales (E O.56.8).

0   5 cm

Fig. 277. Armour scale mould (?) (C86 O.16; Aleppo M 12400).
The photo on the right shows a scale that fits into the mould.

bows.[7] Such an explanation is certainly possible, but the material listed in Tablet T12 might also have been used to make armours.

Indeed, large quantities of bronze and iron armour scales were found in Building C1a and even more in Building E2. Some of them were still arranged in their original position (*Fig. 275* and *276*). They were attached to a leather support, traces of which sometimes were visible on the back of the scales. Armours were thus stored in these buildings. Were they made there? It is not likely. The production process of scales involves either cutting and hammering iron metal sheets or moulding bronze scales in a large number of moulds. No large-scale equipment of this kind was found in these buildings. However, a few small terracotta objects with a depression reproducing in hollow the shape and central ridge of an armour scale were found in Building C1a (*Fig. 277*). These objects might have been moulds used to repair damaged armours, whereas the actual production took place elsewhere. These objects may have been used in the manufacture of scales, but it is difficult to imagine that

they were produced in large numbers. It is more likely that these moulds were used to repair existing coats. Damaged armours could thus be repaired in the excavated buildings, whereas the actual production took place elsewhere.

Actually, two metallurgic workshops have been identified. One was not far from the C1a–C1b–C2 complex. The geophysical survey, conducted under John M. Russell's direction (above pp. 148–152) located a structure about halfway between Hanni's house and the city-wall to the west. An excavation trench opened in this sector (Area CJ4) revealed the western end of a room set against a wall more than 2 m thick, which delimited the construction towards the south-west. The many copper and iron objects, slag and fragments of crucibles found there indicate that it was a metallurgic workshop.

Another workshop was located at some distance from the tell, towards the west, in Area L.[8] It is not known what objects were made there, but the abundance of slag and the presence of crucibles leaves little doubt that bronze was worked there.

The metallurgic workshop of Area CJ4 (Elizabeth Hendrix)

In 2001, magnetic resonance surveys of western parts of the Lower Town of Tell Ahmar revealed the outline of a very large building whose apparent architectural plan does not fall into known types of structures of this size. In 2002 excavations in this building revealed evidence of a metalworking area in levels contemporary with the Neo-Assyrian city of Til Barsib (*Fig. a*). Although the excavation was limited to one season, even the relatively small amount of evidence gathered from the 18 × 4 m trench suggests that metalworking was occurring at an industrial scale for this time period.

The remains found in Area CJ4 can be classed generally as waste debris generated from at least two different kinds of metalworking: smelting and/or forging of wrought iron and small casting of copper or copper alloy.

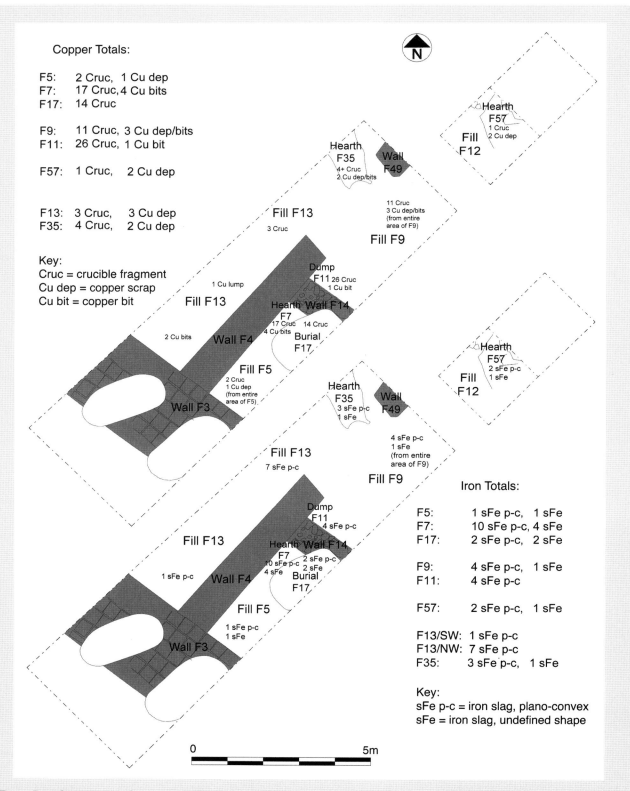

Copper Totals:

F5:   2 Cruc, 1 Cu dep
F7:   17 Cruc, 4 Cu bits
F17:   14 Cruc

F9:   11 Cruc, 3 Cu dep/bits
F11:   26 Cruc, 1 Cu bit

F57:   1 Cruc,   2 Cu dep

F13:   3 Cruc,   3 Cu dep
F35:   4 Cruc,   2 Cu dep

Key:
Cruc = crucible fragment
Cu dep = copper scrap
Cu bit = copper bit

Iron Totals:

F5:   1 sFe p-c, 1 sFe
F7:   10 sFe p-c, 4 sFe
F17:   2 sFe p-c, 2 sFe

F9:   4 sFe p-c, 1 sFe
F11:   4 sFe p-c

F57:   2 sFe p-c, 1 sFe

F13/SW: 1 sFe p-c
F13/NW: 7 sFe p-c
F35:   3 sFe p-c, 1 sFe

Key:
sFe p-c = iron slag, plano-convex
sFe = iron slag, undefined shape

Fig. a. Distribution maps of copper crucibles and iron slag: 1) crucibles associated with copper production; 2) iron slag (drawing: John M. Russell).

The fact that both these sorts of debris were found in the same area suggests that the trench excavated in Area CJ4 was located in a metalworking shop where both iron and copper workers plied their trades, either simultaneously at the same hearth, or at different hearths. Three hearths were found, each of which we may define as a forge, in which fuel and an air supply would have been used to achieve temperatures high enough to manipulate metals.

There is generally one source of air in each forge and it is the control of that air along with the raking up of the fuel that governs the intensity of the heat. Each worker will require specific temperatures for the project at hand, controlled by the arrangement of the fuel and the force of the air. Thus, it is possible that the copper worker and iron worker will share the forge at the same time, each positioning his work at the appropriate heat level. Alternatively, two hearths could be fired up. The distribution maps show that the three hearths in CJ4 Phase 2 all have copper as well as iron-working debris associated with them.

Fig. b. Crucible fragment showing corroded copper on surface (photo: Elizabeth Hendrix).

Copper or copper alloy working

The main evidence for copper working in Area CJ4 came in the form of 67 crucible fragments (*Figs a* and *b*). These rather unassuming bits of fired clay were identified as crucible fragments because of their high chaff content combined with secondary burnt surfaces and especially the visible presence of corroded copper or copper alloy on some of the surfaces. High chaff content in the original clay (chopped straw or other similar organic material) would have burned out in the first firing of the vessel, leaving long criss-crossing voids that allow the clay to expand and contract without breaking when the vessel is again exposed to high heat, creating a refractory material suitable for industrial processes.

The burnt and occasionally vitrified surfaces on the concave (interior) side of the vessels show that there was a secondary application of intense heat focused on that

Fig. c. The three classes of iron slag (photo: Elizabeth Hendrix).

part of the vessel. The best way to produce such a focused heat is by the use of a bellows or blowpipe aimed at the concave surface, forcing the heat from an adjacent flame onto that surface and whatever was placed on it, in this case copper. It is possible that copper ores, such as malachite, were smelted in the crucibles, but it is more likely that copper scraps and/or ingots were melted in these small crucibles, primarily because smelting was most commonly done as close to the ore source as possible to avoid transporting the non-valuable components of the ore.

In order to melt pure copper temperatures of up to 900°C need to be achieved, which can quite easily be done with a small fire and a blowpipe to increase the oxygen at the fire. At 900°C clay will begin to vitrify, that is melt into a glassy phase, which can be seen on the surfaces of some of the fragments. Some of the crucible fragments do not exhibit evidence of vitrification, suggesting that temperatures lower than 900°C were employed. As copper is alloyed with other metals to form different bronzes (such as arsenical or tin brones, perhaps mixed with lead, in various proportions), the melting temperature decreases and properties such as colour, castability and hardness in the finished alloy also change. The metalworker will have known empirically, to a more or less precise degree, what colour combination of copper scraps would yield the desired properties in the final product. Until more evidence can be gathered the provisional explanation of these crucible fragments is that they were used for the remelting of scraps of copper or copper alloy until the metal was liquified and could be poured into a mould for a desired object, such as an armour scale (*Fig. 277*).

Ironworking

Most of the metalworking debris found in Area CJ4 can be classified as slag generated from ironworking processes. Slags consist of silica-rich minerals that were liquified by heat during processes used to make metal, and are important as they absorb minerals readily, thus helping to draw contaminants away from the metal being worked.

In the case of the slag found in Area CJ4, three main classes of the more than 150 specimens retrieved could be distinguished (*Figs a* and *c*):

(Class 1) iron-stained plano-convex or concave-convex lumps (or "hearth-bottoms", referred to as plano-convex buns, or "pcbs"), most about palm-sized or slightly larger;
(Class 2) small (<5 cm diameter) nodules of black, glassy, highly porous slag;
(Class 3) heterogeneous lumps of dense slag, ranging from a few centimetres in diameter to about 10 cm in length, characterized by tiny gas pores, lumps of iron-stained material, rocky material, and lesser amounts of other materials.

The presence of all three classes of slag suggests that smiths at Til Barsib were working with iron ores or semi-refined blooms, not just pure iron billets or bar stock from which they could readily forge tools, weapons, hardware and other items.

Iron ore is essentially a rock that contains a sufficient amount of iron in its mineral form to make it worth smelting. In order to change iron from mineral to metal, iron ore was crushed, combined with charcoal and heated in a furnace with other materials, known as fluxes. The smelter's goal was to create a slag from the fluxes and the minerals in the ore that would melt and pull minerals away from the iron molecules in the ore.

After a time judged sufficient by the smelter, the furnace was allowed to cool down slightly and the heavy mass of iron and slag, known as a "bloom", was pulled out and placed on an anvil where it was given a few gentle blows with a hammer. The iron at this stage is similar to a pile of natural sponges surrounded by slag. The smith must squeeze the slag out from between and within the metallic iron "sponges", consolidating the bloom with repeated reheating and careful hammering to avoid breaking parts of the bloom. Short heats in the furnace or forge (different from the furnace used for the original smelting of the ore in that the forge had an open top) and one or two hammer blows would eject chunks of slag that were dense, heterogeneous and filled with tiny gas pores, and may account for the Class 3 slags.

Eventually, enough of the slag between the sponges was squeezed out to consolidate them into one large sponge so that the smith could heat the bloom for longer periods, allowing the slag to become less viscous (*i.e.* "runnier"). At that point the smith could hammer the slag away from the iron more aggressively, further consolidating the soft but solid iron metal into wrought iron bar stock. These hammerings expelled blobs of slag that became spherical as they cooled, flying through the air. This describes well the second class of slag recovered from Area CJ4.

Meanwhile, as the bloom was repeatedly placed in the forge it lost bits around its perimeter, which fell to the bottom of the forge, combining with pieces of unconsumed charcoal, fragments of forge lining and fuel ash, forming a semi-molten lump, often with a depression at the top from the blasts of heat coming from the bellows or blowpipe(s). If the forge had a rounded bottom it would give these lumps of fallen materials a rounded shape, characteristic of the concave-convex lumps (pcbs) described as Class 1 in our catalogue of slags. Alternatively, pcbs can also form when billets of wrought iron bar stock were placed in the smithing forge, since as they were hammered into objects they too shed debris, consisting mainly of hammer scale (flakes of oxidized iron shattered from the surface of the hot iron at each hammer blow), sand used as a flux in an attempt to keep oxygen away from the hot surface of the metal to minimize the production of hammer scale, and bits of charcoal and forge lining.

The 28 specimens of pcbs (Class 1) from Area CJ4 are of a type known from other metalworking sites in the Middle East,[1] and from modern experiments.[2] and attest to the forging of iron blooms, iron billets, or both. The spherical blobs and heterogeneous lumps of slag (Classes 2 and 3) also suggest that blooms were being worked in Area CJ4. It would be surprising if iron was being smelted at Til Barsib, if only because of the cost of transporting all that extra volume and weight in the ore. It is possible that rough iron blooms were produced at the ore source and were then transported to Til Barsib and further refined there.

Finished products

Copper spear tips, armour scales, fibulae (decorative pins), and other small objects were found in Neo-Assyrian levels at Tell Ahmar but, until analyses are done on all these objects as well as on copper scraps or ingots which may yet be found in Area CJ4, it is not possible to determine which if any of these items were made in the city's workshops and which were imported from other regions. However, several moulds for casting individual armour scales were excavated in Neo-Assyrian levels from Area C.

Building E2 contained, among other things, the remains of a tunic of armour made mostly of iron scales with a small percentage of similar copper scales, all sewn onto a woven backing cloth (long since deteriorated but preserving impressions of the weave in the corrosion products of the metal). The possibility exists that one function of the building found in Area CJ4 was as a workshop for the production of garments of armour like those found in Areas C and E.

Symbolic value

Some residents of Til Barsib also may have placed a special cultural value on certain iron objects and even ironworking itself. Building E1 contained a small closet-like chamber whose contents included a 1 m long iron "trident" (*Fig. 231*), and an open bowl with a solidified pool of material at the bottom that was analysed and identified as iron slag from a smithing operation. The trace minerals in the bowl were also found in the metal of the "trident" but not in the iron armour scales in Building E2.[3] We are left to wonder about the significance given to ironworking, at least in specific examples such as this, when the debris from the process is accorded a status that places it in such a context.

Notes

1   H.A. VELDHUIZEN & Th. REHREN, Slags and the city: early iron production at Tell Hammeh, Jordan, and Tel Beth-Shemesh, Israel, *Metals and Mines – Studies in Archaeometallurgy*, ed. S. LaNIECE & P. CRADDOCK, London 2007, pp. 189–201.

2   G. McDONNELL, A model for the formation of smithing slags, *Materialy Archeologiczne* (Krakow) 26 (1991), pp. 23–26; L. SAUDER & H. WILLIAMS, A practical treatise on the smelting and smithing of bloomery iron, *Historical Metallurgy* 36/2 (2002), pp. 122–131.

3   E. HENDRIX, in preparation.

b. Textile activities

Finds made in Room 15 of Building C1a raise the possibility that the function of the room was that of a weaving workshop. Small slightly fired clay objects of various sizes and shapes – ovoid, cylindrical (sometimes with slightly concave sides), annular or conical (*Fig. 278*) – were found piled up in several places. These objects, whose size seldom exceeded 10 cm, were weights intended to stretch the warp threads – *i.e.* the vertical threads between which the horinzontal weft threads were passed – of a loom. Moreover, three logs – between one and 2 m long and about 15 cm in diameter – were lying on the ground. Their dimensions rule out that they were beams, but they would have been very suitable for a loom. Looms generally consisted of a frame made of two vertical bars held by a horizontal one at the top. Smaller pieces of wood ensured the stability of this frame and allowed the weft threads to pass between the warp threads. The wood, according to Valérie Roitel, was a variety of pine, a species not native to the region but which may have been imported from Asia Minor. Two large jars were sunk below the room's floor. Other jars were found smashed on the floor. Smaller vases were also part of the finds as well as a basalt mortar. The activities performed in Room 15 therefore involved the use of liquids and the grinding of certain substances. This is reminiscent of the dye mentioned in T12 above. Everything concurs to show that Room 15 was a textile manufacturing workshop.

Fig. 278. Clay loom weights.

Fig. 280. Terracotta lamp (C PL4364).

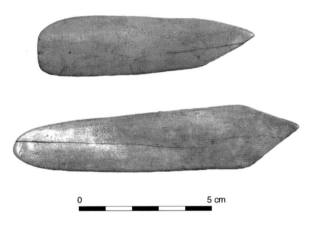

Fig. 279. Bone spatulae (C O.157.2–3).

A frequent category of objects, especially in the "House of Hanni" but also at many Iron Age sites, consists of bone spatulae (*Fig. 279*). They are thin and elongated, pointed at one end and rounded at the other. Their function is uncertain. It is possible that they were used in the production of fine textiles, as suggested by Jean-Marc Doyen,[9] for instance to compact the weft yarns.

Lastly, we must mention another frequent category of objects, namely spindle-whorls, which are also found at Tell Ahmar as well as at other ancient sites. They are small objects in the shape of a flattened cone with a vertical perforation, which were used to give weight to the handle of a distaff. They were generally made of stone and primarily found in domestic contexts.

5. Objects of everyday use

a. Lamps

Several lamps or fragments of lamps have come to light. They consist of small bowls with a wide rim and a pinched spout, usually referred to as "saucer lamps" (*Fig. 280*).[10]

Fig. 281. Limestone stand (C O.84).

Light is produced by the burning end of a wick which, placed in the spout, sucks oil from the lamp's body through the effect of capillarity. The blackish colour of the spout results from the burning of the wick.

From the burial vault of Area C comes a "pedestal lamp", or a "saucer lamp", supported by a hollow pedestal standing in a bowl (*Fig. 220*). A handle connects the lamp to the bowl. The Nimrud excavations yielded a similar object, which, however, is made of bronze and lacks the handle.[11] It is interesting to note that both the Tell Ahmar and Nimrud pedestal lamps come from a tomb.

b. Stands

Another relatively common category of object includes stands consisting of a cylindrical body, a bowl or platter-like top and a disc base (*Fig. 281*).[12] These objects were made of limestone or terracotta. They may have been used as stands to support a lamp or an incense burner.

c. Fibulae

These large safety pins or brooches used to fasten garments were generally made of bronze, less frequently of iron. Sometimes the bow was made of bronze and the pin of iron. Two types are documented at Tell Ahmar: bent or triangular fibulae (*Fig. 282*) and arched fibulae (*Fig. 283*). Subtypes can be defined according to the decoration, which consisted of an alternation of rings and balls arranged in varying patterns. The relative stylistic homogeneity of the fibulae across the empire is better explained by trade than by local production.

d. Cosmetic palettes

Two small bowls, 8.6 cm and 10 cm in diameter (*Fig. 284*), made of white stone – perhaps dolomite – belong to a type usually defined as cosmetic palettes. Unfortunately, they lack an archaeological context as they were found on the surface, but they must date from the eighth/seventh century. The central depression was intended to grind or mix cosmetic substances. The wide edge was incised with a geometric decoration. Such objects were relatively common in Phoenicia and Palestine during the Iron Age, but not much so in northern Syria.[13]

e. Weights

The industrial and commercial activities were only possible with the help of a system of weights and measures. Texts are of little help to determine the standards in use at Til Barsib/Kar-Shalmaneser. Sheqel, mina and talent can be mentioned, but in only one case is it specified that the weight used is the "mina of Carchemish" (T15, 2').

Actual weights were found. Some were duck-shaped. The practice of shaping weights in the form of a duck, often depicted lying down with the head turned back, dates back to the third millennium and was still flourishing in Assyrian times. A small bronze duck was found in a pit dug in the wall separating Room 1 from Room 2 in Building C5 (*Fig. 285*). Its weight, 24.8 g, is worth three light shekels of the Assyro-Babylonian system according to a personal communication by Carlo Zaccagnini. Interestingly, it does not turn its head back. The rings placed around its neck were probably added to give the object the desired weight.

Small stone or iron cubes (*Fig. 286*), as well as stone or terracotta balls (*Fig. 287*), found in various places, may also have been used as weights. The cubes shown in *Figure 286* weigh, from left to right, 20.2 g, 4.3 g and 1.4 g and the balls in *Figure 287*, from left to right and top to bottom, weigh 107.4 g, 34,5 g, 14.4 g, 17.9 g, and 22.3 g

Fig. 282. *Triangular bronze fibula (C O.394; Aleppo M 12420).*

Fig. 283. *Arched bronze fibula (C O.115+68).*

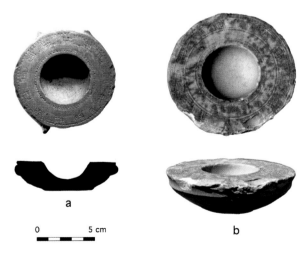

Fig. 284. *Cosmetic palettes (a: Aleppo M 12427; b: Aleppo M 12426).*

Fig. 285. Duck-shaped bronze weight (C O.1557; Aleppo M 10978).

Fig. 286. Iron and limestone cubes (C O.36; C O.522; S O.166).

Fig. 287. Stone and terracotta balls (C O.485; C O.96; C O.487; C O.92.04; C O.1484).

6. Food processing

Bread must have been, at that time as much as today, an essential part of the diet. This is evidenced by the number of grinders and ovens of the *tannur* type that have been discovered in the Assyrian level. On the other hand, it is surprising to see how many animal bones were found in the fills that accumulated in the rooms of the large residential buildings. However, there is a lack of information about where the animals were slaughtered and the process that brought meat to the place of consumption. One thing is striking, however. According to a preliminary study by Geoff Irvin, the animal remains included a large number of pork bones (about 38% in Area C). Less surprisingly, there were also a large number of sheep bones (about 54% in Area C). Cattle, however, lagged far behind with 3.50% in Area C. It can be seen that, in ancient times as today, sheep meat was more prized than beef but, unlike today, pork was also widely consumed.

The objects described in this section are considered in terms of their possible role in food preparation. It should be borne in mind, however, that many of them might have been used in craft activities. This is the case, for example, with grinding implements or large containers.

a. Grinding tools

Three kinds of objects were used for grinding, most of them made of basalt.[14] The most common, intended to grind cereals, was a quern consisting of two parts (*Fig. 288*). The upper part, the "handstone", was an oval stone with a rounded top and a flat base, sometimes manipulated by a stick fixed, often with bitumen, in a groove made in its top. The lower part, the "base", was a larger stone with a flat and slightly concave surface. By pushing the upper stone back and forth on the lower stone, it was possible to reduce to flour a small quantity of grain.

The second kind of grinding tool consisted of large mortar bowls, in which the grain was crushed (*Fig. 289*). This produced a coarser grind, probably to prepare a form of food similar to what the villagers today call *burghul*

Fig. 288. The two components of a basalt hand mill.

Fig. 289. Basalt mortar (C BsL156).

Fig. 291. Basalt pestle (C BsL176).

Fig. 290. Four-legged basalt dish decorated with two bull's heads (CJ4 BsL2; Aleppo M 12430).

Fig. 292. Basalt bowl (C BsL259+650.1.2).

(often known as *bulghur*), *i.e.* wheat boiled, dried in the sun and crushed to be prepared like rice.

A third kind of grinding tool included small rectangular dishes resting on four legs. Two of these legs were often decorated with bull's heads (*Fig. 290*). In some cases, the interior surface of the dish, often slightly hollow, was so smooth that it looked polished. These dishes were another form of mortar used to grind or crush fine substances, perhaps spices or material for make-up. The grinding was made by small, cone-shaped pestles with a convex base (*Fig. 291*).

There were also shallow bowls made of very fine basalt (*Fig. 292*). They may have been used as mortars as well as dishes. Some of them could be mounted on three legs.

b. Ovens

Cooking was done in small ovens usually referred to by the Arabic name *tannur*. These were terracotta cylinders with a diameter of approximately 50 cm. The cylinder was consolidated and held in vertical position by a thick mass of clay. The fuel was placed in the bottom of the oven. Bread could be baked by applying a thin rolled-out piece of dough on its inner walls and cooking could be done by placing a pot on top of the terracotta cylinder, or on a grid or a metal plate covering the opening. This type of oven was not specific to the Assyrian period. It is found in large numbers in all periods and at all sites in Western Asia and is still in use today.

c. Containers for food preservation and consumption

The preservation, preparation and consumption of food must have been done not only in ceramic containers but also in metal utensils, mainly bronze and, in exceptional cases, silver. However, as metal objects have disappeared only pottery remains to give an idea of how food was treated.[15]

Ceramic imitations of models made of other materials can be recognized here and there. For example, an important part of the ceramic crockery consisted of containers, especially plates, covered with a red slip, hence the name "Red Slip" given to this category of ceramics (*Fig. 298e, Fig. b1*, p. 187). The purpose of this may have been to imitate copper or bronze prototypes. Another possible imitation was the so-called "Palace Ware" (*Fig. a5*, p. 187). It was characterized by a very fine paste and very thin walls decorated with dimple impressions at regular intervals. The manufacture of such objects must have been extremely delicate and the decoration was not of the kind that comes naturally to mind when working with clay. One may wonder whether the Palace Ware was not imitating vases and goblets made of other materials such as metal or, perhaps, glass. Also to be mentioned is a fine grey ceramic which reproduced the colour and shapes of similar objects made of basalt, such as simple bowls and tripod bowls.

Concerning the use of the various types of pottery, broad categories can be defined according to their transportability, which, combined with specific attributes, may give information about their possible function. They could be designed to stay in place (storage), to be transported (over a short or long distance), or to be easily manipulated (consumption).

In the first category were large jars, which, even empty, must have been difficult to transport. They are generally regarded as storage devices (*Fig. 293*). Some were sunk into the ground with only the neck visible on the surface, others may have been placed in the niches near the entrance to the living/reception rooms of the large residential buildings. They were intended to contain water that could be drawn for drinking or for washing hands or feet. No clear evidence for the storage of foodstuff, such as cereals, oil or wine, has been found. However, this does not preclude their use for such a purpose.

The second category consisted of medium-size containers. Some were a few dozen centimetres high and therefore easy to handle with both hands. They may have been used for both transport and short-term storage. For example, jars with an ovoid body and a pointed base, which were characteristic of the Neo-Assyrian period (*Fig. 294a*), may have been used to carry wine, milk or water, from their storage place to the consumption area.

The medium-size category also included pots, made of extremely brittle clay, certainly used for cooking (*Fig. 295*). This is clear from the blackish marks left by the fire. They were generally over 20 cm in diameter and height, and could also be easily handled, for instance to fill the serving containers.

Still in the medium-size category were containers, 20 or 30 cm in diameter. Some had small handles and a restricted

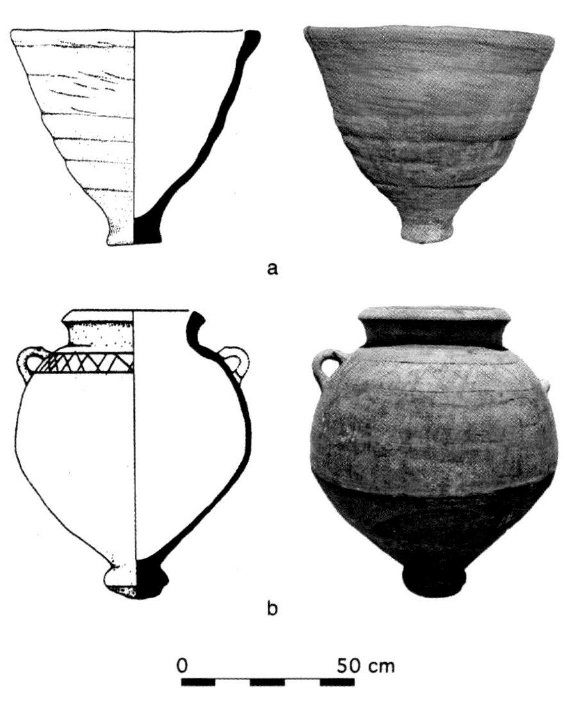

Fig. 293. Large storage jars (a: C PL3289; b: C PL8712) (drawings: Andrew S. Jamieson).

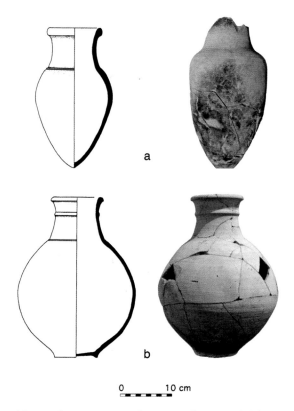

Fig. 294. Medium-size jar with a pointed or rounded base (a: C PL7822 & C PL603; b: C PL4609) (drawings: Andrew S. Jamieson).

opening (*Fig. 296*), others were open bowls (*Fig. 297*). This type of vessel may have been used to present the guests with liquid or semi-liquid food. They may also have contained a drinking liquid, like the Greek craters. It is hard to imagine that they could have been used for the long-term preservation of any food.

The third category consisted of various pottery types that could be lifted with one hand. Some dishes, a few centimetres high and 20–30 cm in diameter, were not without analogy to modern plates (*Fig. 298*). They may have been intended for individual consumption but could also have been used to present portions of various foods from which guests could help themselves. In the same category of easy to carry vessels were small jugs, about 15–20 cm high, which may have been used to pour liquid in goblets or cups (*Fig. 299*).

Small bottles, less than 20 cm high, may have been used in the food consumption process, but not necessarily so.

They had no handle and were best suited to contain a liquid, such as perfume or oil for toiletry (*Fig. 300*).

Last in the third category were small bowls, or goblets, that could be filled with a drink (*Fig. 301a–c*), as is shown on some reliefs. Another category of drinking

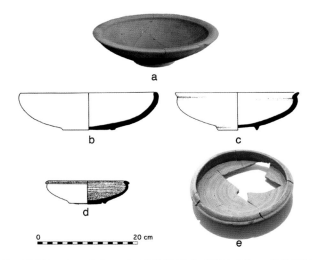

Fig. 298. Bowls and plates (a: C PL7023; b: C PL2555; c: C PL2831; d: C PL3742; e: C PL567) (drawings: Andrew S. Jamieson).

Fig. 295. Cooking pot (C PL685) (drawing: Andrew S. Jamieson).

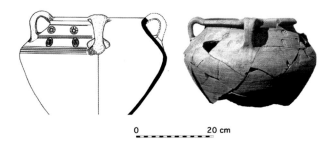

Fig. 296. Medium-size closed bowl with stamped decoration (C PL388) (drawing: Andrew S. Jamieson).

Fig. 299. Jugs (a: C PL7847; b: C PL81.59).

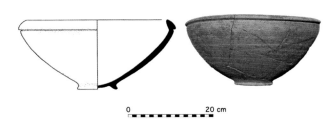

Fig. 297. Medium-size open bowl (C PL3832) (drawing: Andrew S. Jamieson).

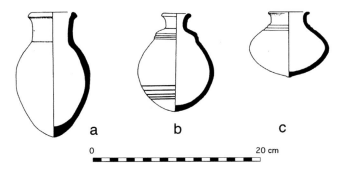

Fig. 300. Small bottles (a: C PL7102; b: C PL7638; c: C PL704) (drawings: Andrew S. Jamieson).

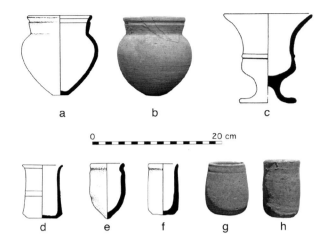

Fig. 302. Pottery stand (C P2087) (drawing: Andrew S. Jamieson).

Fig. 301. Goblets (a: C PL701; b: C PL3529; c: C PL542; d: C PL7849; e: C PL24; f: C PL7849; g: C PL3321; h: C PL8909) (drawings: Andrew S. Jamieson).

vessels consisted of approximately cylindrical cups, about 10 cm high, sometimes referred to as *istikan* after similar goblets used today for drinking tea (*Fig. 301d-h*). Their small capacity indicates that they must have contained a liquid consumed in small quantity. They are not without

analogy with the cups found in the third millennium temple (above, *Fig. 59*, p. 39).

In addition to these groups, we should mention objects in the shape of a hollow cylinder with a flaring base, that were not directly associated with food consumption (*Fig. 302*). They could have served as stands for containers whose rounded base prevented them from being placed on a flat surface.

In concluding this review, it is important to note that all these ceramic forms can be found both in Assyria and in the provinces. They show once again the cultural homogeneity of the empire at its apogee. They also show the interdependence between the heart of the empire and its marches.

Neo-Assyrian pottery between East and West (Andrew S. Jamieson)

The pottery from the Neo-Assyrian residential buildings of Area C comprised 255,825 items, including diagnostic and body sherds, as well as many complete or reconstructable vessels. Key ceramic diagnostics enable this pottery to be dated to the seventh century, and more specifically to the second half of the seventh century. In addition, the uniformity and homogeneity of the pottery corpus reinforces a relatively short period of use.[1]

In all instances, the ware types that were identified at Tell Ahmar relate to known Neo-Assyrian fabrics that are documented at other Neo-Assyrian sites. The different technical attributes of the Area C pottery also reflect different systems of production.

Typology

The Neo-Assyrian pottery from Area C may be readily divided into seventeen ware types, which can be grouped into three main groups.

1) The first group is characterized by low firing temperatures, soft hardness and hand-made methods of construction suggesting localized levels of production. It includes Coarse Ware (COW) and Cooking Pot Ware (CPW) (*Fig. 295*).

2) The second group consists of wheel-made fabrics that are characterized by high rates of uniformity. They appear to be highly utilitarian and probably produced by large-scale pottery industries. Such are the Common Ware (CW) (*Fig. a1*), Tall Jar Ware (TJW) (*Fig. 293b*), Stamped Ware (STMW) (*Figs 296* and *a2*), Tell Sheikh Hamad Ware (TSHW) (*Fig. a3*), and Plain Crisp Ware (PCW).

3) The third group, although appearing relatively infrequently, is characterized by wheel-made, high fired products that exhibit considerable investment in the application of different surface treatments. They include Red Slip Ware (RSW) (*Figs 298e* and *b1*), Palace Ware (PW) (*Fig. a5*), Fine Ware (FW)

(*Fig. a6*), Grey Ware (GW) (*Fig. a4*), Painted Ware (PATW) (*Fig. b2*), Incised Ware (INCW), Glazed Ware (GLZW) (*Fig. b3*), Cypriot Ware (CYPW) (*Fig. 270*), Bi-Chrome Ware (BCW) (*Fig. b5*) and Phoenician Ware (PHOW) (*Fig. b4*).

Many of the pottery types are of a highly domestic nature and most vessels appear to have been used to cook, store, prepare, serve or transport various foods and liquids. Vessels that are not of a specific domestic nature (*e.g.* RSW, PW, FW, GW, TJW), particularly vessels of specialized methods of manufacture (*e.g.* GLZW, PATW, INCW, STMW), and vessels of external origin (*e.g.* CYPW, PHOW, BCW, PCW, TSHW), occur less frequently and have less immediate domestic functions.

It is apparent that the Tell Ahmar Area C assemblage of Neo-Assyrian-style pottery was enriched by ceramic imports from Anatolia, Cyprus, Phoenicia and Northern Mesopotamia. In some instances, it is possible that the presence of these external products at Tell Ahmar relates to contents of these vessels.

Relations with Assyria

The greatest and closest parallels of the Area C pottery are with the ceramics from the Assyrian heartland. The pottery from Fort Shalmaneser and the private dwellings in Area TW at Nimrud is most like the Area C material.[2] The pottery from these areas at Nimrud has become the best known assemblage associated with the end of the Assyrian empire. The grit tempered Common Ware, Cooking Pot Ware, Red Slip Ware, Palace Ware, Fine Ware, Grey Ware, Glazed Ware, Stamped Ware and Painted Ware are all represented in the Neo-Assyrian assemblage at Nimrud. Within these wares, many of the individual types find exact parallels with the pottery from Area C at Tell Ahmar. The high number of similar wares and shapes, particularly within the Common Ware that display classic Assyrian forms, suggests that the occupants of the buildings in Area C at Tell Ahmar were closely connected with the Neo-Assyrian heartland, at least in terms of the pottery.

However, it is important to note that despite the strong correlations with Nimrud and the Assyrian heartland sites, there are some important differences. The capital cities, like other sites in the north Mesopotamian region, lack the imported pottery which is characteristic of Neo-Assyrian sites located in the south-east and coastal Anatolian region, and the sites in the Orontes valley, and along the Syrian and Lebanese coast, and which are well represented at Tell Ahmar, albeit in disproportionate quantities.

What this pattern suggests is that the process of "Assyrianization" was in many ways selective and did not only operate in one direction. It is likely that certain sites, locations or regions, were specifically selected by

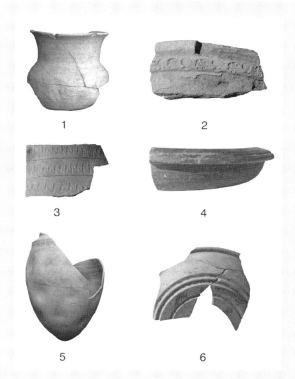

Fig. a. Pottery with monochrome surface; 1) Common Ware (CW); 2) Stamped Ware (STMW); 3) Tell Sheikh Hamad Ware (TSHW); 4) Grey Ware (GW); 5) Palace Ware (PW); 6) Fine Ware (FW).

Fig. b. Pottery with painted decoration: 1) Red Slip Ware (RSW); 2) Painted Ware (PATW); 3) Glazed Ware (GLZW); 4) Phoenician Ware (PHOW); 5) Bichrome Ware (BCW).

the Assyrians as a focus for their activities and administration. Assyrian influence appears to have pervaded all localities to some degree but at some sites this interest is far more evident and pronounced than in others. It is also apparent that at some sites, such as Tell Ahmar, a strongly Neo-Assyrian-styled assemblage could be enriched by external ceramic imports, which are not encountered in the capitals.

The material found at Tell Ahmar demonstrates the degree to which Assyrian culture could be strongly transmitted and replicated in the peripheral regions of the Empire, whilst at the same time the situation at Tell Ahmar also maintains elements unique to that location and specific to that region.

Notes

1   For more details see A.S. Jamieson, *Neo-Assyrian Pottery from Area C*, Tell Ahmar III, Ancient Near Eastern Studies Supplement 35, Leuven-Paris-Walpole (MA), 2012.

2   A.S. Jamieson, Processes of Assyrianisation: Identity and connectivity in Neo-Assyrian ceramics and the Tell Ahmar Area C pottery, *Identity and Connectivity: Proceedings of the 16th symposium on Mediterranean archaeology* (Florence, Italy, 1–3 March 2012), I, ed. L. Bombardieri, A. D'Agostino, G. Guarducci, V. Orsi, & S. Valentini, Oxford 2013, pp. 75–88.

* * *

Both the Hanni archives and the artefacts found in the large residences of the Assyrian period show a society involved in business transactions – lending money, buying slaves – and craft activities, particularly textile production and metallurgy. The general framework is that of a cosmopolitan society in relation with the heart of the empire as well as the Mediterranean regions and Asia Minor. Pottery, most of all, illustrates these interactions.

However, as the material recovered comes from large residences, it mainly concerns an economic and presumably also political elite. We do not know how the peasants and small craftsmen lived. We also do not know what role the army played in local life, although the military presence in a provincial capital – and, moreover, at an important station on the road from Assyria to Egypt – must have been significant. Anyhow, we see that military equipment was kept and repaired in the city.

Tell Ahmar was definitely at the crossroads of multiple interfering cultural paths.

Notes

1   S. Dalley, Neo-Assyrian tablets from Til Barsib, *Abr-Nahrain* 34 (1996–1997), pp. 66–99; P. Bordreuil & F. Briquel-Chatonnet, Aramaic documents from Til Barsib, *ibid.*, pp. 100–107; F.M. Fales, K. Radner, C. Pappi & E. Attardo, The Assyrian and Aramaic texts from Tell Shiukh Fawqani, *Tell Shiukh Fawqani 1994–1998*, ed. L. Bachelot & F.M. Fales, Padua 2005, pp. 607–610; A. Lemaire, *Nouvelles tablettes araméennes*, École pratique des hautes études, Sciences historiques et philologiques II, Hautes études orientales 34, Moyen et Proche-Orient 1, Geneva 2001, pp. 127–129; K. Radner, A Neo-Assyrian tablet from Til Barsib, *Nouvelles asyriologiques brèves et utilitaires* 2004, no 26, pp. 25–27, and no 82, p. 83. The texts are available online at <http://oracc.museum.upenn.edu/atae/tilbarsip/pager>.

2   A.R. Millard, with a contribution by R. Whiting, *The Eponyms of the Assyrian Empire 910–612 B.C.*, State Archives of Assyria Studies II, Helsinki 1994.

3   J.E. Reade, Assyrian eponyms, kings and pretenders, 648–605 BC, *Orientalia* NS 67 (1998), pp. 255–265.

4   PNA 2/I, s.v. Ḥannî 7, p. 454 (R. Mattila & M. P. Streck).

5   *Til-Barsib*, p. 131 (G. Dossin).

6   F.M. Fales *et al.*, *art. cit.* (n. 1), p. 608.

7   S. Dalley, *art. cit.* (n. 1), pp. 80–82.

8   V. Verardi, A metallurgist workshop at Tell Ahmar, Syria, *Akkadica* 128 (2007), pp. 109–116.

9   J.-M. Doyen, L'outillage en os des sites de Tell Abou Danne et d'Oum el-Marra (campagnes 1975–1983): quelques aspects de l'artisanat en Syrie du Nord du IIIème au Ier millénaire, *Akkadica* 47 (March/April 1986), pp. 30–74.

10 A.S. Jamieson, *Neo-Assyrian Pottery from Area C*, Tell Ahmar III, Ancient Near Eastern Studies Supplement 35, Leuven-Paris-Walpole (MA), 2012, p. 76.

11 J. Oates & D. Oates, *Nimrud: An Assyrian Imperial City Revealed*, London 2001, fig. 48, p. 88.

12 A. Squitieri, *Stone Vessels in the Near East During the Iron Age and the Persian Period (c. 1200–330 BCE)*, Archaeopress Ancient Near Eastern Archaeology 2, Oxford 2017, p. 44 (see especially fig. 5.5.a, p. 48)

13 A. Squitieri, *op. cit.* (n. 12), pp. 58–59.

14 A general description of the stone implements from Tell Ahmar can be found in A. Squitieri, *op. cit.* (n. 12), pp. 164–166.

15 The ceramic material from Area C is extensively discussed by A.S. Jamieson, *op. cit.* (n. 10).

Epilogue

The end of Tell Ahmar

1. The end of the Assyrian city

The Medes, allied with the Babylonians, captured Nineveh in 612. This did not mark the end of the Assyrian kingdom. The administration and the court withdrew to Harran and the region between the Euphrates and the Habur, that is to the area where Tell Ahmar was located, where they perpetuated for some years the fiction of a powerful Assyria. It is therefore unlikely that the site had to suffer violence when the heart of the empire fell into the hands of the Medes and the Babylonians. The war between the Egyptians and the Babylonians in 605 in the region of Carchemish, and thus very close to Tell Ahmar, does not seem to have dramatically affected the site either. Neither the palace on the Acropolis, nor the residential buildings excavated in Areas C and E show traces of fire in the levels corresponding to the last occupation phase of these buildings. The only exception is the residential building of Area D, close to the West Gate of the site. The overall impression, however, is that the site was abandoned.

The most likely explanation is that Tell Ahmar had lost all geo-political significance by the end of the seventh century. The city was no longer a bridge between western regions and an empire centred on Upper Mesopotamia. It had acquired this role in the ninth century, because Carchemish, who controlled the region, was still too powerful to be attacked head-on. It had maintained it because the empire needed it. It lost it at the end of the seventh century, because the empire no longer existed. Carchemish, as shown by the Egyptian–Babylonian war, was regaining its place, even if only for a short period.

Be that as it may, Tell Ahmar lost its status as a regional centre with the fall of the Assyrian empire. A good indication of this is that its fate under Babylonian rule is unknown. Both written documentation and archaeology are silent on this point. However, the last and ill-defined occupation phase of the "House of Hanni" (Phase C/2a) may point to the survival, in the early days of Babylonian rule, of a lifestyle that can still be regarded as Assyrian.

Such was the case in Dur-Katlimmu, on the lower reaches of the Habur, as is demonstrated by tablets that are Assyrian in appearance but date from the Babylonian period.[1]

2. The Achaemenid period

The Achaemenid domination is only represented by a few graves. Seven tombs dated to the Achaemenid period have been recognized on the Acropolis by the Thureau-Dangin expedition,[2] which included four jar burials, two burials in bathtub sarcophagi and one grave of undefined nature. The material deposited in these tombs consisted, among other things, of various bronze utensils, ornamental objects such as rings and fibulae, semi-precious stone beads as well as stamp seals and scarabs, sometimes engraved with inscriptions in Aramaic or Egyptian hieroglyphs.

In the Middle Town, three tombs, or installations that may have been tombs, can be mentioned. One, Tomb C2 F4, had been dug in the south-west wall of Room 2 of Building C1b (*Fig. 303*). It consisted of a round, downward-flaring pit, about 1 m deep, covering a second, narrow, elongated pit in which a body could have been placed. This pit, however, was completely empty. The fill in the upper pit contained pottery sherds and a bronze bowl from the Achaemenid period (*Fig. 304*).

Another installation that might point to the presence of an Achaemenid burial was uncovered in the C5 building complex (*Fig. 305*). A terracotta bathtub (C62 F1942) had been buried in Room 3 from a later level than the level of the building complex. Although it did not contain any bone remains, it was probably a sarcophagus of the type already encountered in the Assyrian burial vault of Area C.

The only indisputable Achaemenid grave found in the Middle Town was discovered in Area CJ4 (Tomb CJ4 F.32) (*Fig. 306*) in the remains of the metallurgy workshop described in the previous chapter (pp. 175–179). It was an in-ground burial consisting of an oval of mud-bricks lined

Fig. 303. Area C: Achaemenid burial (?) dug in the SW wall of Room 2 of Building C1b (C2 F4).

Fig. 304. Area C: Achaemenid bronze bowl from possible Burial C2 F4 (C O.118).

with stones, within which a quadrangular pit also lined with stones had been dug. The body had been laid down in the central pit. A few objects were retrieved from the tomb, namely a small jar (*Fig. 307d*), a bronze bowl (*Fig. 307c*), a fibula made of the same metal (*Fig. 307a*) and a marble cylinder seal, which still had its bronze setting (*Fig. 307b*). The seal was engraved with a scene representing a king pulling a shackled prisoner and holding a wild goat by one of its hind legs.

Other pits had the appearance of tombs although they contained neither bones nor offerings. Such was the case for a rectangular pit with smooth mud-plastered walls (C4+9 F49), which was dug in the fill of Room 2 of Building C1b (*Fig. 308*). One of the shorter sides had a kind of rounded recess as to make room for the head. Another example was an elongated oval-shaped pit with bricks along its side, which was dug in the fill of Courtyard 3 of Building C1a, along the wall of Room 4 (C21 F241a) (*Fig. 309*). Both these pits were large enough to accommodate a body and, despite the absence of corroborating evidence, it is difficult to imagine what other function they might have had.

The place of residence of the living is unknown. This lack of evidence must undoubtedly be seen in the light of a global change in the structure of settlement in Western Asia, which began around the middle of the first millennium. The tells had hitherto formed the heart of the habitat which, in the case of larger settlements, extended to the surrounding area. For unknown reasons the tells were progressively abandoned. The concentration of the habitat seems to have been replaced by a more extensive or scattered occupation.

a   b

Fig. 305. Area C: Achaemenid burial (?) with a "bathtub sarcophagus", dug in Building C5 (C62 F1942) (drawing: A.S. Jamieson).

Fig. 306. Area CJ4: Achaemenid burial (CJ4 F32).

Fig. 308. Area C: Pit whose walls were coated with mud plaster (C4+9 F49).

Fig. 309. Area C: Pit in the shape of an elongated oval (C21 F241a).

Fig. 307. Area CJ4: Objects from the Achaemenid burial CJ4 F32: a) Triangular fibula (CJ4 O.32; Aleppo M 12431); b) marble cylinder seal (CJ4 O.33; Aleppo M 12432); c) bronze bowl (CJ4 O.26; Aleppo M 12433); d) jar (CJ4 PL88; Aleppo M 12434).

Today the tells are often used as cemeteries for villages situated some distance away and these villages themselves, even if they are centuries old, no longer form a tell. This profound change in land use is reflected in the few post-Neo-Assyrian remains found at Tell Ahmar and makes it difficult to locate related settlements.

3. The Greco-Roman period

On the Acropolis, the French archaeologists found carefully carved stones, some of them embossed, which would have belonged to a platform on which stood a mud brick construction.[3] Most of the blocks were scattered in the debris that covered the Assyrian palace and a few were still aligned in a north–south direction. According to Maurice Dunand, the working technique of these blocks reminded that of the small Hellenistic temple of Arslan Tash.[4]

Also found on the Acropolis, a small monetary treasure, figurines, especially moulded clay figures, ands fragments of lamps also date from the Hellenistic period. However, as was the case for the Achaemenid period, no settlement that could be dated to the Hellenistic period has been found at Tell Ahmar.

The Roman period does not seem to have left any trace on the Acropolis. In Area C, however, Roman period floors were found immediately above the Assyrian period buildings. They formed Stratum C/1. The walls associated with them were very poorly preserved. The material consisted of a few badly worn coins, fragments of glass and ceramics, among which a few pieces of terra sigillata.

The nature of the occupation appears to have changed in Roman times, not only at Tell Ahmar, but throughout the region. It seems to have intensified. Traces of occupation are indeed omnipresent on both banks of the Euphrates until the beginning of the Byzantine period.[5] It can be assumed that settlements consisted of villages, *i.e.* grouped settlements, and rural settlements, *i.e.* farms scattered throughout the countryside. A systematic occupation policy may have been undertaken by the imperial authorities, including the settlement of veterans in the area. An inscription found on the right bank of the river opposite Tell Ahmar, in a place known as Shaqleh, was the epitaph of a Roman soldier (*Fig. 310*):[6]

> Here lies Marcus, son of Goras, standard-bearer of the First Cohort of the Ascalonites, of the Century of Claudianus. He served twenty-five years in the army (and) lived fifty years, a native of Emesa.

He may have been, as Pierre-Louis Gatier assumed, a soldier who died during operations on the Euphrates. He could also

Fig. 310. Funerary inscription of a Roman soldier (Aleppo).

have been a demobilized soldier who had received land in the region. The inscription would date from the late first or early second century CE.

The role of the Euphrates, both as a border and as a buffer zone between the Roman and Iranian empires, does not seem to have prevented the development of occupation in the region. It may even have favoured it. The name Til Barsib, in the form *Bersiba*, was still known to Ptolemy in the second century CE.[7] The changes in land use, observed after the fall of the Assyrian empire, may thus have intensified during the last centuries of antiquity.

4. Eclipse, flood, rebirth and chaos

From the Islamic conquest to the nineteenth century, Tell Ahmar's fate is shrouded in darkness. A few sporadic finds are not sufficient to attest a continuous occupation. The existence of the modern village can be traced back until the nineteenth century, but we do not know when the tell received its name of "Red Hill", which, as we saw, probably comes from the colour of the bricks that consolidated its sides during the Neo-Assyrian period.

The completion of the Tishrin Dam in July 1999 caused the flooding of part of the village, while most of the houses that had not been flooded were abandoned. The villagers carried away everything they could, in particular doors, window frames and the logs that supported the roofs. Only walls remained (*Fig. 311*). In 2000, the village had the desolate appearance of a bombed village. The still standing walls started to collapse. Mud-bricks returned to mud. Craters formed where once there had been houses. Life, however, did not give up. A few craters were levelled to allow trees to grow. Vegetable gardens sprang up. New houses were built.

Violence, however, came back. Troops fought for the control of the village during the recent civil war. Houses just rebuilt were destroyed again. The inhabitants were driven out. The Acropolis was bulldozed and became a military station. The geographical advantages that had made the prosperity of ancient Tell Ahmar caused the ruin of the modern village.

Fig. 311. The Lower Town seen from the modern road in year 2000.

After the excavations: The conservation of archaeological finds (Andrew S. Jamieson)

A problem that every archaeological mission has to face is the conservation of the various objects and finds that the museums, due to lack of space, cannot accept in their storage facilities. This material is, however, of great interest for archaeological research and should be available to anyone interested. A Syro-Australian initiative is seeking to solve this problem.

A Syrian-Australian Archaeological Research Collaboration Project commenced in 2008: a joint partnership involving the University of Melbourne and the National Museum of Aleppo.[1] One of the project aims is to develop an artefact repository for archaeological collections from the Euphrates River valley in northern Syria. The combined salvage excavations conducted by Syrian and other international missions in the Euphrates valley generated large quantities of archaeological artefacts. Many of the most significant finds from the excavations from the Tabqa and Tishrin Dams are on display in the National Museum of Aleppo, where a special permanent exhibition is devoted to the finds from this region. However, it was not possible for the museum in Aleppo to accommodate all the material generated from these rescue operations. So that the Euphrates valley material is available and accessible in the future, an alternative location was needed for the storage of these important archaeological collections.

A potential repository was identified by the late Hamido Hammade at Qalaat Nejem (Qalat Najm, Qal'at Nağim), located on the right bank of the Euphrates River, overlooking the Tishrin reservoir, approximately 20 km from the modern town of Menbij (Fig. a). The large Arab fortress at Qalaat Nejem marks an important crossing point on the Euphrates River. The Syrian Directorate General of Antiquities and Museums (DGAM) have carried out major restoration works at Qalaat Nejem over many years. The extant remains of Qalaat Nejem largely date from the thirteenth century CE rebuilding of the fortress. Whilst it is

Fig. a. The fortress of Qalaat Nejem (photo: Andrew S. Jamieson).

Fig. b. Qalaat Nejem: Tell Ahmar pottery stored in a room of the fortress (photo: Andrew S. Jamieson).

widely acknowledged that the Arab military architecture of Qalaat Nejem is historically significant, its full potential, for tourism and other adaptive reuses, has not been fully investigated or explored. The large galleries and chambers at Qalaat Nejem have the potential and capacity to accommodate the archaeological collections from the excavations in the Euphrates valley that cannot be housed by the museum of Aleppo, thus providing a much needed artefact repository.

Before the Syrian conflict, the Syrian-Australian Archaeological Research Collaboration Project developed a broad research framework involving the following four stages.

Stage one: The establishment of an archaeological collections repository

In 2010 work began on the first stage with creation of the repository. As a pilot study, the stratified Neo-Assyrian pottery from the excavations in Area C at Tell Ahmar was relocated to Qalaat Nejem (Fig. b). It is planned to use this diagnostic well-dated seventh century corpus as a model of one curated collection to be applied to other collections to be deposited at Qalaat Nejem.

Stage two: The creation of a research centre for archaeological reference collections

In 2010 preliminary work also began developing a regional historical research framework. In managing the archaeological collections, such as those from the Euphrates valley their significance must be assessed not only with reference to the research design of the archaeological project that recovered and created them, but also from an understanding of wider regional and national research frameworks to which they may be able to contribute new information. The development of a research framework may be used to identify research priorities, thereby situating site-specific projects in a broader context and providing access to cumulative knowledge about particular site-types and artefact assemblages. Importantly, research frameworks can inform judgements about the relative significance of archaeological sites and collections. This information assists heritage agencies and antiquities organizations to manage repositories and to justify the allocation of resources. Artefact collections that can provide data for rarely addressed areas of research should be considered to have greater research potential than those that provide data for more commonly published, and possibly exhausted, research topics.

Stage three: The promotion of education, interpretation and public programs

Unfortunately, owing to the crisis in Syria it has not been possible to return to Qalaat Nejem to continue with the implementation and development of the project. However, when it is safe to do so, it is envisaged that Qalaat Nejem may serve as a research and education facility in which a variety of learning and interpretation activities could inform local and international visitors about the history of the Euphrates valley. It is envisaged this would include displays on selected key sites and selected archaeological collections from the Euphrates valley and information on Qalaat Nejem reinforcing and enhancing the site's historical importance within the context of the history of the region. It is also planned to include material and information about the culture and heritage of the modern era inhabitants who have added an important dimension to the life along the Euphrates valley.

Stage four: The identification of community engagement opportunities and tourism-related activities

With the modern inhabitants of the Euphrates valley in mind the Qalaat Nejem project aspires to offer opportunities for local communities and acknowledge the importance of integrating local historical knowledge, by bringing this knowledge to the foreground and acknowledging these groups. It is hoped that the project at Qalaat Nejem will provide local communities an opportunity to manage the cultural heritage in their area and attract tourists in a project aimed at developing the local economy and raising awareness about managing and preserving the archaeological heritage of the Euphrates valley region. The project would provide training opportunities and promote the importance of Qalaat Nejem across Syria, encourage sustainable tourism, and develop ways to generate income for the local community using the archaeology of the region through interpretation and presentation at the historic site.

The Syrian-Australian Archaeological Research Collaboration Project believes that the proposed objectives at Qalaat Nejem are considered to be highly complementary to the sites historical importance providing benefits not just for the castle but also for the storage of archaeological collections of the Euphrates valley region as well as providing opportunities for tourism-related activities and engagement with the local communities.

Note

1   A.s. JAMIESON & Y. KANJOU, Archaeological research by the University of Melbourne in the Middle and Upper Euphrates Valley, North Syria, *The Artefact* 32/1 (2009), pp. 1–30; A. JAMIESON & D. FITZPATRICK, Sustainable management strategies for Near Eastern archaeological collections, *Proceedings of the 8th International Congress on the Archaeology of the Ancient Near East 30 April–4 May 2012, University of Warsaw*, III, ed. P. BIELIŃSKI et al., Wiesbaden 2014, pp. 251–268.

Notes

1   The tablets are published and commented by H. KÜHNE, J.N. POSTGATE, W. RÖLLIG, J.A. BRINKMAN & F.M. FALES in *State Archive of Assyria Bulletin* 7/2 (1993), pp. 75–150. The archaeological aspect is dealt with by F.J. KREPPNER, The collapse of the Assyrian empire and the continuity of ceramic culture: The case of the Red House at Tall Sheikh Hamad, *Ancient Near Eastern Studies* 45 (2008), pp. 147–165.

2   Til-Barsib, pp. 75–80 (M. Dunand).

3   Til-Barsib, pp. 81–83 (M. Dunand).

4   Til-Barsib, p. 81.

5   A. EGE VIVANCOS, 'Eufratense et Osrhoene': Poblamiento romano en el Alto Éufrates sirio, Antigüedad y Cristianismo 22, Murcia 2005.

6   P.-L. GATIER, Une inscription latine du moyen Euphrate, *Syria* 71 (1994), pp. 151–157.

7   PTOLEMY, *Geographia* 5.17.5.

Field work at Tell Ahmar: Selected bibliography

First research

BELL, G.L., The east bank of the Euphrates from Tell Ahmar to Hit, *Geographical Journal* 36 (1910), 513–537 (513–515 for Tell Ahmar).

BELL, G.L., *Amurath to Amurath*, London 1911 (2nd ed. 1924), 26–34.

BELL, G.L., Her letters, diaries and photographs are available at <https://research.ncl.ac.uk/gertrudebell/gertrudebellarchive/>. See in particular the *Diaries* of 17, 18 and 19 February 1909, and the letters dated 17, 18 and 19 February 1909.

HOGARTH, D.G., Carchemish and its neighbourhood, *Liverpool Annals of Archaeology and Anthropology* 2 (1909), 165–184 (177–183 for Tell Ahmar).

LAWRENCE, T.E., Letter Carchemish, Sunday about April 16, 1911 (formerly available at <http://www.telstudies.org/writings/letters/1911/110416_family.shtml>) and Carchemish, May 16, 1911 (formerly available at <http://www.telstudies.org/writings/letters/1911/110516_family.shtml>).

PERDRIZET, P., Les travaux de la mission Perdrizet en septembre 1925, *Syria* 6 (1925), 299–300.

THOMPSON, R.C., Til-Barsip and its cuneiform inscriptions, *Proceedings of the Society of Biblical Archaeology* 34 (1912), 66–74.

French excavations

DUNAND, M., La décoration d'un palais assyrien au VIIIe siècle avant notre ère, *Gazette des Beaux Arts* 1930/II, 205–215.

THOMAS, A., *Les peintures murales du palais de Tell Ahmar: Les couleurs de l'empire assyrien*, Dijon-Paris 2019.

THUREAU–DANGIN, F., Tell Ahmar, *Syria* 10 (1929), 185–205.

THUREAU–DANGIN, F., Un spécimen des peintures assyriennes de Til-Barsib, *Syria* 11 (1930), 113–132.

THUREAU–DANGIN, F., L'inscription des lions de Til-Barsib, *Revue d'Assyriologie* 27 (1930), 11–21.

THUREAU–DANGIN, F. & DUNAND, M., *Til-Barsib*, BAH 23 (2 vols), Paris 1936.

Australian and Belgian excavations

Tell Ahmar I = BUNNENS, G. (ed.), *Tell Ahmar 1988 Season*, Supplement to Abr-Nahrain 2, Leuven 1990.

Tell Ahmar II = BUNNENS, G., *A New Luwian Stele and the Cult of the Storm-God at Til Barsib-Masuwari*, with a chapter by D.J. HAWKINS and a contribution by I. LEIRENS, Publications de la Mission archéologique de l'Université de Liège en Syrie, Publications of the Archaeological Expedition to Tell Ahmar, II, Leuven-Paris-Dudley (MA) 2006.

Tell Ahmar III = JAMIESON, A.S., *Neo-Assyrian Pottery from Area C*, Ancient Near Eastern Studies Supplement 35, Leuven-Paris-Walpole (MA) 2012.

ABBATE, L., Wall-paintings from a Neo-Assyrian building at Til Barsib, *Abr-Nahrain* 32 (1994), 7–16.

BACCARIN, C., Burial practices in the middle Euphrates area during the early Bronze Age: The contribution of the hypogeum of Tell Ahmar (north Syria), *Broadening Horizons 3. Conference of Young Researchers Working in the Ancient Near East*, ed. F. BORRELL TENA, M. BOUSO GARCÍA, A. GÓMEZ BACH, C. TORNERO DACASA & O. VICENTE CAMPOS, Bellaterra (Barcelona) 2012, 137–149.

BACCARIN, C., The Hypogeum of Tell Ahmar: An analysis of the monumental burial complex in the context of the Early Bronze Age funerary practice, *Ancient Near Eastern Studies* 51 (2014), 213–225.

BACCARIN, C., Child burials from Tell Ahmar (north Syria): A few examples from the Early and Middle Bronze Age, *Akkadica* 136/1 (2015), 1–16.

BACCARIN, C., Consumption in a temple? An interpretation of the ceramic repertoire of the Early Bronze Age temple at Tell Ahmar (north Syria), *Proceedings of the 9th International Congress on the Archaeology of the Ancient Near East* 3, *Reports*, ed. O. KAELIN & H.–P. MATHYS, Wiesbaden 2016, 163–175.

BUNNENS, G., Carved ivories from Til Barsib, *American Journal of Archaeology* 101 (1997), 435–450.

BUNNENS, G., Til Barsib before the Assyrians, *Annales Archéologiques Arabes Syriennes* 45–46 (2002–2003), 163–172.

BUNNENS, G., Facial mutilations on the Til Barsib wall paintings, *Fundstellen: Gesammelte Schriften zur Archäologie und Geschichte Altvorderasiens ad honorem Hartmut Kühne*, ed. D. BONATZ, R.M. CZICHON & F.J. KREPPNER, Wiesbaden 2008, 145–153.

BUNNENS, G., Assyrian empire building and aramization of culture as seen from Tell Ahmar/Til Barsib, *Interaction entre*

Assyriens et Araméens, ed. C. Kepinski & A. Tenu, *Syria* 86 (2009), 67–82.

Bunnens, G., Tell Ahmar in the Middle and Late Bronze Age, *Proceedings of the 6th International Congress on the Archaeology of the Ancient Near East, May, 5th–10th 2008, Sapienza – Università di Roma, Volume 2, Excavations, Surveys and Restorations: Reports on Recent Field Archaeology in the Near East*, ed. P. Matthiae, F. Pinnock, L. Nigro, & N. Marchetti, with the collaboration of L. Romano, Rome 2010, 111–122.

Bunnens, G., Sealing practices at Neo-Assyrian Til Barsib: Cylinders – stamps – *sissiktu* – seal box, *The Ancient Near East, a Life! Festschrift Karel Van Lerberghe*, ed. T. Boiy, J. Bretschneider, A. Godderis, H. Hameeuw, G. Jans, & J. Tavernier, Leuven-Paris-Walpole (MA) 2012, 75–89.

Bunnens, G., Looking for Luwians, Aramaeans and Assyrians in the Tell Ahmar stratigraphy, *Syrian Archaeology in Perspective. Celebrating 20 Years of Excavations at Tell Afis*, ed. S. Mazzoni & S. Soldi, Pisa 2013, 177–197.

Bunnens, G., Til-Barsib. B. Archäologisch, *Reallexikon der Assyriologie* 14/1–2 (2014), 38–42.

Bunnens, G., A 3rd millennium temple at Tell Ahmar (Syria), *Proceedings of the 9th International Congress on the Archaeology of the Ancient Near East 3, Reports*, ed. O. Kaelin & H.–P. Mathys, Wiesbaden 2016, 187–198.

Bunnens, G., Unfinished work at Tell Ahmar: Early and Middle Bronze Age finds, *Archaeological Explorations in Syria 2000–2011* (Proceedings of ISCACH–Beirut 2015), ed. J. Abdul Massih & S. Nishiyama, in collaboration with H. Charaf & A. Deb, Oxford 2018, 31–38.

Bunnens, G., A stela of the moon god from Tell Ahmar/Til Barsib: Contribution to the iconography of the moon god in the Neo-Assyrian period, *Travels Through the Orient and the Mediterranean World: Essays presented to Eric Gubel*, ed. V. Boschloos, B. Overlaet, I.M. Swinnen & V. Van der Stede, Orientalia Lovaniensia Analecta 302, Leuven-Paris-Bristol (CT) 2021, 99–110.

Bunnens, G. & Russell, J.M., A bit-hilani at Til-Barsib? Clarifications and further evidence, *Ugarit–Forschungen* 43 (2011), 31–35.

Bunnens, G., Dalley, S.M., Bordreuil, P., Briquel-Chatonnet, F & Hawkins, J.D., New inscriptions from Til Barsib, *Abr-Nahrain* 34 (1996–1997), 59–117.

Dugay, L., Early Bronze Age burials from Tell Ahmar, *Si un homme... Textes offerts en hommage à André Finet*, ed. P. Talon & V. Van der Stede, Subartu XVI, Turnhout 2005, 37–49.

Jamieson, A.S., The Neo-Assyrian ceramics from Tell Ahmar and associated research projects relating to the study of the ancient pottery, *Bulletin of the Archaeological and Anthropological Society of Victoria* 1992/6, 4–9.

Jamieson, A.S., Neo-Assyrian pottery from Tell Ahmar, *Iron Age Pottery in Northern Mesopotamia, Northern Syria and South-Eastern Anatolia*, ed. A. Hausleiter & A. Reiche, Munster 1999, 287–308.

Jamieson, A.S., Identifying room use and vessel functions: A case-study of Iron Age pottery from building C2 at Tell Ahmar, north Syria, *Essays on Syria in the Iron Age*, ed. G. Bunnens, Ancient Near Eastern Studies Supplement 7, Leuven 2000, 259–303.

Jamieson, A.S., A painted Eye-Vase from Tell Ahmar and the Syro-Cilician painted ceramic tradition, *Si un homme... Textes offerts en hommage à André Finet*, ed. P. Talon & V. Van der Stede, Subartu, XVI, Turnhout 2005, 79–83.

Jamieson, A.S., Processes of Assyrianisation: Identity and connectivity manifested in Neo-Assyrian ceramics and the Tell Ahmar Area C pottery, *Identity and Connectivity*, SOMA 2012, ed. L. Bombardieri, A. D'Agostino, G. Guarducci, V. Orsi & S. Valentini, Oxford 2013, 75–85.

Perini, S., Frequency and distribution of ceramic functional categories at Tell Ahmar (Syria) during the Middle Bronze Age II (*c.* 1800–1600 BC), *Proceedings of the 7th International Congress on the Archaeology of the Ancient Near East 3*, ed. R. Matthews & J. Curtis, Wiesbaden 2012, 235–248.

Perini, S., Organic remains from Middle Bronze Age ceramic vessels at Tell Ahmar, *Horizons 4: A Conference of Young Researchers Working in the Ancient Near East, Egypt and Central Asia, University of Torino, October 2011*, BAR S2698, Oxford 2015, 195–200.

Radner, K., A Neo-Assyrian tablet from Til Barsib, *NABU* 2004/26, 25–27; /82, p. 83.

Roobaert, A., A Neo-Assyrian statue from Til Barsib, *Iraq* 58 (1996), 79–87.

Roobaert, A., Continuity and discontinuity: Pillar figurines from Tell Ahmar, *Travels Through the Orient and the Mediterranean World: Essays presented to Eric Gubel*, ed. V. Boschloos, B. Overlaet, I.M. Swinnen, & V. Van der Stede, Orientalia Lovaniensia Analecta 302, Leuven-Paris-Bristol (CT) 2021, 111–119.

Roobaert, A. & Bunnens, G., Excavations at Tell Ahmar–Til Barsib, *Archaeology of the Upper Syrian Euphrates: The Tishrin Dam area*, ed. G. del Olmo Lete & J.–L. Montero Fenollos, Sabadell (Barcelona) 1999, 163–178.

Roobaert, A., Jamieson, A.S. and Otto, A., New Middle Bronze Age funerary evidence from Tell Ahmar (Syria), *Abr-Nahrain* 35 (1998), p. 95–134.

Trokay, M., Le matériel de broyage en basalte du Tell Ahmar (Area C, fouilles de 1989–1996), *Proceedings of the First International Congress on the Archaeology of the Ancient Near East*, ed. P. Matthiae, A. Enea, L. Peyronal & F. Pinnock, Rome 2000, 1665–1677.

Verardi, V., A metallurgist workshop at Tell Ahmar, Syria, *Akkadica* 128 (2007), 109–116.